THE

F

WORD

35 Lessons at 35

Clarisse C. Frazier

THE f WORD
35 Lessons at 35

Written by Clarisse C. Frazier

Foreword by Lauren Jones

First Edition, 2016
Published in the United States of America

Published by Radically Rouge
Atlanta, Georgia

All rights reserved. No part of this book may be reproduced or transmitted in any form or by any means, electronic or mechanical, including photocopying, recording or by any information storage and retrieval system, without written permission from the author, except for the inclusion of brief quotations in a review.

Copyright © 2016 by Clarisse Frazier
First Edition, 2016
Published in the United States of America

ISBN- 978-0-692-79908-6

Front and Back Cover Design by Lydia Kashaka

Dedication

This book is in honor of my beautiful mother, *Ellen Marie Shields Frazier*. She represents the voice I lost but the courage I gained. I love you for the woman you inspired me to be. "For God has not given us a spirit of fear…" To my father, *Clarence Frazier, Jr.*, may your "F", FRAZIER, always live on through you and the words of this book.

"I could have failed, BUT GOD! I could have hated, BUT GOD! I could have been bitter, BUT GOD! I was sometimes scared, BUT GOD! I was sometimes discouraged and overwhelmed, BUT GOD! I was alone some nights balled up on the floor like a child wanting my mom and my grandma, BUT GOD! Today, I praise GOD for the BUT GOD situation and I hope that yours is just around the corner."

~*Clarisse Frazier*
Author, The f Word

The f Word
35 Lessons at 35
By Clarisse C. Frazier

01
Faith

No matter what, keep going
Every now and then, be still
Learn the lesson and pass the test
Read and apply
Pray
Guard your mental
Share your testimony

02
Family

Family is everything?
My parents did their best
Let things go
Set the stage for others to win
Make traditions
Never give up on love
Do your own research

03

Friendship

Don't be afraid to tell people you love them
Surround yourself with people who make you better
Learn when to speak vs. when to listen
Be consistent
Proximity does not define importance
Embrace your differences
Reciprocity

04

Finance

Save your money
Invest in you
Be cheap
Leave work at work
Find the job you want and plan to have it
Learn to say no
Be creative

05
Freedom

Discipline your body
Know your worth and live accordingly
Pay it forward
No day is promised
Sometimes you have to face your mountain
Go get it!
Love your body and teach others to do the same

FOREWORD BY LAUREN JONES

To the Reader of this Work:

Throughout the entirety of my 7th and 8th grade school year, Ms. Frazier, my English Language Arts teacher, has given and demonstrated her many life lessons to the class. Besides teaching me how to properly identify figurative language, she has also told me and my classmates some of her earliest childhood memories and how they affect her now. Because I am still very young, hearing these good and bad experiences from a woman of her caliber has taught me that if you would like to bear the sweetest fruit, you must absorb all of the nutrients you can first. At her present age of 35, Ms. Frazier has decided to disperse her seeds of knowledge unto the minds of the public in the form of a novel. With this novel, many people will also have the chance to realize what you must learn and experience first-hand so that you too will also bear the sweetest, juiciest fruit. "Share your success and help others succeed. Give everyone a chance to have a piece of the pie. If the pie's not big enough, make a bigger pie." ~ Dave Thomas

Lauren Jones
8th Grade Student at Atlanta Heights Charter School

FOREWORD BY CLARISSE FRAZIER

You want to give people a reason to hate you? Write a book.

-Clarisse Frazier

I wrestled with an explanation as to why this book was so necessary for it involved many different layers of my life and would require me to be naked in front of the entire world when I was uncomfortable being naked within the privacy of my own home. When the idea to finally buckle down and chronicle my life's lessons popped into my head, it was motivated by many things I had endured at the hands of the men I loved. Then, it shifted to serving as a road map for single mothers who found themselves discouraged by the challenges of life. The problem I continued to encounter was the groups of people I would omit if I forced myself into a box. So, I dug a little deeper and posed the question to myself; what can be a universal truth most can relate to which will encompass every one of our personal journeys? Then it came to me...each of us will come to a point when we will have to shift our thinking from things trivial, grow up in our mentality and embrace a more mature perspective. The bible says this; "When I was a child, I spake as a child, I understood as a child, I thought as a child: but when I became a man, I put away childish things." I Corinthians 13:11 King James Version (KJV). It was from this perspective I decided to take the thoughts from my brain and commit them to the pages of this book.

I hope for several things with this published work. I hope with each verbal drawing that accompanies each chapter will allow my readers an opportunity to embrace the memories of their own childhoods whether they be good or bad. I hope the beginning anecdotes, many written from my younger years which feed into a more adult interpretation of each lesson, will guide each reader through a learning cycle of relatable material. Finally, in response to our overwhelming dependence on social media, my follow up questions gleaned from my adult connections are designed to spawn conversations at book club meetings our spark debates at leisure "kickbacks." It is my belief that we should not live our lives in solitude wasting all of the priceless nuggets presented to us through our interactions and experiences. We are meant to grow and help those we love to grow by communicating the lessons we have learned and how they are the glue holding our society together. When more of us have meaningful dialogue, we will realize we are experiencing similar things in our respective lives.

I hope at the conclusion of this piece, my parents will be proud of the courage it has taken after 35 years to share my life with the world. I hope they will laugh, cry and share each story as they were up front and center for most of the events which formed my life's lessons. I hope my daughter will get to know her mom just a little better by walking through the pages of my life. I urge more people to share their lives with others; you never know who is watching as you dance effortlessly on your stage.

faith

chapter 1

"No matter what, keep going"

I would quit allowing my life to be defined by my total surrender to the needs of those around me. I would quit focusing on all of the things I did well which began to serve as a mask for the things I needed to improve in my life. I would quit devoting every ounce of myself to increasing the levels of happiness in the lives of others and I would quit putting my own personal desires on the back burner. For the first time in my life, I would quit being everyone else's hero and I would be strong enough to be my own. -C. Frazier

Chapter One
No matter what, keep going

> Let everything happen to you
> Beauty and terror
> Just keep going
> No feeling is final
> — **Rainer Maria Rilke**

I told myself I would never teach anyone's bad a** kids. Who in their right mind would willingly decide to pursue a career where they would be overworked, underpaid, questioned, micromanaged, disrespected and treated as disposable? Teaching was never an attractive profession and was certainly not one anyone was breaking down doors to experience. In fact, when I was in college, education was one of the least checked boxes on the page of intended occupations. However, there was no other profession where you could be a mentor, doctor, sister, coach, motivator, mother, confidant and nurse all on a Monday, so after trying my hand at the hotel industry and even banking, I found myself in front of children.

My third year as a teacher was one of the most interesting as we began to experience high teacher turnover and an influx of students. We found ourselves having classes on every inch of the campus in an effort to maintain our positive academic performance record. During that time, it was not uncommon to walk into work only to be told another one of our comrades had bowed out of the race sending the administration into scramble for an emergency substitute. Our instructional coaches sprang into gear and began to plan staff development sessions designed to boost our morale. Each week, we would have to gather during our planning and be met with everything from Chicago-style popcorn to grab bag giveaways. It wasn't enough to persuade many not to jump ship but for the rest of us who still believed in the profession, it was enough to keep us going.

One particular session met our group on overload after a series of tireless visits from instructional gurus who all but pulled our classrooms apart at the seams. It seemed everything we thought was great proved we had no business standing at the chalkboard and it was evident they had lost faith we could grow the children. We plopped into our chairs, ripped into the tempting chocolate bowls on each table and did our best to fake the fact we wished we could be anywhere but there. The coordinator simply clicked on the projector and our eyes fell on some young men on a football field. As true Southerners, we enjoyed the connection to football given our undying devotion to the New Orleans Saints and the LSU Tigers but the lesson we were to learn at the end of the clip would change most of us for the rest of our lives.

The clip was a simple one. A group of high school football players were horsing around after practice as their head coach began to share with them the statistics of their upcoming opponent. At the mere mention of the team's name, the demeanor of the players changed. Unlike the huddles made popular on television by team captain greats like Ray Lewis and Drew Brees, these young men hung their heads in defeat long before they had even taken the field. Their team captain noted how much bigger and better their opponent had been in past match-ups against rival teams and also informed his soldiers he felt they would not fare well against them. The head coach agreed the opposing team might be bigger, better and stronger, however, he prompted the captain to agree to give his best effort despite the possible outcome. Haphazardly, he conceded to give his best, but the smirk on his face revealed his deception.

The coach decided to kick things up a notch and asked the captain to do the "death crawl" with a smaller teammate on his back. The captain chuckled yet got into position and began the task of crawling on his hands and feet toward an unknown destination. To add a little twist, the coach blindfolded the captain so all he could depend on was his determination. As the captain began to crawl inch by inch, yard by yard, the coach stood on the side of him encouraging him to dig deeper. When the captain began to fatigue, the coach sprang into gear and the real lesson began. The captain began to complain of pain and exhaustion, yet the coach got down on his own hands and knees and emphatically prompted the captain not to quit. As they moved further and further down the field, the intensity of the situation grew; with every painstaking motion, the captain and the coach were in sync and the goal was clear. The coach needed the captain's commitment and the captain needed the coach to believe in his ability to accomplish an impossible task.

As the intensity of the scene increased, I could hear the sniffs coming from my colleagues. As many of us allowed the tears to flow freely, the room was filled with the release of pressure which had been boiling from the pits of our souls. As the coach tucked his captain away in the end zone having gone 100 yards with his teammate on his back, the message was clear; our task would be daunting, our job would be thankless but if we could build our students to the point they would blindly trust us to get them into the end zone, we could win the game. The key was we would have to keep GOING if we were ever going to have the victory; for there is no glory in quitting before you make it to the end zone!

As an adult, I fought hard never to allow myself to be labeled as a quitter. In every aspect of my life, I could be called many things but a quitter would never be a modifier to describe me personally or my work ethic. I would forgo sleep if my job needed me to complete a task without question. It was almost understood that sleep deprivation was required to complete a task with great precision. I would go so far as to refuse invitations if it meant I would not be able to make good on what I had committed to do for someone else. It was important for me to set a standard for myself which would label me as dependable because I would never leave a job undone. For many years, I had no life because I chose to sow into the lives of others. I would miss hair appointments and opt for a ponytail if I needed to help a friend set up for a birthday party. I would allow clothes to pile up all over the house if my laundry time could be better spent handcrafting gifts for my sorority sisters' parties. I was obsessed with
 proving to the world I was, in the words of the great poet, Beyoncé, irreplaceable.

Then...one day, I woke up. I looked at my ceiling with NOTHING to do one Wednesday. My daughter had gone for a visit to Louisiana, it was the summer time so I didn't have to go to work and for the first time, there was no place I had to be with any urgency...my world was quiet. I had nothing to do with myself and I was afraid. For the first time in my life, I was afraid of not being needed. I had learned to shoot validation into my veins and much like an addict, I laid in my bed and felt the first pains of withdrawal. Almost equivalent to cold sweats, I began to feel my perceived purpose pulsing from my pores as I struggled to define myself without the approval of the fiends whom I had learned to supply. As their pusher, I had that thing that they needed. Much like American Gangster, the product, Blue Magic, prided itself in being a guaranteed brand. There was a quality one could expect should they elect to subscribe to the effects of mass-market branding and the promised expectations had never disappointed its customers. I had been pushing my own brand of Blue Magic, only now, I find myself looking for my buyers.

Perhaps if I had to pinpoint the day I realized I had an addiction to being needed, I had found my day. In that moment, I was not happy with my discovery. Almost instantaneously, I decided to quit for the first time in my life. I would quit allowing my life to be defined by my total surrender to the needs of those around me. I would quit focusing on all of the things I did well which began to serve as a mask for the things I needed to improve in my life. I would quit devoting every ounce of myself to increasing the levels of happiness in the lives of others and I would quit putting my own personal desires on the back burner. For the first time in my life, I would quit being everyone else's hero and I would be strong enough to be my own.

I can't say you will be the most popular person on the block when you make a decision to cut the apron strings. Those who learned to lean on you because you had given them permission to do so will view you as a Judas and deny you ever contributed anything of value to their lives. They won't understand your process even if you make a gallant attempt to explain it in great detail.

I can connect this process to the comical scene in the movie, "E.T." In this scene, Elliot returns home from school to find E.T. dressed in full drag and sharing the few words he had learned that day from television and Elliot's little sister. E.T. continued to repeat, "E.T. phone home." Although he had gone through the trouble of learning their own language to communicate better with his new, earthly family, they continued to repeat his words with confusion. In the moments when I made the attempt to share the importance of my refocusing, I found myself in E.T.'s shoes. I felt I had gone through the trouble of sharing my passion and purpose, however, my friends and family would often stare at me with a big, blank look on their faces.

The reality is, when you decide to quit something, it doesn't make you a bad person. No matter what someone tells you, know that such a decision is absolutely necessary multiple times of your life. It doesn't make you any less of who you are, in fact, it can prove to make you better. I have learned at 35 that sometimes I will have to quit things if I am going to win. I am willing to quit all of my hindering bad habits if they don't benefit me in the long run. Now, I am happy to be called a quitter. Each time I choose myself over someone else, I have a sense of pride knowing the courage it takes to focus on my own best interest. So when I think about the lesson in the phrase, "Keep Going," I equate its message to the simple fable entitled, "The Farmer's Donkey."

The Farmer's Donkey: A Fable for Our Time

One day a farmer's donkey fell down into a well. The animal cried piteously for hours as the farmer tried to figure out a way to get him out. Finally he decided it was probably impossible and the animal was old and the well was dry anyway, so it just wasn't worth it to try and retrieve the donkey. So the farmer asked his neighbors to come over and help him cover up the well. They all grabbed shovels and began to shovel dirt into the well.

At first, when the donkey realized what was happening he cried horribly. Then, to everyone's amazement, he quieted down and let out some happy brays. A few shovel loads later, the farmer looked down the well to see what was happening and was astonished at what he saw. With every shovel of dirt that hit his back, the donkey was shaking it off and taking a step up. (Shifting)

As the farmer's neighbors continued to shovel dirt on top of the animal, he continued to shake it off and take a step up. Pretty soon, to everyone's amazement, the donkey stepped up over the edge of the well and trotted off!

Moral: Life is going to shovel dirt on you. The trick to getting out of the well is to shake it off and take a step up. Every adversity can be turned into a stepping stone. The way to get out of the deepest well is by never giving up but by shaking yourself off and taking a step up.
What happens to you isn't nearly as important as how you react to it.

Author Unknown

In the next phase of my life, my survival will be largely dependent on my ability to continue to move forward and to keep going. As long as we use each lesson, each struggle and even each pleasurable moment to shape our path, we will always find ourselves moving forward to greatness. All we have to do is to subscribe to the importance of continuous movement. Just because you make the decision to quit a few things along the way does not mean you ever stop moving. Even when it costs you relationships or even career aspirations, you must continue to move with the flow of your life. Perhaps the blessing with be in your decision to move with purpose until you reach your promise.

chapter 2

"Every now and then, be still"

So, in this next phase of my life, whether it be for a second, minute or an entire season, I will take in the world, live a bit of nature and lose myself in the air. I will smell success and crave more of it. I will ignore reality for just a moment, enjoy being free for just a whisper of time and feel at peace with being blissfully still. -C. Frazier

Chapter Two
Every now and then, be still

Take some time in a quiet place to contemplate
the balance between being of service -
both to this generation and to generations yet unborn -
and renewing your vitality with play and celebration.
Without play, one becomes old and dry.
Without service, life becomes meaningless.
- **Jonathan Lockwood Huie**

Have you ever thought what it would feel like to have your limbs ripped from your body during a ferocious attack at the hands of a circus lion? I am sure many of you lay awake at night wondering such things…or maybe it's just me. Either way, I am sure, many of us have purchased tickets to the circus trusting that the handlers and trainers have the beasts properly educated not to kill us as we enjoy what has being named, "The Greatest Show on Earth." Unbeknownst to us, we sit only a few feet away from inevitable mutilation. I, however, always remained ever so mindful that these beautiful creatures possess an instinct given to them at the time of their birth and the likelihood of them lying in wait to rip our heads off our necks always prevented me from enjoying my $38 ticket. During the entire show as everyone else lets off their "Ooooo's" and "Ahhhhhh's," I sat with sweaty palms wondering when one of the lions, tigers and bears will decide to make one of us their own personal pan pizza with extra sauce.

The lion is the most ferocious animal known to man. It is bold, powerful and relentless which has coined it the respected King of the Jungle. The lion, when in its true habitat, is feared and revered because of its ability to dominate its prey. I watched many YouTube clips involving the lion and how it hunts its prey. I learned many interesting facts about the beast by watching it interact with other animals and its own group. One of the most disturbing videos I watched showed a lion chasing a gazelle. The lion had done the impossible; he had cornered one of the fastest animals on the planet. The lion wrapped its arms around the gazelle and pushed it down to the ground. For the first few moments, the gazelle tried to use the one thing it had going for it to assist with an escape plan; its legs. His legs sprang into motion as he tried his best to master the art of running against the air but he was going nowhere. He found himself trapped and his annihilation seemed clear.

The lion was clearly basking in the defeat of his dinner to the point he placed one paw on the ribcage of the gazelle as if to symbolize he had climbed Mt. Olympus. As I continued to watch the clip wondering how much of the encounter the director would show, in entered another lion. In true predator fashion, the lion with his hands on the food growled at his competition letting him know what time it was. The hungry adversary was not planning to back down possibly feeling as if there was enough precious carnage to go around. As the two inched closer and closer to one another, both were prepared to go head to head for the right to prove they were an unnatural force to be reckoned with. As they exchanged a series of growls and fighting stances, the unfathomable happened. The gazelle lifted its head and peeked at the argument unfolding just a few yards away. The gazelle eased its head back down on the ground for a few seconds, then in one lightning quick motion, it took off in the opposite direction. The two competing lions were none the wiser as to what had occurred behind their backs, but by the time they turned around, the entree had exited the scene. One thing was learned from the gazelle, sometimes if you want to escape an impossible situation, you just have to take the time to be still.

I almost died when I was about seven years old at a friend's birthday party. I hadn't received many invitations to anyone's birthday party outside of family although I was forced to invite the entire school to my birthday parties. I was elated to finally have a folded card in my hands asking me to attend a pool party. When the invitation came in the mail addressed to me, I felt I had finally arrived; I was finally going to be a part of the elementary school social scene. Gone were the days I would have to play with my Barbie dolls all alone. I was tired of trying to tell the story of romance and courtship between Barbie and Ken in solitude. Now, I would have an additional set of individuals to help me tell the story.

My mom and sisters were excited as well and we made an entire day of shopping for all the essentials needed for a Southern pool party. Louisiana is a different type of heat. When it is hot in Louisiana, it brings on an attitude that can lead to altercations and the commission of crimes. The Louisiana heat is unforgiving and laughs at everyone's air conditioning units which can never manage to defeat the beast. For this pool party, we would take on the moist heat in an effort to fight for our right to PAAARRRRTTTTTAAAYYY!

When we left the neighborhood Wal-Mart with sunscreen, beach towels, flip flops, swim cap and goggles, I was confident I would not stand out as an over-eager weirdo who had never been to a party. From there, we went to Dillard's department store where we picked out an orange and white striped all-in-one swimsuit with a big, yellow flower on the shoulder. Now that I was squared away, we walked the mall to find the perfect gift for the birthday girl. I enjoyed shopping for her because my mom taught me the rule to purchasing gifts; never get someone a gift you wouldn't want for yourself. I settled on a cute shirt with matching bracelets and hair bows. It had been a great day and I was looking forward to the party.

Surprisingly enough, the birthday party was in my neighborhood so I didn't have far to travel for a day filled with fun. Although I was going to a pool party, my mother made me sit still and get my hair done. This was a tedious process as I did not have the most cooperative hair in the world. My hair would often take on its own personality and my scalp would deviously divide itself into regions. The front of my hair, the bang, would often subscribe to stick to my forehead in a distracting manner often making it impossible to see in front of my face. The nape of my neck would curl up tightly and mock my mother's comb by refusing to allow it to pass through without a fight. The right side of my head would always show me love and hold beautiful curls while its adversary would do the complete opposite. As my mother struggled to initiate perfect harmony between them all, precious party time seemed to be slipping away.

She took tags off one of my summer short sets and picked out the shoes she wanted me to wear. I put my swimsuit on under my outfit but I was instructed to make sure when I took off my birthday outfit, I placed it neatly in the floral beach bag placed on my shoulder. I followed a very detailed step-by-step instruction as to how I was to prepare to get in the pool and I engraved each directive in my mind to ensure if ever in receipt of another invite, I would be granted permission to pass "Go." My sisters sacrificed a few hours before leaving for the mall to see me off. Both of them acted like they didn't care but I know there was no other place they would have been. Instead of my mom taking me to the party, my dad decided he wanted to be the one to accompany me. As I went to jump in his car, he informed me he wanted us to walk to the party. I never hesitated. I was so happy I could spend time with my daddy. I knew on that walk, all of his attention would be mine. With each one of his confident steps, I took three smaller steps doing my best to stay side by side with him. He seemed to have a little more pep in his step than usual reminding me of being truly proud and carefree. I was not sure of what I had done to make him so incredibly proud as we walked through the neighborhood but I vowed then and there to spend the rest of my life trying to duplicate my accomplishment. The day was already shaping up to be the best day ever.

We arrived at the house and it was covered in banners and balloons. I was in awe and my dad allowed his admiration of the time and attention the family had devoted to their child's celebration to show in his eyes as they widened in approval. He grabbed my hand and knocked on the front door of the house. I looked up at him blinded by the sunlight but I am sure he could see the diamonds sparkling through my pupils. When the door opened, we were greeted by a smiling woman who my dad knew from work. He introduced her as Ms. Gail and I reached my hand out to offer a handshake much like my dad had done. As I attempted to give her a firm handshake, Ms. Gail laughed a bit and give me a hug. I hugged her back then allowed my hands to grope the air until they reconnected with my dad. We were invited in the house and I, instinctively, took my position behind him. My dad twisted me around and guided me through the door first and he followed after.

The decorations continued all over the house showing they spared no expense. All along the walls were balloon bouquets and stuffed animals all meshing with the party theme, "All the World's a Stage." My dad and I greeted everyone seated in the formal sitting area and living room introducing ourselves over and over again with our names, address and my dad's occupation. It was almost as if we had to give our family resume to prove we had not been invited in error. Once we had been grilled to their liking, we were ushered to the backyard for the poolside fun. The other kids were already in the pool hitting a big ball over a new net stretched across the width of the pool. All of them seemed to be having a ton of fun and I felt if I didn't hurry and get in on it, there wouldn't be enough leftovers for me. I began to whip off my outfit and then I was reminded by my dad of the instructions my mother had given. I slowed down a bit, folded my clothes, applied sunscreen, tucked my hair into the cap and slid on the goggles. I didn't really care that I probably looked like an idiot. I feared my dad would report back to my mom if I had not done what she had told me to do down to the letter and I would be forbidden from being able to attend another party.

Once my dad saw I was okay, he informed me he was going to go back to our house and he would return to pick me up in two hours. I was surprised he was going to leave me by myself but I felt comfortable knowing Ms. Gail had been left in charge of my well-being. Once he was out of my sight, I approached the pool. I had never been in a pool before and I was very excited. I walked down the stairs of the 3 feet area ready to have some fun. I noticed all of the other kids were splashing around further toward the middle and opposite side of the pool so I decided to walk over to the group. As my steps brought me closer, they also took me deeper. I had not been told that so I stopped in my tracks and then started to walk backward. One of the girls at the party came to my side of the pool and introduced herself as Ashley. I was happy she had chosen to come to me because I was feeling a little lonely by myself being a chicken in the kiddie side of the pool. She asked me if I could swim and not wanting to be an outcast, I lied and said I could. She looked relieved and we started playing with some of the floating objects strewn around the pool.

After a while, I felt more and more comfortable in the pool. I even decided to climb atop of one of the floating devices. I laid myself out and looked up at the sky. There wasn't a cloud or bird in the sky above me. The sky was a special shade of periwinkle made just to commemorate the huge step I had just taken in my life. I tuned out everything around me and focused on allowing my hands to drag the water. It was still cool to my fingertips and this experience was more than I could have asked for. Then...it happened. One of the boys grabbed my hand and pulled me in the freaking water!

Now normally, having a young man playfully dunk me in the cool water would have been a fun interaction had I been tucked safely in my little 3 feet area where my feet could still detect the flooring beneath the gallons of chlorine-rich of water. However, as I was rolling on a river like Tina Turner, I had drifted down to the deepest end of the pool and now, I was in trouble. I immediately sank to the bottom of the pool and began to fight my way back up to the top. As I got up to the sun, I only had about two seconds to get air, look around, ask for help and get ready to do it again. The first time I managed to get my head above water, I yelled out, "Hel...," and then I was back under again. Through the water propelling me under, I could hear sound waves of the other kids laughing and playing. The brilliant young man who had decided to dunk me had then moved on to something more exciting; typical of men, right. Then, I was on top again doing my, "Help me," monologue. Down I traveled again kicking and flailing with all I had in my body. I hated birthday parties. I hated balloons and animals and gifts and sunscreen and ice cream and anything else associated with it. There was only one thing I loved about birthday parties, and that was Ms. Gail.

Out of nowhere, I felt arms around my legs just as I had nothing left to help me fight the water. The arms swept me toward the top of the water and my arms broke through the barrier and I was able to breathe again. My arms continued to punch the water over and over again and my legs, fought to escape the clutches of my lifeguard. I kept boxing and boxing realizing my next breath could depend on my ability to knockout my opponent which was the pool water. As I continued to fight, I finally heard someone say, "Just be still."

I realized there was a partygoer in the water within arm's length so I climbed over his shoulders and held on for dear life. I finally stopped fighting and allowed them to save me. I heard Ms. Gail say, "She's not playing. She's drowning." With the help of Ms. Gail and most of the other kids, I was pulled from the water and laid out on the side of the pool. I began to vomit and cough up the water I had ingested. I noticed Ms. Gail was soaking wet. She had jumped in the pool to help me in her clothes; shoes and all. As she came over to check on me, I grabbed on to her and wept in her arms. I had no more fight left in me. I was done and so was the party.

When my dad came to pick me up after the cake cutting and gift opening, I was afraid of the story he would be told. When the knock on the door came, I braced myself for his reaction. I heard him exchange greetings with the others in the front sitting area and I heard when he teased Ms.

Gail about getting in the pool with the kids. Ms. Gail asked him to step in the foyer where I was sure she was telling him in the nicest way possible that I had almost killed myself at her house because I had lied. I hated the fact my dad would be embarrassed but there was nothing I could do.

My dad was directed to me in the kitchen where I was seated over a barely touched piece of chocolate cake. Any other day, the cake before me would have been nothing shy of a masterpiece. I had managed to score a corner piece with a pink rose sitting on top of a moist and delicious slice of Devil's Food. Today, however, the thought of cake turned my stomach on its head. I couldn't even look at my dad. He moved to stand in front of me and I finally looked up into his eyes. The sparkle was gone and what remained was something I had not seen before. Deep in my father's eyes was fear. My dad was actually afraid. The tears fell from my eyes as he grabbed my hand and my swim bag. I didn't say anything, I just followed him out the front door of the house. The walk home was the longest of my life as we walked in silence. My dad's footsteps were strong and his stride remained powerful; I had to triple his step to keep up. When we got to the house, he opened the back door and ushered me inside. He followed me, locked the door and told me to go and take a bath. I did as I was careful not to interact with my family members until he gave me the clearance.

Once I was done with my bath and in my pajamas, my mom came in my room. After I walked her through what happened, she had the same look in her eyes as I had seen in my father. I didn't understand what was going on with my mom and dad but I didn't ask. Instead, I went to bed as I was told. About thirty minutes later, my sisters came into my room and turned on my light. I sat up in bed and realized they both had a similar look on their faces. They explained how mom and dad had been devastated I had almost drowned. They explained how they had been in a very bad car accident with an 18 wheeler only a year prior which landed both of them in the hospital. They told me the story of how mom had to stay at the house with me while daddy had to come to the accident site with each detail. I finally understood what I had done and it made me sad.

I remembered overhearing the story of how my dad thought someone had died in the accident based on the condition of the car. When he realized all of the kids in the car were going to make it, it finally hit him how bad things could have been. My sisters felt my parents had never recovered from the scare the accident caused. What happened to me at the party was another reminder of how quickly things could happen when children were out of the sight of their parents. I felt awful but promised them I wouldn't lie anymore and I wouldn't hurt my parents.

What I learned from the experience of almost drowning at a birthday party was sometimes, if I don't learn to be still, I can hurt myself and those around me. If I am not honest with myself that sometimes I will need to be rescued from my own mistakes, I will run the risk of suffocating myself. Every now and then, when you learn to be still, you will find there are lifelines all around to pull your head safely above water.

As an adult, I remember the chart-topping song, "Saving all my love for you," by Whitney Houston. In this song, Houston tells the narrative of an unrequited love affair where the "side chick" shared the love she had for a married man with the world over a delicate melody. She was clear that she desired to break the hold he had on her but sadly, she could not find anyone who could give her what she needed better than he. As the story reached its climax, the main character would find herself recalling his promises:

> *You used to tell me we'd run away together*
> *Love gives you the right to be free*
> *You said be patient, just wait a little longer*
> *But that's just an old fantasy*

The lyrics made one thing clear to me, I did not want to live a life where I was being saved for anyone not meant for me. As reflected on my failed relationships, it was obvious that I had been saving the right thing for the wrong people. Oftentimes, I was saving my heart for men who didn't want it, I was saving my ambition for occupations that couldn't develop it, I was saving my impact for a world who wasn't ready for it. Ultimately, I decided I didn't want to be saved anymore and in my stillness came my revelation.

As I continue to evolve as a woman, I realize, there are things I have yet to give to the world and those around me. In my stillness, I have learned to become one with the things I want in life and sometimes, instead of forcing myself to move too quickly, I made the decision not to save anything. Even when being still, one can make a huge impact, for stillness allows for careful contemplation and planning. Without the presence of those two things, it is almost impossible for any plan to be effectively implemented. So, in this next phase of my life, whether it be for a second, minute or an entire season, I will take in the world, live a bit of nature and lose myself in the air. I will smell success and crave more of it. I will ignore reality for just a moment, enjoy being free for just a whisper of time and feel at peace with being blissfully still.

chapter 3

"Learn the Lesson and Pass the Test"

Now, any black woman knows, good hair is hard to come by so I was faced with a huge dilemma; do I leave the hair on the ground and let it go to waste or do I scoop down and pick it up in hopes of using it later? In that instant, I learned who my real friends were for one of my buddies, Amy, bent down and retrieved my hair concealing it in her purse. Now, that was a FRIEND. –C. Frazier

Chapter Three
Learn the lesson and pass the test

In school, you're taught a lesson and then given a test. In life, you're given a test that teaches you a lesson.
-Tom Bodett

"Don't look at me like I have poop on my shoe!" screamed my brain as I looked at a classroom filled with judgmental, unfocused and unmotivated teenagers. As a first year teacher, I remember one of the first lessons I ever taught to my 7th graders which I felt would finally spark their attention like it was yesterday. After weeks of feeling as if all the curriculum jargon was an ancient form of Greek language, I had finally been released from the clutches of my instructional lead teacher and was trusted to construct my own lesson and try it out on my little guinea pigs. I had done a lot of meaningless research but wrote the appropriate responses thus proving my ability to decode educational pedagogy to the point my mentors finally felt I was ready to take off the training wheels. I was happy to finally put my eager passion to educate into practice. On that fateful Monday, I was going to be ready to put on the full armor of God and tackle my task head on. What was my task in a nutshell? Simple. Get one hundred and ten 8th grade students from an urban background to love literature.

I decided I would teach a dynamic lesson on figurative language which I was certain was just as important and discovering a cure for cancer. I had stayed up all weekend preparing the individual puzzle pieces the kids would need to complete their jigsaw and I was careful to pack each group's work in nice little Ziploc bags I had scored from the Dollar Tree. Most of the weekend, I went over and over my checklist of items I would need for each group and by Sunday night, I was prepared to show up and show out. I was certain after that lesson, the administration would be ready to promote me into some leadership position made for awesome teachers who oozed ambition. I was on my way to being great and everyone would know it.

When I walked into the school that day, it was almost as if the theme to "Shaft" was playing behind me. I threw open the front doors of the building and a delicious wind propelled me into the front office amidst teachers who looked as if they still had one side of their body nestled sweetly under their comforters. My hair caught that Beyonce-bellow and I catwalked all the way from the front door to the back hall. I chuckled a bit because inside, I knew all my colleagues were oblivious to the havoc I was about to wreak on our building. No one would be safe, everyone would be susceptible to the creative innovation I was about to bestow upon our great place of learning. I walked with a little limp down the hall knowing I was the bomb and I was about to explode.

My classroom had a different feel that morning. Over the weekend, the cleaning crew had finally buffed our floors only months after their expected date of completion. The glow from the floors reflecting the lights from the overhead fixtures seemed to create an angelic, luminescent hue which I was sure would waft itself down the hallway. I knew, instantly, the day was going to be perfect and I began to set up my classroom for the day's lesson. Once all pieces were in place, I revealed the coup de grace; assorted bags of chocolate and Jolly Ranchers! Yes, ladies and gentlemen, I was a-shoo in for Teacher of the Year and everyone would be wise to take notes.

As my teammates and I exchanged inappropriate details of our weekend which often included behaviors once forbidden for those practicing our profession, I was just a bit anxious to get started. Once you've heard one sordid story of promiscuity, you've heard them all and today, I wasn't interested in the vivid details. Four classes of students would be my real-world assessment and being the scholar I was, I was going to pass with flying colors. As the kids began to pour onto the hall, I knew the day of reckoning had finally come. The students exchanged their own inappropriate details of their weekends which, alarmingly enough, sounded a lot like ours. After all of the slamming of the lockers and slapping of the hands, they finally settled themselves into their respective classrooms.

I performed my usual duties of checking the role, taking up assignments, distributing letters from the office and taking up cell phones before the morning announcements. Only two kids were missing so I would have to adjust the groups in my mind, so far, so good. Finally, after our school news reporters took us through the lunch menu for the day, practice schedules and upcoming club and organization meetings, it was time to begin instruction. Finally.

It was go time. I put on my game face and I was ready to propel my students well into the next stratosphere of their educational pursuits. I stood proudly at the front of the classroom and announced we would be learning about Figurative Language. My excitement was met with blank stares and it was almost is if the beginning of my lesson was a sleeping pill as I watched the life drain from the faces of my scholars. I, however, was unbothered by this response because they had no way of knowing the tremendous things I had planned for them. I explained each one of the examples moving effortlessly between each one. I was impressed by my own knowledge and I was confident my kiddos would leave having added figurative language to their arsenal of knowledge. However, it happened, one of the kids passed gas...this was not going to come as easily as I had anticipated.

An hour into the lesson, the kids could care less about hyperboles, metaphors, similes, idioms, personification and definitely did not care about onomatopoeia. Many had started the annoying game of "hide the cell phone from the teacher" doing their best to use books and backpacks to keep it out of plain sight. I gave them the planned test at the end of the period and as I walked around the classroom and glanced over their shoulders, I watched my excitement for my lesson diminish with every stroke of their pens. They had learned absolutely NOTHING for an entire hour and a half. One thing was clear; when you learn the lesson, you should be able to pass the test.

I was fortunate to be a strong test-taker as a kid. When others would shield their big, red grades from the eyesight of others, I would proudly leave my papers on the desk for all to see. After all, I had sacrificed sleep to ensure I knew my material so I had earned the right to gloat just a little bit...right? Many of my classmates bragged about hanging out after school at the mall and in each other's neighborhoods while I elected to spend my time going back through algebraic expressions. Since I paid the price of greatness, I deserved to pass the test.

My senior year, I remember having my weave pulled out during a fight I had with a friend. The weave I was wearing had been given to me by a friend of mine named Jessica who had learned the trick to blonde hair streaks; blonde weave pieces. Wanting to mimic her style, I dropped hints ranging from my dissatisfaction with my look and my lack of funds waiting for her to offer a few of her tracks to the needy...me. However, after about a week of beating around the bush, I finally asked her to bless me with a little faux gift. Thankfully, she slipped me two blond tracks one morning during breakfast. I felt like Charlie and the Chocolate Factory now that I had my "golden ticket."

On the day of my altercation, I had a bang and swoop over my right eye. I had used a rattail comb to strategically lay my own brown hair over the peaks of blonde cleverly pinned beneath. Now, as an amateur weaveologist, I failed to secure my tracks with the normal tools; weave and glue. Instead, I opted to pin both sides with bobby pins confident they would last the day with no problem. Everyone noticed my new highlights and even made reference to my imitation taking a silent tally of who had worn it better. Nonetheless, I felt good and my confidence was through the roof.

Sitting in the cafeteria with my friends, I cannot even remember the topic of conversation leading to our disagreement however I remember a combination of canned peaches in my new hair and a nasty attitude. The next thing I knew, we were fighting in and out of the cafeteria. The fight went on for what seemed like hours finally ending when our friends intervened. At the end of it, we both stood panting for air with our hair all over our heads but for me, it would not be as simple to recover from the fight. On the ground laid my new blonde tracks. Now everyone knew my secret. I was exposed!

Now, any black woman knows, good hair is hard to come by so I was faced with a huge dilemma; do I leave the hair on the ground and let it go to waste or do I scoop down and pick it up in hopes of using it later? In that instant, I learned who my real friends were for one of my buddies, Aariel, bent down and retrieved my hair concealing it in her purse. Now, that was a FRIEND. Although I would face three days of a suspension, I would return with my blonde streaks secured TIGHTLY in my head. I had learned the lesson and I would never fail the test of securing my weave again.

Yes, I find humor in the situation now, but as an adult, I have learned the importance of taking a reflective moment to learn something new from each experience I have encountered. Even in an impossible situation, there is something valuable to be learned. With each failed relationship, I have learned to change the bait I use to attract men. If I don't want to attract sexually-driven men, I have to stop leading with sexual innuendo. With each strained encounter at work comes a lesson in teamwork. Sometimes, no matter how many degrees one might have, there is still much to be learned from collaborative work projects. I have learned to value everyone's opinion and to require the same in return.

In life, once we focus on the learning in the lesson, there is no test we cannot pass. I have learned God will give the same test over and over again until we earn a passing score. Now, I don't want to have to go through the same trials and tribulations over and over again. Instead, I want to learn the lesson and pass my test so I can be free to move on stronger and wiser than before.

chapter 4

"Read and Apply"

In my adult life, I found myself deviating from God's script more than I cared to admit. My mother always told me there was nothing new under the sun and under the Son, yet I always found myself trying to create some new and innovative way to cure heartbreak, eliminate mediocrity and cancel out despair. -C. Frazier

Chapter Four
Read and apply

...to learn and not to do is really not to learn. To know and not to do is really not to know.
— **Stephen R. Covey**

The first time I tried to cook macaroni and cheese was by accident. Quite frankly, I was never a fan of the instant macaroni and cheese as it never seemed to taste quite like the delicious dish with the crunchy crust served at special occasions. My mom boasted a special recipe for macaroni and cheese which she only broke out of its glass case when it was time to impress a crowd. When I was finally graced with the secret family recipe at twenty-five, I realized I had finally been forged by fire and had crossed the burning sands into Frazier land. Her mac and cheese, as I came to learn, was a heart attack waiting to happen. It was packed with butter and cheeses sure to clog any artery with ease. It was the one dish we never seemed to have enough leftovers of at the conclusion of family dinners. It was that one thing perfect dish found perfect in any combination. It didn't matter if you put it with turkey, sweet potatoes, broccoli and cheese rice…hell, you could put it with pecan pie and it would fit like a glove.

The taste of instant macaroni and cheese was shameful on most days as we tried our best to doctor it up with plenty of pepper, butter and as much salt as we could stand. The truth is, it was probable one would have to make a science of doctoring it up without needing to drink a gallon of water due to the heavy hand of most amateur cooks. So, on the day I decided to bite the bullet, my decision was made strictly out of a necessity for nourishment.

Earlier in the day, the cafeteria workers must have decided they were going to ruin the rest of my night by serving chicken fried so hard each piece deserved its own funeral procession. The overwhelming thickness of the bland batter used to coat our once feathered friends was an embarrassment to Southern cuisine but sadly, those of us whose mothers didn't love us enough to make us a special lunch with sandwiches minus the crust of the sandwich edges had no choice except to pick our way through the muck and mire in hopes of uncovering something remotely edible. After much time complaining at the lunch table with others facing the same challenge of obtaining one bite of food acceptable to our taste buds, I finally decided to ask for an extra milk and piece of blue banana cake.

In true "cafeteria lady style," they all but threatened me within an inch of my life not to tell any of the other students I had been blessed with the periwinkle colored square of pure sugar as I am sure they wanted to take some chunks home and enjoy them over ice cream while watching reruns of their favorite show. I graciously accepted their generosity hiding it on my orange tray behind two cartons of milk measuring only an hour shy of its expiration date and returned to my class table for the few minutes remaining in our lunch period. I was well aware the final classes of the day were going to be an upward climb but what choice did I have?

With each passing hour, my stomach and my mental capacity to focus on something other than my fleeting energy were at war with one another. Each teacher who called my name for validation of my comprehension became my arch nemesis and for the first time in my life, I was praying my bus would pull out of the lane first and deliver me home. I remembered my mother had cooked the night before and based on my calculations, minus the unknown variable that now existed where sensibility once lived, and I was excited to revisit the menu one more time. If my memory served me right, there would be two juicy pork chops waiting on me to jump off the big bird.

Finally, my teachers let me out of prison and I made a mad dash for the bus waiting for me at the top of the bus lane. I was thankful my bus driver had been on time and jumped us to the front of the line so we would be the first ones to make the drive home. I found my seat at the front of the bus where most of those afraid of a little old fashioned ribbing sat under the watchful eye of the bus driver who they never seemed to understand was keeping his eye on the road. I watched the mailboxes go by like small interstate markers showing progress. Finally, we pulled up to my stop and I bounded from my seat grabbing for my key as I walked down the stairs of the bus. I felt my ability to multitask would cut down some of the time it would take for me to get to my food. I had begun to belch what tasted like the bile from the bottom of my stomach and they only thing I could pray was I would not chip a tooth on the chop bone as I inhaled my first real meal of the day. As I fought with the sticky lock my dad had as a permanent fixture on his "honey do" list, I breathed a sigh of relief when I finally found myself on the other side of the door. I dropped my backpack next to the sofa and went straight for the refrigerator.

Once inside the doors of heaven under the soft glow of the cascading light, I searched desperately for the leftovers I had anticipated all day. I moved the lettuce back and forth on the second shelf hoping my treat was lurking behind but I had no luck locating the meat I craved. After shifting everything around and not finding any sign of my pork chops, only one thing could explain where it had gone; my dad. The bottomless pit known as my dad had struck again and my dreams of a full stomach had been shattered in a matter of minutes. It was then I realized I had to fend for myself so I began to rummage the cabinets in search of something I could cook safely without burning down the house before my mother and father came home.

Nothing caught my eye except for one lonely box of Kraft mac and cheese. The box mocked me but one thing was certain, the only thing standing between me and something on my stomach was some boiled water. I began to get to work. After following the simple directions, I found myself in eager anticipation of my culinary masterpiece. Minute after minute I stood before the great stove where so many works of art had been created at the hands of my mother. So many days she had shaved hours off large meals to present skillful concoctions to her family after a long day at work. As I witnessed the boiling water funneling around the large pot, I wondered had she somehow blessed me with the inherited ability to wow a crowd with something as simplistic as noodles and cheese.

As the noodles neared completion, I decided to reread the directions one more time to ensure my steps had been ordered correctly. It looked as if I had done all I could do and I would now have to trust the step by step explanation. I removed the pot from the heat immediately halting the boil, strained the noodles as instructed and allowed them to dangle helplessly over the kitchen sink until the final drop fell from the silver tool made especially for this job. Once sure all water had been drained, it was time for me to place the noodles in the bowl, add the milk, butter and cheese and give it all a thorough tossing. It was almost time for me to dine!

With only plating standing between me and my meal, I elected to go off the script just a bit by adding some seasoning from my mother's impressive cabinet of spices. Now, I had seen my mother reach in this cabinet over a thousand times and, for some reason, whatever she sprinkled always seemed to make things just a little bit better. This time would be no different as I would work to add a little flare to my dish. I grabbed for the salt and cayenne pepper...looked good to me. Suddenly, the smell from the cayenne pepper, which was now thrown over my dish, pinched me in the nose and the sneezing ensued. I knew I had made a grave mistake and regretted the fact I had deviated from the plan trying to do things my own way.

As I shoveled most of the mac and cheese in the trashcan, I could have kicked myself in the teeth with a steel work boot. Had I simply followed the plan as laid out in plain English, I could have avoided the feeling of disappointment, failure and hunger all racing through my body. If only I could have trusted someone else to lead me in the right direction, I would not have wasted time and energy trying to fix a problem I had created for myself. Such is life.

In my adult life, I found myself deviating from God's script more than I cared to admit. My mother always told me there was nothing new under the sun and under the Son, yet I always found myself trying to create some new and innovative way to cure heartbreak, eliminate mediocrity and cancel out despair. I can remember having the instructions in front of my face many times only to find myself doing it my own way. Most times, the decision to deviate cost me time, patience and money proving my way would never be the right way.

Ikea is known for its lack of explicit directions. While the furniture powerhouse prides itself on being one of the best options for those wanting to improve the décor in their homes, the low prices were made possible by the mandate that all pieces came in boxes and assembly would not be included. Time and time again, I would roam the aisles in search of new pieces to add to my home only to find myself ruining them in the process.

I purchased a set of drawers for my daughter's bedroom for about $110.00 which was a drastic discount from Haverty's who wanted a minimum of $230.00 for a similar piece. My pockets voted for Ikea although my brain petitioned on Haverty's behalf. As I pushed the box of miscellaneous wooden pieces into the trunk of my Honda, I was excited about my savings and none the wiser as to the time and effort it was going to take to finally enjoy my purchase.

Three hours, one million screws and six hundred curse words later, I sat in front of a structure I could not depend on to hold socks or even cotton balls because the bottom of the drawers continued to fall to the floor each time any weight was added to the drawer. I tried to read the directions over and over again but the brackets never seemed steady and the matching of screws to holes was beyond my comprehension so I began to force piece together with random fasteners I had thrown in to my kitchen drawers. Hours later it was clear to me the importance of reading the directions and applying my knowledge. I was so upset with myself for cutting corners and longed for the days when Haverty's would be delivered to my home by big, sweaty men armed with tools who would not leave until my piece was installed perfectly.

What I have learned in these 35 years is that the word of God has the key to each lock in our lives. Each parable, psalm and interpretation of God's instruction is a blueprint for us to follow. Instead of inventing a bolt cutter, if we simply asked for the key, we could walk through some doors in our lives without such strain. Our issue is that we never read the directions accurately because many of God's instructions require each of us to pay a price of praise or sacrifice. Both of these requirements are based on decisions we have to make to submit to the directions in their entirety without interjecting our own random fasteners to hold things together. If we read the Word and apply it to our lives, maybe we can stop ruining our mac and cheese and finally feed our souls.

chapter 5

"Pray"

In my adult life, I found myself deviating from God's script more than I cared to admit. My mother always told me there was nothing new under the sun and under the Son, yet I always found myself trying to create some new and innovative way to cure heartbreak, eliminate mediocrity and cancel out despair. -C. Frazier

Chapter Five
Pray

I pray because I can't help myself. I pray because I'm helpless. I pray because the need flows out of me all the time- waking and sleeping. It doesn't change God- it changes me.

— **William Nicholson**

Submitted to Facebook on November 30, 2012--This morning's prayer call was all about the way we should pray. Did you know that ALL prayers should/must begin with reverence to God. Tell Him how awesome He is, how faithful He is, how loving He is, how much He protects you like no other, how He healed your body or spared your life? Who wouldn't like to hear a little bit of the resume they have built with you? According to my pastor, when you begin to lift Him to glory, that problem you intended to pray about seems smaller and smaller! Lord, teach us to pray.

My prayers as a child were always very simple, sweet and to the point. They began with "Now I lay me," and ended with, "if I die." It hadn't taken my mother long to teach it to me as a rite of passage in my southern Baptist Church home. I can remember how proud she was when I finally stumbled my way through its entirety without her prompting. I actually felt these words pouring from my lips like pudding and this must have meant something because little I had done prior seemed to have the same effect on my mother. I even began to look forward to bedtime so I could earn her praise all over again.

Each Sunday in church, a section of the service would be reserved for one of our seasoned deacons to kneel down on a wicker chair placed to the right of the communion table. It would take him quite a moment to get down there given the frailty of his legs, and I was often afraid one day he would get stuck down there but he never took the easy way out by standing at the podium. He would deliver the Lord's Prayer each Sunday through tears; he never added a word, changed a word or omitted any of the words taught to each of us. I never understood what about the same prayer delivered each Sunday as routine made him so emotional and I often questioned its authenticity.

As I got older, prayers seemed to have less focus as the youth department at my church began to move more into the idea of developing a "relationship" with God. I was quite confident it must have been a great idea but there was one big hole that had not been filled. In my conversations with other members of the MCYD, many of us lacked an understanding of what the word "relationship" meant. Based on our interpretation, a "relationship" was that thing we had with each other on the back rows of the church van on the way on one of our youth conference trips. If you and your beau happened to christen your "relationship" with a kiss indicative of your passion for one another, you were a respected couple among the good church-going kiddos. Somehow, lumping a relationship with the church drummer and an intimate relationship with our Lord seemed like comparing apples to apples in my book.

During one of our summer camps, we were allowed to travel south of the state to attend seminars geared toward teaching young adults how to foster a real relationship with God. The first time down, it was almost as if we had traveled across borders because we watched young people praising God perfectly. It was as if they had studied the behaviors of their pastors and parents because they had the script down pat. Young worshippers would stomp their feet in a series of taps while others would lift hands to the sky uttering various phrases. Although it was interesting to watch, I felt as if I had no idea of the inner connection they were having with God and I questioned if I had ever felt Him or if He was real to me. Night after night, when we returned to our church, I spoke freely to my youth director and told her I wanted to know how I could have a relationship with God that would help me to cry and lift my hands like the other kids. She responded with the truest comment I have heard to date. She simply said, "Life will teach you how to pray."

It is not uncommon to hear people praying on a daily basis. In fact, the more intentional I was in terms of paying attention to petitions made to God I found some were just habitual. For example, when my students would do something silly in their Math class, the teacher would often say, "God help us all." Even at the gym, it was common to hear someone declare in spin class, "Whew, thank you Lord." Such trivial examples seem to be disconnected, but I have learned that a prayer life is just as regular as air and can show up anywhere.

As an adult, I have learned the importance of praying about everything and to make it a part of my daily routine. Imagine God is just like a best friend you simply call to discuss the events of your day. The only difference is, no matter what you tell this friend, you don't have to worry about hearing your business in the street the next day. You don't have to worry about this friend getting mad with you and throwing your secrets back in your face. This friend does not judge you or forget to acknowledge your feelings. Sometimes, this friend simply listens and keeps His opinion to Himself.

My mom was always great at praying. Before Thanksgiving meals, no matter who joined hands with us around the incredible spread she would lay on the table, she would begin to pray. I can recall inviting two of my former students to Louisiana with me to experience true Southern living. As they stood with hands joined in our family circle, my mother began to usher in the spirit of God with thanksgiving for blessings of protection. She always thanked God for protecting us from dangers "seen and unseen" proving she understood the importance of Him orchestrating His angels to surround us. She would thank God for not allowing our bed to be our "cooling board" demonstrating her appreciation for the fact she woke up that morning. As she would climb higher and higher into her prayer, the tears would begin to fall freely from her eyes and the beauty of her connection to the living God was an amazing glow in the room.

My students found themselves overcome with emotions as the room was filled with a realization most had overlooked all year. In that moment, we basked in awe of a God who had been moving the chess pieces of our lives and landing us in safe places where we could truly enjoy life. At the final "Amen" my mother would be washed down in tears and most of us would be in the same condition. There was just something about my mother's prayers...I always felt like her prayers had the ability to penetrate the very eardrums of God...there was just something about my mother's prayers.

When researching the definition of prayer, I stumbled upon a response to the inquiry written by the founder of the Christians Apologetics and Research Ministry. In the article, prayer is noted in the following quote:

"Prayer changes the one praying because in prayer, you are in the presence of God as you lay before Him your complete self in confession and dependence. There is nothing to hide when in quiet supplication we are reaching into the deepest part of ourselves and admitting our needs and failures. In so doing, our hearts are quieted and pride is stripped and we enjoy the presence of God. James 4:8 says, "Draw near to God and He will draw near to you."

There is another benefit of prayer: peace. "Be anxious for nothing, but in everything by prayer and supplication with thanksgiving let your requests be made known to God. 7 And the peace of God, which surpasses all comprehension, shall guard your hearts and your minds in Christ Jesus," (Phil. 4:6-7)."

Although a simplistic concept of petitioning a higher power for guidance, protection and healing, the issue of faith becomes the piece most often overlooked. When in prayer, the absence of faith becomes an insurmountable mountain standing in between the effectiveness of our prayer. My mother often prayed for our safety and protection but, as I grew older, I began to pray for the revelation of purpose and direction in my life. The beauty of having a prayer life is it grows with you and becomes a passenger on the roller coaster of life.

At the age of 35, I have learned to appreciate the prayers of my mother. I realized that my mother's prayers have a completely different basis as my own. In my mother's prayers there lies a confidence in the one in whom she is petitioning. She has no doubt in her mind that her prayer will be answered. She would say, "Lord, I know you might say yes and you might say no, but I know you hear me and for that, I am thankful." There was always such an appreciation for God in my mother's prayers. Now, when I pray, I am careful to focus on the connection I hope to make with God. I spend a lot of time losing myself in Him before I begin to speak. Prayer has built my faith and as I move forward in life, I know a strong and consistent prayer life will be my firm foundation.

chapter 6

"Guard Your Mental"

Similar to Lloyd and Harry, most women I have met over the years have encountered men with the same "dumb" mentality. For some strange reason, someone on the freak train had sold each man a dream of a better life. Many of the men in our lives found themselves surrounded by beautiful, confident and successful women yet seemed be holding out for the bigger, better deal."
-C. Frazier

Chapter Six
Guard your mental

If you talk to a man in a language he understands, that goes to his head. If you talk to him in his language, that goes to his heart.
-Nelson Mandela

November 2, 2014--Just got slapped in the face by my pastor! I have to renew my mind! I have been detached from my spiritual focus, hence the chaos in my head. We have to see ourselves through the eyes of God or we will allow foolishness in our lives worried about opinions that don't matter. I care what God thinks of me and I know He is not well pleased with my thoughts and reactions as of lately. Even when it seems unfair, I will rise above as He has required of me. I will uphold my character and be stronger than my adversity. Time to transform my mind! She's back!

Louisiana people are funny. If you have never been around a group of people from the "boot" you are truly missing a treat. The true Southerners hailing from Louisiana say the craziest things and give the most outlandish reasoning for the things going on around us to the point it will actually begin to make sense. My mom would say things like, "Chile, people are dying who ain't never died before." The first time I heard it, I laughed so hard I cried. I think even funnier than the saying was the seriousness in which it was delivered. My mom did not crack a smile or bat an eye. Pure comedy. I can recall one of the funniest things my mother shared with me which was about the Crazy Christmas Ham and this story solidified my conclusion that being truly Southern is a badge of honor.

Ok, I know it sounds absurd and trust me, it is, but the concept stuck with me so vividly I had to research its validity for myself. My mom always told us the story of Mitchell Jefferson, a local man who sang a song of peanuts advising others to indulge in the treat. His song went something like this:

"*Hooooottttttt peanuts.*

Get you hoooooottttttttt peanuts.
You betta get em, for they all be gone.
I got em here now. Hooooooootttttttt peanuts"

Now, this man made a living selling...yes, that's right, hot peanuts. Please understand, these weren't any ordinary ol' peanuts. These peanuts had a special saltiness to them with a hit of old hickory smoke. Each hull served as an ingenious cover for some of the most delicious nuts one had ever tasted. The shells seemed to crack perfectly and the delicate covering on each peanut would fall gently from each treat to the Earth below. Our distributor would pedal them around on a bike he would all but walk around using his right leg as an additional set of wheels. The bottom of his shoes told the tale of a less than lucrative business venture however, he continued to encourage the city to enjoy the timeless treat. Now, my mother never seemed to want any peanuts from Mr. Jefferson although on many occasions, she could be found pouring the contents of a peanut bag from the corner store into her ice-cold Pepsi. I never asked why, but one day, my mother offered a little bit of an explanation that seemed to confuse me even more.

It was rumored that people who were classified as "crazy" were given a bad reputation in the town. None of those labeled this way were ever referred to as having an official medical diagnosis. Instead, most of them had the bottle to blame for their imbalances. Funny thing is, almost everyone knew each "crazy" person's drink of choice which had led to the diminishing of their mental capacity. Now, take Mr. Jefferson, for example, JB Scotch had been the culprit which had robbed him of a wife, kids and a home years before. As the story went, Mr. Jefferson was arrested in front of the Super 1 Foods store wearing socks, a Santa hat and a black trash bag hanging from his wrist filled with Community Coffee cans. He stood in front of the store for at least a half an hour showing the world his business before the authorities had been called to "talk" to him about his choice of attire in a public place.

According to eyewitnesses in my family, none of whom could confirm whether they had actually witnessed this themselves or had been told the story so many times they simply believed it to be true, but he just stood in front of the store with his left leg posed to the side with his weight resting on a pointed toe. Yes....they said the toe was pointed like Misty Copeland. People, accustomed to minding their own business, continued to carry on with their shopping as normal except for those with children whose eyes needed to be shielded from the burlesque show taking place free of charge. He seemed to be minding his own business, not engaging anyone in conversation of explanation so the world continued to revolve as if nothing was happening. When the cops finally arrived, they simply had a quiet conversation with him informing him of his attire and him, almost like the king is the popular fable, "The Emperor's New Clothes," found himself scurrying to hide his most prized possessions from plain sight. The cops let him off with a warning concerned he had perhaps blacked out or suffered some sort of mental trauma. However, when he showed up at the summer concert on the river again bearing it all, it was clear his behavior would have to be addressed…URGENTLY.

My mother and the cackling hens of the family always managed to guide us to the story of crazy Jefferson at some point of every family event. There was even some speculation of his participation in the fathering of one of my sisters although we all knew there was no truth to the playful allegation. All in all, what was most important was his relationship to the Christmas ham. It was rumored that everyone classified as "crazy" was given a $14.00 check and a ham for Christmas. Now, the combination never seemed to fit together in the recesses of my mind, however, everyone seemed comfortable with such compensation for being completely and totally off one's rocker. My family joked each holiday about inviting Jefferson and some of the other known crazies in the area to our annual family dinner counting up their meaty contributions as the making of a feast.

I remember the day when I heard the story of Mr. Jefferson and when he disappeared from the local spotlight. He had been spotted near the mall performing one of his lewd and lascivious acts when the cops had finally determined they had turned a blind eye to his behavior for the last time. After again running him through the normal drill of putting his clothes back on unbeknownst to him, they added some handcuffs to his wardrobe. He simply hung his head and began to cry uncontrollably. He began to apologize and ask them to help him to be normal like everyone else. When everyone stopped teasing him and began to dig a bit, they discovered he had lost his wife and his job after failing several certification tests. With the loss of his wife came a strained relationship between Mr. Jefferson and his children. He could no longer attend family functions in fear of the shame that preceded his arrival so it left him without many options. He sold peanuts because it was what everyone expected a bum like him to do given his circumstance. Also, his peanut route ran right by his children's school which had been deemed off limits for him or so he had been told by the courts. He had bouts with depression which revealed itself through his inappropriate acts. He shared that he did those things because he felt people were scrutinizing him on a daily basis behind his back and he wanted to put it out in the open. His story was my first exposure to the phrase most African-American people refused to utter…mental illness.

Recently, my pastor began preaching a series on the armor of God. For those who follow the Bible, the scripture makes mention of putting on the "helmet of salvation." When I realized his direction upon giving the masses his focus for the biblical teaching one Sunday, I was relieved to see someone realized the importance of the mind and how it must be protected at all cost. He went on to talk about the various pieces of the armor worn by warriors in biblical times. William J. Brown, in his analysis of the helmet of salvation, goes further to describe it as more of a symbolic piece of the soldier's uniform. As a Christian, the helmet symbolizes our confident belief in the process of salvation. The guarding of our heads is in fact, the protection of our minds so doubt cannot penetrate. This explanation of the importance of our mental state proved true as I began to go through things in my life; I learned to process of protecting my head and therefore the importance of guarding my mental.

I loved watching Dumb and Dumber many years after developing a love for Jim Carey in his Ace Ventura role. I loved the freedom of his comedy and his piano key-sized teeth. I took to Dumb and Dumber because it seemed to be filled with idiocy much like things I witnessed each day working with "adults." I found myself laughing uncontrollably at the two friends who just couldn't seem to make sense of the most simplistic things in life. One part I thought to be hilarious involved Harry being used by the FBI to lure an unsuspecting villain into the arms of the law. During the dramatic exchange involving a gun, Harry was asked," What if they shot you in the face." Harry seemed to ponder this possibility with great concern for his life only to find it was a risk the FBI was willing to take. For that brief moment, Harry realized just how close he had come to being killed all because he had not guarded his head, however, the fact the risk factors had never been shared which gave him a false sense of security.

This simple omission of vital information and an unrealistic belief that he could put his trust in a stranger presents a completely different perspective.

Harry and Lloyd, the two main characters in the movie, had always been presented as everyday idiots often settling for the bottom of the barrel. When they lucked up on money and the chance for love, they became slaves to an ideal which convinced them they could be normal and live a normal life. Although their lack of common sense seemed to puzzle most onlookers, for most of the movie, they seemed none the wiser. It was not until the two of them were presented with what seemed like a better opportunity, they decided their lives were no longer good enough.

Similar to Lloyd and Harry, most women I have met over the years have encountered men with the same "dumb" mentality. For some strange reason, someone on the freak train had sold each man a dream of a better life. Many of the men in our lives found themselves surrounded by beautiful, confident and successful women yet seemed be holding out for the bigger, better deal.

Many women were bred to hate the "freak train." When I first heard the term, I was extremely interested to learn more details as it related to this lewd locomotive. I am embarrassed to say, the first time I heard anyone make mention of it was on the popular sitcom, Martin. In the episode, Pam and Gina struggled to understand why men were so reluctant to enter into a commitment with a woman. Similar to these women, my girlfriends and I seemed to have almost identical conversations trying desperately to figure out what we were doing wrong when it came to the men we were dating. What in the world was going on in their mental?

I can recall the story of my friend, Lauren, who broke down unexpectedly over our Sunday brunch just as the drinks were being placed on the table. We hadn't been discussing anything emotionally jarring so her reaction to a simple mention of the new Mac fall colors threw us all for a loop. In true "girlfriend" fashion, we allowed her to weep a bit realizing her dam had finally broke and for her to openly display her vulnerability in front of a restaurant filled with strangers was a necessary release. About a minute into her release, she was finally prompted to share the origin of her hurt. Of course, none of us were surprised to hear her tears were centered on her boyfriend, Jay.

Now, each of us had been a little skittish of her relationship with Jay. He was a pretty cool dude but not one we figured to be the "boyfriend" type. He was a free-spirit who loved to pick up and go at a moment's notice without having to consider the needs of a significant other. Mentally, he did not seem a proper fit for our friend but we remained cautious not to overstep our bounds. Now, Lauren, on the other hand, melted at the thought of matrimony and it was no question what she wanted for her life. In our minds, knowing both of them, the relationship would hit some major snags if it would work out at all. However, we learned to mind our own business and to allow adults to do whatever they wanted to do without the opinions and suggestions of each of us.

On this particular day, we discovered our fears were now realized as Jay had finally decided to drop the "act" where he forced himself to be something he wasn't. He picked up and left for a football game in New York with his college fraternity brothers. Now, this would not have been a problem except he had not discussed it with Lauren and now was not responding to text messages or phone calls. Doing our best to play the devil's advocate, one of the ladies at the table asked, "Are you sure he is okay? Maybe something happened to him." Each of us lit up thinking the best thing for him was if he was somewhere in the hospital. If he had been in some freak accident, we could work to calm her fears and address the concerns with a more logical explanation.

However, almost immediately, she whipped out her cellphone sharing recent Instagram posts with Jay plastered all over each one. He was sporting the biggest smile in each picture where he stood amidst his fraternity brothers and various women in tight leggings and puff jackets. Some of the ladies were throwing up their own Greek sorority symbols which we could easily explain away as a college reunion-type trip. However, as we continued to scroll, the same face continued to photo bomb each one of Jay's images. In the earlier images, the face was a mere insignificant person peeking in at the time of the flash. Several pictures later, the same face was now a full body shot nestled in between Jay's body and his arm. The most recent picture was the same body having a cocktail with Jay and his friends. From the look of things, this unidentified figure was ensuring Jay had a great time on his impromptu trip.

As we looked into Lauren's eyes, we realized she needed us to assure her nothing was going on with Jay and the unfamiliar woman but none of us wanted to put our stamp on the situation. The catch 22 as her friends was to determine if we should be honest or thoughtful. If honesty was our selection, we would have to outline each one of the relationship codes he had violated which would no doubt end their relationship. If we elected to be thoughtful, we would advise her to wait until he returned and give him a chance to explain the situation. Now, we did what any group of previous scorned women would do, we advised her to act a fool...man, why did we do that?

A week later, we helped her move her things out of his townhouse in downtown Atlanta after learning their confrontation about the situation had resulted in a few broken items and a bunch of words that could not be taken back. We wondered if we had done the right thing. Realizing she would be starting over at 34, it wasn't clear if we had done more harm than good. After moving all of her things back into her parent's house, we sat around the living room with bottles and bottles of wine and any other spirits we could find. Our reflective period sounded much like the conversation between Gina and Pam on the hit show, Martin. Each of us questioned why men would pretend to want something they knew they were not ready for. We wondered what we were doing wrong by sharing our desires from the onset. Everyone questioned if we were just spinning our wheels realizing the "side chick" era has us all losing at the end of the day. Mentally, we had been bruised and our brains were about to explode all over one another.

One of the younger girls in our crew shed light on a mistake those of us five to seven years her senior had missed. She said, "instead of guarding your heart, you need to be guarding your head."

Man.

We hadn't even thought of that! For so many years, we had looked at women like Jasmine Guy in Harlem Nights as a fictitious creature who had managed to do the impossible. She had connected with Eddie Murphy weeks prior to their sexual encounter and decided she would have him in the only way she wanted; between the sheets. He did his best to impress her with flowers, kisses on the hand and flattery however, she was not moved by any of his gestures. In his conversations, he was intrigued by her beauty and wanted to test her boundaries justifying his pursuit by saying, "Suga, she came onto me."

Finally, she invited him over to her home with very little conversation and no expression of expectations. Once they were finished participating in the act she had been looking for the entire time, she commenced to do what she had intended which, unfortunately in this case, was to kill him using a dainty gun tucked under her silk pillows. It was clear his feelings were hurt to see she was actually prepared to execute her plan which he had foiled as he stashed his own concealed weapon under the same silk pillow despite the connection he felt they had shared. As he retaliated by shooting her after clarifying her intent, one thing was clear, "Dominique Lareaux" had done something most women were not equipped to do; she had successfully guarded her head although, sadly, he blew it off with his gun.

Now, back to the whole concept of a "freak train." The freak train is symbolic of the man's mentality that there is always something better waiting around the corner. The reasons are best summed up by an article written by an anonymous source which states the top four reasons a man does not want to commit as:

1. Labels
2. Past Hurts
3. Physical Hang Ups
4. Men are dogs.

Men are frightened by labels. As long as they are not labeled as your husband, fiancé, boyfriend or even your lover, they are comfortable with whatever relationship you have fostered. Now, is this because they don't want to be loved or want to love? I don't think so. According to the article, men are afraid of labels because with labels come expectations. When we purchase meals at the grocery store with labels glued around the can, we expect the contents on the inside to match the description on the outside. Such is true for a relationship label. If a man is your boyfriend, he cannot redeem his ticket on the "freak train" because it will hurt our feelings and ruin the relationship. They can't have a random one-night-stand after a fun night at the bar because we won't be happy about it. Now, the funny thing is, they might not even have intentions of engaging in such behavior but with the label, they feel restricted should the opportunity present itself and, much like caged beasts, the thought of confinement is far worse than the actual process of restraint.

Relationships seem to work the best for men and women when there is no real accountability. In a situation where one of the parties does not embrace the title, the absence of accountability adds to the comfortability. For the one in the relationship with the hope of creating a cake from mud pies, they are sure to find labels to be their worst enemy. When a man feels he has a leash around his neck tugging him down the aisle, he is likely to resist it kicking and screaming. In many respects, the ideal of a label is much like that leash forcing a man into a situation he is not sure he is ready for. As long as a woman is willing to forego the process of illustrating a label, one would argue she stands a greater chance of keeping her man...wait, is that another label? Man, that mental is serious!

Men are from Mars, Women are from Venus. No, I don't know if that is true, but one thing is for sure, we don't handle breakups the same way. For women, breakups are almost as common as the changing fashion trends. In a woman's lifetime, it is not uncommon for her to have her heart broken multiple times and occasionally, by the same man. The expectation of a woman is to withstand each breakup and continue to get back on the saddle. Although each time a piece of her is ripped from her soul, she is forbidden to carry any of her past hurts into the next relationship or she runs the risk of being labeled by the affectionate name made popular by Erykah Badu, "Bag Lady."

In the chart topping song, Badu croons her advice to emotionally scarred women who would find themselves looking for love again. In her lyrics, she cautioned women to ditch their emotional baggage because most men would not stick around for her to get all of her bags off of the baggage claim turnstile.

> *Bag lady you gone hurt your back*
> *Dragging all them bags like that*
> *I guess nobody ever told you*
> *All you must hold onto, is you, is you, is you*
> *One day all them bags gon' get in your way*

Now, on the other hand, men and their ability to survive a breakup looks quite different. On the other side of the spectrum, a heartbroken man experiences a plethora of emotions as he attempts to cope with the failure of a relationship. Many men rest on the feeling of anger which prompts them to question why they even tried to enter into relationship in the first place. Others cry for a moment and then get angry at themselves for allowing a woman to reduce them to tears. Other men fake a passive approach where they act like they never cared in the first place and then they get angry when they have to put on the faux face for their friends. In fact, the emotional roller coaster of a lost love for men circles back to anger and that feeling is one they seek to avoid at all cost as they move on. In other words, they put some muscles on their mental.

A woman who finds herself dating a man who refuses to share his true emotions, a man who makes her guess what he is thinking, a man who disappears from the relationship when things seem to be going well or a man who will only give the physical part of himself is most likely a man who has been hurt in a relationship. The only problem is, a woman will find herself hard pressed to identify these men before her emotions are involved. These men, unfortunately, want the comforts of a secure relationship where the woman is performing wifely duties only to find she would not receive a return on her investment. What a world it would be if these men would have a flashing sign on their foreheads to let us know who they really are when it comes to their availability.

You think your man likes the small dimple in your left butt cheek? Did he tell you it looked like your booty was always smiling at him? Did you believe him? Shame on you. Want to find out what he really thinks about it? Ask him to make a commitment and he will use any and everything he can think of as a justifiable reason not to put the proverbial ring on it. Now, what is funny is, a woman will overlook a man's pot belly, his financial status and even those frequent pairs of underwear with the chocolate remnants in them all to accept him for who he is. A woman can change herself in two hundred different versions to appeal to her man's visual cravings only to find that small cut behind her left ear still haunts him because it reminds him of when he had to get his ears cleaned out as a child. A woman will find herself with a look of sheer confusion on her face listening to him tell the vivid details of the accident and why it is the reason he can't tell her she in the "one." Basically, the man puts a mask on his mental.

The older we get, the more it seems that men demand perfection from us but expect us to be patient and understanding as they work on their own areas of deficiency. Perhaps worse than that is the man who has been hoisted to a pedestal where the women in his life have persuaded him to believe he is perfect; God's gift to a woman. That man, charming as he may be due to his overabundance of self-confidence, will never work on a relationship because he will always feel the other person is the problem. When women encounter either one of these men, the outcome for the hopeful, doting bride seems impossible as she will never be enough to keep him but will have enough imperfections for him to let her go.

Simply put, men run from relationships because they are dogs. The end. Harsh? Yes. True in most cases? Yes. Mentally draining? Absolutely!

In the grand scheme of things, a guarded head gives protection to thoughts. The Bible confirms that as a man thinks, so is he. This means we control ourselves by the thoughts we conjure. Whether it is a relationship with a significant other or a relationship with ourselves, we have an obligation to protect the head which allows love into the heart.

Thoughts of hurt creates an unstable foundation for a relationship. Thoughts of self-loathing creates for a relationship filled with presumed infidelity. Thoughts of happily ever after can create a relationship filled with expectations never meant to be met. If we protect our head and free our minds, the rest will, indeed, follow.

chapter 7

"Share Your Testimony"

"It is vital for us to create a space and place where our life's story can be shared. Sometimes it feels good to see you aren't the only one to go through struggles." - C. Frazier

Chapter Seven
Share your testimony

We've been called to share Jesus with the lost and give our testimonies anytime we have the opportunity to tell another person of our hope. We've been called to pray. We've been called to disciple others, teaching God's Word and ways. We've been called to resist the devil as Christ did, with the spoken Word of God. We've even been called to speak to some mountains and tell them to move!
— **Beth Moore**

Submitted to Facebook on November 20, 2013--So, this morning I examined the things going on around me and evaluated the conversations I have been having with those close to me. It became clear to me that the things I have encountered have not just been for my growth, but so that I could give sound advice to those around me. I find myself reflecting on times when I thought I wouldn't make it and realizing that I came out of my own proverbial wilderness with war wounds, but with stronger faith as well. I can now thank God for the "trial by fire" because I am one of the lucky ones; one of the ones that lived to tell my story. I am one that can stand firm and proclaim that God is bigger than ANY circumstance in your life. He is able to provide all of your needs and to direct you if you trust. My friends are going through some things, but I am so glad that we all know that same God. It is He that sustained me, and He that will prove Himself mighty for them! Great morning!

Black, helium-filled balloons wrapped themselves around patio furniture on Friday evening in the heart of Atlanta's Buckhead strip. Thirty-six ladies dressed in sexy, tight and short dresses gathered over dinner and wine for the purpose of celebrating my upcoming book release. The smell of various perfumes and pheromones decorated the air with femininity and the stage had been perfectly set for a night of "girl talk."

During the big reveal of the book's title and possible book covers, a rich discussion began without real intention. During that time, the "cookie jar" became a topic of discussion as I began to share my decision to practice abstinence. As the ladies listened to my transparent explanation of my decision, I realized through their approving nods I had released my testimony into the atmosphere and it was being absorbed. I crawled deeper and deeper into my monologue allowing the words to free me from my emotional seclusion brought on by my need to hide from the judgmental eyes of others. With each recollection of past hurts shared with my table of beauties, I realized I had had been given a chance to share the intimate parts of my testimony with ears ready to hear.

Perhaps one of the best and worst inventions in the world was Facebook. Although it was an ingenious creation initially created for college students to connect, the door was opened for everyone to take part in the flood of familiarization. Strangers began to pose as friends based on their access to the intimate movements of those on the other end of the social media profiles. It was almost as if the need to chronicle every movement in everyone's life took the place of personal conversations and face to face meetings.

In addition to being an outlet for people to share their world with many strangers whom they would see in crowded rooms and still not exchange pleasantries, social media outlets such as Facebook and Instagram quickly became a place for each of us to come clean and wait for the posts of approvals through Likes and Shares to give us the validation each of us needed but would never admit. What each of us seemed to negate was the reality that each of us was telling pieces of our own testimony each day and possibly saving someone's life.

"I am so embarrassed about my life that I can barely look at myself in the mirror," I shared with my mother one day. I realized that I no longer cared what people said about me because I had become my own, personal judge and jury. I had done so much I perceived as "wrong" in my life that I was ashamed to even stare into my own eyes for they now held so much pain and inner turmoil. I couldn't bear to be reminded of it anymore. At only 32 years old, I had deemed myself one of the most horrible individuals to walk the Earth. I had given up. So, during that period of time, I avoided all mirrors; I often dressed in my bedroom away from any possibility of catching my own image in any reflective mirror or window.

I struggled with putting my testimony to paper for many years. My mom often encouraged me to face some of my demons and to release them into the atmosphere; she thought it would be therapeutic for me but I was too busy trying to forget some of my past indiscretions. So, to put them to paper meant they would be forever recorded and therefore given life over and over again. I wasn't sure that I ever wanted to face that person ever again once I had rid myself of her. I was sure that I wanted to bury her in the deepest darkest hole and hope that she would disappear into an unknown abyss never to be seen or heard from again. For many years, I wasn't ready to be honest and accept that fact that I had to be that horrible person to move toward the woman God intended for me to become....until today.

My story is one that revealed seven different women with many different emotions all wrapped up into one vessel that would be used to show forth God's glory. I never imagined when I raised my hands to God in total surrender to His will and His way, it was going to be serving as a living sacrifice. God never said He was going to give me a testimony without giving me tests. Many of these tests found me in a dark, dank wood with only God to be the light in my valley. It is my hope and prayer that my desire for freedom and my journey from my wilderness to my worship will inspire others to fight their way through their own wilderness experience.

Each testimony is written with a pen of promise and highlighted in hope. Each page a prompting of promotion and each chapter a conundrum of chaos used to form our experiences. It is vital for us to create a space and place where our life's story can be shared. Sometimes it feels good to see you aren't the only one to go through struggles. Sometimes is it healthy to know you can make it. Sometimes it is therapeutic to believe all things will line up perfectly for your life even if it never happens. Sometimes...

family

chapter 8

"Family is Everything?"

"Although I didn't like the idea of the violence that accompanied battle of the families, I loved the idea of having people with you to support you even when you were wrong. There is just something about taking on the world when you have a strong team beside you." - C. Frazier

Chapter Eight
Family is everything?

> The family is the cornerstone of our society. More than any other force it shapes the attitude, the hopes, the ambitions, and the values of the child. And when the family collapses it is the children that are usually damaged. When it happens on a massive scale the community itself is crippled. So, unless we work to strengthen the family, to create conditions under which most parents will stay together, all the rest — schools, playgrounds, and public assistance, and private concern — will never be enough.
> **-Lyndon Baines Johnson**

Can one live a full and productive life without family? Is it possible to wander this world separate and attached from those who share your bloodline? If this is possible, could a life be meaningful and purposeful without such influence? Many would blame the issues of the world on the lack of parental influence or lack of social interaction but when it's all said and done, is it realistic of us to believe one must belong to a tribe to be relevant?

In many indigenous countries, belonging to a tribe was necessary for survival. As a norm, tribal members would hunt together, fight other tribes together and determine the lineage would remain pure as defined by tribal regulations. The harshest punishment during those times was to be exiled from the tribe because it meant one could be subjected to harm and even starvation. If such practices were prevalent in American culture, it would be justified to believe family is required, but in a society leaning towards individualism, that need no longer seems to exist.

Perhaps one of the most timeless stories demonstrating the influence of the family is found within the various scenes in "Romeo and Juliet" where the Montagues and the Capulets collided on the stage all in the name of defending the honor of their family name. When it was all said and done, poor Romeo and Juliet found themselves choosing death over their family allegiance. One thing was evident in the physical interactions between the two families; whether right, wrong or indifferent, the families were willing to die for one another. They were willing to make the ultimate sacrifice in the name of family.

When I was growing up, there was one family of siblings you didn't dare step to. Oddly enough, their last name was Bruiser and each one of them lived up to their name. It was understood if you got into a fight with one, it was almost as if they all had a spider-sense because the others would swoop in and knock you on your butt before you even realized what had happened. No one from the clan ever asked for the details of the disagreement, they simply entered swinging. The only relevant information was the fact their family needed them and they were obligated to show up.

Perhaps the worst one of all was the youngest girl, Myla, who had all the mouth in the world. At only six years old, she was known to curse people out with words she must have learned from sitting in on heated games of spades because her ability to put them into her verbal lashings was poetic. She had a gift for combining expletives in such a clever way even the adults would marvel at her talent. Now, the child could barely read or write, but that never seemed to stop her from sharing what she thought of a situation and where she wanted you to get off. It was clear she feared no one because she had no problem going up against anyone. It was also understood her sisters and brothers would always be in the vicinity and that assurance added confidence to her swag.

The one day family probably meant the most to the Bruisers was the day Medgar, Myla's older brother, had encountered a boy bigger and badder than him during his gym class. The boy had fattened his lip for calling his mom a horrible name neither of them probably knew the meaning of, but it was said in such a way, Medgar knew he should be offended. Medgar realized in that moment what it felt like to be without his brothers and sisters and did his best to hold his own with his aggressor. Despite his best attempts, the altercation ended with Medgar on his back and his body cringing under the weight of the victor who had him pinned until the gym coach instructed them to break it up. Medgar was furious more than embarrassed and as the other students cautioned his new enemy about the probability of having to fight again after school once the rest of the Bruiser clan learned of the fight, the young man stood tall and said, "I ain't scared."

Little did any of us know but the confidence displayed was because the young man knew he had a secret weapon of his own. His last name was Prince and he and his family had just moved to our town from New York. Along with him, he brought two older brothers and they had joined their cousins who all matriculated through the school sooner or later. This promised to be a showdown for the ages as both sides had one thing going for them; family. Needless to say, when the Bruiser family assembled themselves in the bus lane and all the students who had purchased their ticket to the big fight positioned themselves within view of the unfolding debauchery, the crowd finally steadied itself and everyone secured their bets.

As the Prince family began to reveal themselves, one thing was clear, neither side had an advantage and it was going to come down to which family wanted to preserve their family's good name. After the dust cleared and the school staff worked hard to pull all of the kids apart, each participant retreated to check on one another. When all was calm, they had done their families proud by sticking up for one another.

I thought a lot about that fight for weeks to come knowing full well I would have never been able to survive such an ordeal. In my case, my sisters were older than me and I never had one of them at my school during any of the years I found myself rushing to class to beat the bell. I had moved away from my hometown so I never had cousins or family friends with me, either. My reality was simple; if I ever got into a fight, I would be on my own. When the fight between the Prince and Bruiser families happened, the reviews from the critics was the most interesting part of the entire ordeal.

Medgar was criticized the most for being a chicken who had to get his brothers and sisters to fight for him after he had gotten his butt kicked one on one. For Medgar, this was the worst thing that could have happened because his weakness had been exposed. He challenged his opponent to a rematch but the damage to his reputation had already been done. As his days rolled on, he didn't have as much mouth as baby sister, but he had a lot of confidence that he had a team of people who would be there to protect his yellow behind if he needed it.

I, on the other hand, knowing I did not have such backing, learned not to go looking for conflict because being alone in any situation did not promise a favorable outcome. Although I didn't like the idea of the violence that accompanied the battle of the families, I loved the idea of having people with you to support you even when you were wrong; there is just something about taking on the world when you have a strong team beside you.

When asked if family is everything to me, I can say it is. When asked, what defines a family, that connotation is when my entire outlook differs from those who have what is labeled at the "traditional family." Yes, I was born to a married mother and father who brought two additional children into the world. Yes, we lived under the same roof, ate the same food and enjoyed the same memories as a family unit. As I grew up, I learned to include additional people in my definition of family which only made me feel even safer and secure than before.

My definition of family is an ever-changing and ever-evolving group of people serving the purpose of teaching, loving and motivating one to be their best self. With such a definition, my family grew to include my grandparents, aunts, cousins, teachers, church members, friends, sorority sisters and even students who all contributed to teaching me the harsh lessons in life. Much like Martin Lawrence in the comedic movie, "Welcome Home Roscoe Jenkins," I, too, learned to recreate myself for the purposes of escaping many of the unfortunate memories from my childhood. I threw myself into things designed to build me up as an important contributor to the fabric of this world to escape all of the times I was made to feel disposable. However, there were many people...family...who reminded me of who I was and the history of those who had been the architects of our family structure. Funny thing is, although many of them had gone on to glory long before I was born to this world, I always felt a connection to their expectation of me as a part of our lineage. It was something about knowing I had a charge to keep that moved me forward in discouraging times.

Family is not a thing to be taken for granted. Those honored enough to have a connection to those who share their strands of DNA often fail to realize the gift that comes with sharing your world with family. Usually, those people find themselves fighting and arguing over the most trivial things often due to the fact they know their family members will always be there to support them. Everyone else longs for that connection and searches for it in others. So, what do we do to preserve the family in a day and time when it is often so dysfunctional and fragmented? If we say the family structure, even if now unconventional in its makeup, is vital to the fabric of our society, how do we bring it back to a position of importance?

As a professional educator, I have seen many effects of the family on our children. Those who have what we consider to be the "traditional family" with the two working parents, the flourishing children and the dog playing around in the yard of their ranch-style home seem to fare well in today's school system. These children seem to become readers at a young age and have a different respect for the opportunities afforded by education.

On the other side of the spectrum, those who are being raised by mothers who work tirelessly and who share beds with siblings who don't share the totality of their blood line appear to have so many other things on their minds, they could care less about what we are teaching each day. Some of these children see education as pointless while others in their same situation see it as their only ticket to a new and better life. These children are the ones I have seen vomit on standardized tests or even break down in a panic attack knowing the severity of their failure.

What do we do when the family is the cause and not the cure? If we are to believe in the family again, we have to believe in our individual roles as a part of our family's puzzle. If we all do not play an active role in the productivity of the family, they will continue to do more harm than good. Either way, the need for family is ever present and a missing piece to any life's puzzle. Until we acknowledge its potential impact, we will all remain in pieces like our good friend, Humpty.

chapter 9

"My Parents Did Their Best"

"Many of the things I learned from my parents might seem dated but I have found many of those fundamental lessons I learned have set me apart from my colleagues. The demonstrations of respect for others has set me above many of our counterparts both in social and professional arenas. Even though my daughter is often teased for our practices, she continues to reply to adults with the proper, "yes, ma'am," or "no, sir." She does this, not as a sign of submission or some "slave mentality," but as an awareness that until you have your own or own your own, you will have to respect hierarchy."- C. Frazier

Chapter Nine
My Parents Did Their Best

Parents can only give good advice or put them on the right paths, but the final forming of a person's character lies in their own hands.
— **Anne Frank**

Rows and rows of pages, stacks and stacks of theory, aisles and aisles of beliefs stood before me one Sunday afternoon. I searched diligently through card catalogs, search engines and scholarly articles for the proper references and each time it seemed as if I had found the perfect one, it was always missing something. Minute after minute, hour after hour, nothing seemed to connect the dots perfectly showing there was no straight way to get from point A to point B. I solicited the assistance of everyone from the cashier to the stock team to the manager and no one could help me find what I was looking for. I was baffled. Why was it so hard to find a book explaining to us how to be the best parent possible?

I received many gifts during my pregnancy. Some were practical, some were clearly ones re-gifted by those in a rush to attend one of my two planned showers. I remember getting several clothes hampers and a confusing thing called a "Diaper Genie" which, to date, I have not been able to use. Sorting through each token, I realized a lot would be necessary to care for this one, little bundle of skin I was to bring home in a few weeks. Although I received many things, I noticed I received two copies of what was to be the new mother's bible, "What to Expect When You Are Expecting." As I flipped through the pages, I learned what had become common knowledge to most women across borders and boundaries of the physical changes I would undergo as my body worked to accommodate the development of my little jumping bean identified on my sonogram.

The book went from trimester to trimester and from month to month hoping to provide insight into this new and unfamiliar experience for both me and the life growing inside. The book told of the labor process and even the few months after the baby was tucked safely at home in their new habitat. What I didn't notice, however, were any chapters about what to expect when they were teens or even young adults. It was almost as if we would be left to our own devices as if parenting suddenly dropped off a cliff. One thing was clear, I would have to do the best I could with what I had.

My mom was the worst hairstylist in the world. Bless her heart. Her process made no sense to any rational person in the world but no one could question her method. Up until the age of 11, my mother refused to allow me to go to a beauty salon or to get a perm. Now, let's be clear, there is nothing "good" about my hair. I am black on both sides of my family and my hair was clearly passed down from generation to generation leaving me to believe I was a true descendant of the most authentic African tribe. When water would hit my hair, it would immediately soak up all the moisture into tight tufts. If one did not move quickly, it would be a painstaking process to loosen my curls enough to get through them. My mother knew this. There was no secret about it. However, for some reason, she continued to wash my hair on Saturday night, plat it, grease it with way too much grease and send me to bed. Overnight, my hair would air dry and prep itself for the next part of the process which would be the equivalent of Chinese water torture.

Early Sunday morning, my mother would wake me up SUPER early and place me in the torture chamber between her legs. The stove would already be heated and the metal comb would be resting on a plate removed from daily usage allowed to only serve as a cooling rack for the pressing comb. There was always one more item to finish off the set up; she would always have a tub of Country Crock on the counter. Now, why she would need margarine was always an enigma but it wasn't until the first time the melted grease hit the tip top of my ear did I learn the importance of keeping it on hand. As soon as I jumped from the initial contact, my mother would crack the seal the dip her finger in the cool, creamy product and apply it to my charred skin. After she had slathered it on my injury, she would get back to work. Although the butter only cooked itself on my ear because it trapped the heat in place, I had to allow it to sizzle until the skin died a million deaths. In her mind, she had administered the top of the line treatment to my ailment.

The stage for my turn on the gallows had been set. There was no judge, no jury; my fate had been decided. My mom positioned me and it was understood I'd better not move if I didn't want to nurse a third degree burn to my ears and neck. As she unraveled each braid, I winched each time I realized she would be allowing this fiery iron to run through my locks. Many times, I would hear the frying of the grease but I had to sit quietly for it was part of the process. My dad would walk by and see the tears in my eyes brought on each time the small-toothed comb would scream its way through each section. I knew he felt sorry for me but there was nothing he could do as this was the process. I remember being upset with him for not helping me in some sort of way but I figured, he didn't want to find himself in our seat.

After she was done with each section, the torture was not over. She would then take a bristle brush and allow it to scrape my brain's sulcus over and over again stamping the experience as my first introduction to the phrase "beauty is pain." In that moment, I had thoughts of taking the sharpest object I could find and digging it into my mom's ear canal to dig out her eardrum so she could understand how I was feeling. It reminded me of the scene in "Throw Mama From the Train," when Owen had finally had enough of his mother's overwhelming demands which often caused him to forego his own plans to fulfill her needs. At that moment, a firmly pressed pair of kitchen shears to her ear seemed justified.

After the brushing came the parting. Lord, help me, the parting. She would take the tip of the rat tail comb and draw a line over and over from ear to ear until both corners seemed to meet at the same spot. It was almost as if she was cross-eyed how many times she continued to work to perfect her lines and at that point, I could care less if she cork screwed each section of my hair and topped each one with baby doll bows of fluorescent colors. I just wanted it to be over. After she found the perfect part, she would take three pink, sponge rollers and place them across the front of my hair to make my bang. I guess she was tired at that point because she would just pull the rest of my hair into a ponytail and put one roller at the end. Poof! Her masterpiece was complete.

My mom had never been to cosmetology school, never sat through a seminar instructing her on the proper technique to care for natural hair. She had never learned about proper temperatures to use on hair nor ways to moisturize different hair textures. Her method was simple; do what you have learned from your mother or watching others and her rationale was practical; don't let your children leave the house looking any type of way.

She might not have possessed the right tools to build the house, but she had the willingness to learn the process. One thing was for sure, no matter how many hours she had to be on her feet, she would not rest until we all looked ready for the world.

As a mother, I learned not to fry my daughter's hair thanks to our technological advances but had these mediums not existed, my daughter would have found herself in the same, identical torture chamber. It's funny how it goes with parenting; we can only share with our children what we know and, Gods-willing, what we know is what's best for our offspring.

Although many things I have tried over the years as new, cutting edge parenting techniques, I have found myself reverting back to good 'ol faithful. Now, don't get me wrong, I no longer put the hot comb on the stove but I have an electric version of the same. For some reason, nothing else seems to work. Many of the things I learned from my parents might seem dated but I have found many of those fundamental lessons I learned have set me apart from my colleagues. The demonstrations of respect for others has set me above many of our counterparts both in social and professional arenas. Even though my daughter is often teased for our practices, she continues to reply to adults with the proper, "yes, ma'am," or "no, sir." She does this, not as a sign of submission or some "slave mentality," but as an awareness that until you have your own or own your own, you will have to respect hierarchy.

One failed lesson that taught me the most as a parent came when my daughter had her first school project due. I read the instructions over and over to myself to make sure I understood what the teacher wanted me to demonstrate. I toiled day and night over the materials I would need to do my best work. I put my daughter to bed early several nights in a row so I could have enough time to work on my assignment. Each day, I worked my plan and when it was time to put my final stamp on it, I called my daughter to the room asked her to put her name in the corner. She did as she was told and I wrapped the project in a trash bag to make sure my work didn't get damaged on her transport to school the next morning. When it was time for bus to come, I just couldn't trust the bumping of the school bus not to ruin my hard work so I piled my daughter into my car and drove her to the front doors of the school. I parked at the front door, turned on my hazard lights and carried my project through the doors. I asked the receptionist if my daughter's teacher had arrived yet and she informed me she had not checked in yet. I began to panic as I realized I would have to trust my daughter to turn in my work. I instructed my daughter to sit very still in the cafeteria and to make sure the project made it safely to class. I left for work proud of the job I had done and stuck my chest out knowing I was now a contender for Mother of the Year.

At about 2:20, I got the email no parent wants to receive:

Dear Ms. Frazier,

Thank you so much for being such an involved parent in your daughter's life. It is truly a daunting task to bridge the gap between home and school and you are a true demonstration of the support our students need from home if they are going to be productive citizens. Your child's project was submitted today and I must say, it was one of the best I have ever seen in all my years as an educator. While the work clearly exceeds the standard, I expect nothing less when the majority of the work submitted was so heavily influenced by the parent. Imagine the difficulty your daughter had today trying to expound upon the work she submitted knowing little to nothing about the process involved to arrive at the final product. She was embarrassed and ultimately learned nothing from this project which was designed to extend her understanding. I am going to give her an additional week to re-submit this assignment and I am asking whether it is right, wrong or indifferent, you allow her to discover learning through her eyes. Please assist her by helping her to obtain the supplies she will need but I would love to see what she will construct. Thank you for all you do and will continue to do to support your daughter's learning.

Sincerely,

Ms. Jones-Franks

I was mortified. My first reaction was to be insulted. How dare she imply I had not allowed my daughter to have input in my project? Before I hit "send" on my completely obnoxious reply, proofreading taught me one thing; one should always read a reply from the perspective of the recipient. In this case, although my intentions were to make sure my daughter earned an A and could see how important education was to me,

I had missed the parental piece. It was my job to allow her to do her best and support her during that process. My job was to allow her to take the lead and trail behind her to make sure she made it safely to her destination. Although my daughter never complained, much like I hadn't during my hair sessions, I realized I had a lot to learn as a parent and much of it would be trial and error.

The lesson in this is that no matter what we do as parents, we might miss the mark despite the fact our intent is to provide our children with our best interpretation of what we deem right for their lives. Our comprehension might require further explanation but we never stop writing that book because the lessons inside will be priceless. Whether it involves the styling of their hair or the progression of their educational pursuits, one thing is for certain, there has never been a manual written to fit the needs of each child. The reality is, many parents are raised along with their children. Much like the children are learning how to be infants, babies, toddlers, children, teens, young adults and adults, parents are learning how to be something they have never been. Because I had never been a parent before, I had to learn to possess those qualities much like I had learned to be an adult. My only concern remained whether or not I would be a good parent and if my life lessons would afford me the stories I would need to tell to shape my daughter's future.

What's learned? I have learned to give the best I have at all times. I trust that with God, it will always be enough. I learned to trust my daughter's process. Even in her shortcomings will be her victories. I learned so stand as a support and to allow the lessons I had imparted to take root. She could fail, but my God, she could CONQUER!

chapter 10

"Learn to Let Things Go"

"The problem with most of us who elect to hold onto things in our lives is the fear of vulnerability. When you enter into the phase of your life when you begin to understand the importance of revelation, you have to be one with the fact that you will have to endure some embarrassment if you are going to ever be healed. You won't be able to conceal your pain from the world if God intends for you to be used to heal others in the process." - **C. Frazier**

Chapter Ten
Learn to let things go

To let go is to release the images and emotions, the grudges and fears, the clingings and disappointments of the past that bind our spirit.
-Jack Kornfield

I loved blueberry Blow Pops when I was growing up. Prior to the school year ending, local business owners would open the snow cone stands and begin advertising their new flavors. The summer before my 6th grade year, the one within walking distance of my house unveiled its new line of flavors all focused on recreating each of the Blow Pop flavors. Now, to understand how monumental this was, one must understand what snow cones are why they are the perfect summer treat in the South.

A snow cone is at its best when it begins with the perfect grade of shaved ice. Perfectly shaved ice is soft and powdery with a hint of air tucked between each layer. After an initial layer was set by a skilled snowball-atician (yes, I made that word up), the preparer would pour a sweet-flavored syrup onto the ice and then add more ice on top. This would be repeated until it reached the top of the cup. After that, a plastic cone would be placed over the top and ice would be added. The final application would be added and, if you really wanted to ensure you would have a cavity sooner than later, you could add evaporated milk. Man, that was a PERFECT day all for under $3.00!

Now, with the inclusion of Blow Pop flavors, the stage was set for a deliciously sweet summer of fun! A Blow Pop was best with stuck straight down the center of a big, juicy dill pickle, but to imagine the infusion of such flavors was unimaginable. The mixture of sweet and salty was a delicious treat after a perfectly made snow cone. Summers in Louisiana was the best for it was when the most simplistic things would make your days perfect. For $5.00, one could have a memorable day when nothing else mattered as long as there were snow cones and Blow Pops in abundance.

One normal day as my friends and I made our daily trip to the closest snowball stand located just a few neighborhoods past our own, we discussed the order we would place when we reached our destination. Today, we would be a bit more adventurous and add some new flavors to our summer repertoire. With each step and each passing mailbox, we grew more and more excited about our enjoyment which was getting closer and closer. An outsider would think we were on our way to pick up a million dollars and in our opinion, it was just the same.

Once we placed our elbows on the cold, metal shelving hanging off the mobile home cleverly disguised as a reputable business, our eyes darted back and forth over the menu. We had to make some last minute adjustments to our plan as we noticed certain flavors had been crossed out with a large black marker. Unfortunately, many of the flavors were ones on each of our lists and as we questioned the workers to verify there had not been a clerical error, we were grateful so see many of our second choices in rotation.

With requests entrusted to the pleasure professionals, we began to count our money. Each of us had secretly robbed each of our piggy banks and our parents' junk drawers to fund our habits. I had exactly three dollars and, as I searched my pockets for my additional quarter which would pay for my Blow Pop, I found myself fumbling aimlessly. As my friends paid their tabs and tucked their suckers in their pockets for later, I began to realize I would be at a loss if I didn't have mine for our afternoon excursions.

As I stepped up to the cashier to offer my coins as payment, my friends convened at the end of the lot prepared to make the trip back to our familiar territory. The worker had her back turned to me and the Blow Pop I wanted was dangling in an orange tub within my grab. Without even thinking about the consequences, I quickly grabbed a treat and tucked it in my pocket. In that moment, I didn't know if I was feeling relief or disgust but as I scrambled to decipher between the two emotions, I would enjoy my snow cone. I paid my bill and the cashier thanked us for our business. Her customer service made it even more unfathomable that I had just stolen from them and she was none the wiser.

On the walk back home, the Blow Pop began to bore a hole in my pocket. With each step taking me further and further away from my place of redemption, the small, sweet circle seemed to be getting heavier and heavier in my pocket and in my heart. It seemed small, but for some reason, the magnitude of what I had done made me sick to my stomach.

I watched my friends enjoying our time together but I secretly wondered if they would vote me off our island if they knew I had demonstrated felonious tendencies right under their noses.

When the time presented itself for each of us to reveal our second treat of the day, I was the last one to uncover my deception. The sound of slurping and munching was deafening and, as I began to dodge questions regarding my reluctance to indulge, I felt I was obligated to fake an upset stomach to avoid having to eat my stolen goods. After a long day, my buddies began to go our separate ways prepared to tackle our daily chores before our parents made it home. I, on the other hand, took a detour through the lake and set my direction back to the snowball stand.

My feet seemed to get caught on each crack in the road as I threatened to take a dive toward to gravel. It would have been befitting to earn a bloody knee cap after what I had done but I couldn't be so lucky. I made it to the counter just as the team was wiping down the last few machines. I stood motionless for a few minutes hoping they would not turn around and I would just slip the Blow Pop back into the orange bin where I had found it. Of course, I was not going to get off that easily as the same cashier I had duped earlier that day turned to face me.

She informed me the stand was closed and provided me with their hours of operation. I stood in front of her, shrinking with each breath. I soaked in a few precious particles of H20 and began to spill the beans to the cashier. In the midst of my explanation, I retrieved the Blow Pop from my pocket and offered it to her as a living sacrifice. I continued to apologize all over myself and finally, she leaned out of the window and told me, "Don't worry. Just let it go."

She went on to offer the treat to me in exchange for my honesty but I refused her gesture confident it would not taste the same with a sprinkle of sin on it. Instead, I vowed to return the next day with a quarter to reimburse the business for the sucker I was sure they would not want to resell after it had been in my sweaty pocket all day. She chuckled a bit but agreed to accept my love offering. To this day, Blow Pops have lost their luster...I guess I haven't been able to let it go.

Driving to church one Sunday morning, I recall a popular minister discussing his fall from grace. Like so many men of the cloth before him, he found himself undressing before the world by admitting his indiscretions to a judgmental world. As he addressed each tabloid rumor, each speculation and each accusation, he made sure to share the steps he had taken toward full retribution. He openly admitted taking court-mandated group therapy courses to solidify his cleansing and the reporter kindly allowed him to elaborate on the things he had learned through his process.

There were many nuggets of encouragement I gleaned from his supplication, however, the most profound thing he said was, "God cannot heal what you won't reveal." I almost ran off the road trying to grab my phone to record the phrase so I would not forget it for later review. I even let out a, "Good God," in response to his statement realizing his point would soar over most heads undetected much like a UFO. People would simply pass it off as a play on words, but I immediately reached for the deeper connection he was making between his remedy and his cure. I reached for a direct link to his revelation.

I did not have to go back too far to realize exactly what he meant. I had grown accustomed to hiding a lot of things in my life realizing what it would cost me to reveal the truth. More specifically, I hid a burn I received shooting guns on a spicy date. My date's name was Damon and I met him at a place I will continue to deny I ever stepped face in but he was adorable so it was time well spent. In an effort to impress me and to determine if I was a girlie girl or not, he sent me the address of a local gun range for our first date. Now, I have to admit, I was intrigued and I could not wait to see how he was support me once I revealed I had never shot a gun before.

My firearm immaturity must have been incredibly obvious when I grabbed the biggest gun I saw and asked for a full magazine to unload on an unsuspecting target. Damon laughed and asked me to swap out my street sweeper for a more appropriately-sized handgun which would have tucked nicely into my handbag. We went into the shooting area and began to suit up with ear muffs which, by the way, did nothing to compliment my tight-fitting back V-neck shirt. I was happy I had on combat boots, however, because I was ready to go to war to win this guy's heart.

As he unloaded round after round, I watched his powerful shoulders absorb each recoil and I began to salivate. Clearly, he was a regular with the iron because his aim was almost perfect with each shot. However, in an effort to make me feel good about myself, he commented he was not pleased with his performance and he showered me with confidence that I would be able to hit each target with ease. I chuckled and did my best to toss my hair beneath the oversized ear protectors while secretly wanting him to walk me, slowly, through each second of a shooting tutorial.

True to form, we slowly moved through his tutorial careful not to miss an inch of detail he felt would catapult me to sniper status. I enjoyed feeling his strong hands and allowed them to touch any area he deemed necessary to ensure I would not shoot my eye out. When he was confident I was ready to unload, he stepped away and nodded his permission in my direction. Much like he instructed, I pointed the gun toward the waving sheet of paper with the harmless robber photocopied on its center and squeezed the trigger. Almost immediately, the gun jumped up and punched me in the nose while it scalding, hot shell landed on my left breast which was peeked out of my "V." As the shell settled on my skin, the smell of burning flesh wafted into the room.

My beau moved quickly assessing the damage. In his eyes was a fear which had to be associated with the possibility this would ruin his chances of any "act right" at the end of the night. Once I check my nose for broken bone particles and realized all was well with the world, I assured him he was still a front runner with a flirtatious peck on the cheek. He looked down at my chest and suggested we tend to my injury, however, I put my big girl panties on and assured him it was no big deal. I felt my skin boiling beneath my smile but I didn't want Damon to feel as if his brilliant idea would scar me for life so I elected to hold onto my smile for dear life.

The remainder of the date went on forever as I did everything I could to sneak a peek at my dead skin cells. The burn had already passed the swelling stage and I could see a bubble had formed a layer of puss just beneath the surface. I continued to smile and each time I checked in on my little "ouchie," I provided the smile on demand. Damon was clearly convinced he was hosting the best date night in the world because he continued to drag me from building to building in an effort to expose me to every inch of Atlanta in one night. Finally, I could not hold onto my smile any longer and I decided to come clean. I revealed to him the true depth of my injury knowing it would bring our evening to an abrupt ending. He praised my courage for enduring such pain for hours and apologized continuously that he had not noticed my discomfort.

When it was all said and done, the only way I was going to be able to nurse my wound would be to let go of my powerful act and reveal my pain to my knight. There would be no way to heal myself without revealing the truth so I could finally let it go once and for all. The lesson was clear.

The problem with most of us who elect to hold onto things in our lives is the fear of vulnerability. When you enter into the phase of your life when you begin to understand the importance of revelation, you have to be one with the fact that you will have to endure some embarrassment if you are going to ever be healed. You won't be able to conceal your pain from the world if God intends for you to be used to heal others in the process.

The bible speaks of a man with a withered hand in the book of Luke. In this parable, Jesus agrees to heal the man but the man must first reveal his deformity to all those who will mock and ridicule him. The man had been hiding his imperfection from plain sight for many years because he did not want to be teased for enduring a test of his faith. In this case, however, Jesus wanted to teach us the importance of letting go of our own fears to embrace a true healing in every area of our life. What happened in this case was everyone was able to see the power of our Lord and it forced them to believe in Him all the more.

The same is true for each of us today. We must learn to let go of the things we cling to in life if we are going to be healed and elevated to a new level. Let's open our hands, loosen our grips and be okay with letting go!

chapter 11

"Set the Stage for Others to Win"

"I have not done my part to drive home the proper way to handle things, I realize it will be an ongoing construction site in our lives. I have put my hammer to the nails many times to build what I have considered to be a strong, healthy foundation trying my best to set a good example for my daughter by walking her through the times I have walked away from unhealthy situations. However, at other times, I have been the first one at the microphone and sang my own song spewing venomous poison at those I love all in the name of being "right."- C. Frazier

Chapter Eleven
Set the stage for others to win

Life is not a stage on which we were created to struggle — it's the place where we are daily invited to dance in the spotlight.
– Dr. Shannon Reece

My first and only family reunion is very vague in my memory. Not only was I very young, but it was the only one we ever attended as an immediate family. I remember it being in some country, backwoods area because it took us FOREVER to get there early one Saturday morning. As my father forced us all into one car and drove us to a large gymnasium filled with random people, we remained unbothered by the thought of meeting our relatives. As I looked around at the people all different shades of brown, different sizes in the same blue t-shirts with a big tree pressed on the center, I realized each one of us only had one commonality, the fact we were a part of the Duncan-Jones clan. As a kid, the extent of my obligation was to know my parents' names, my grandparents and who was my link to the family lineage. All in all, other than knowing the basic information, all I had to do was run around with other kids and eat as much as I could knowing my family didn't plan to spend any money on food for the rest of the day.

The details escape me as it seemed like any other day of having a play date with my neighborhood friends until the inevitable fight between my aunts which occurred shortly after the family tree presentation. I recall sitting with my "cousins" on the floor learning how to play jacks when a conversation taking place a few tables over began to grow in volume. Although I couldn't make out the particulars of the conversation, nor did I care, I found the flailing arms to be a bit entertaining as my aunt, Deborah, looked as if she was getting ready to take flight. After a few moments, some of the men began to get involved coaxing the women to calm down and go in different directions, however, other female family members encouraged the interaction to continue allowing the women to finally get things "off their chests." I admit, I was intrigued to see where the conversation would end up and why so many people sat around shaking their heads in judgement.

I had often heard stories of my wild and crazy family members as if we should wear our "take no junk" reputations as a badge of honor. The story I enjoyed the most was of my cousin, Shanda, who seemed to be the one who was determined to carry on our "beat your tail" approach to conflict resolution to the grave. My mother recalled a time when my cousin had been sitting at a red light minding her own business when the light changed to allow her to proceed to her destination. Well, apparently, she was not moving fast enough for the car behind her because the driver laid on her horn prompting Shanda to take her car out of gear. Now, anyone who knows my cousin either through personal interaction or the reputation which preceded her, they know this was a suicidal move on the part of the naïve motorist who had just written a check her butt couldn't cash.

According to my mother, Shanda politely put her car in park, unhooked her seat belt securing her safely in her car, unlocked the car and stepped out onto the pavement. Her large body must have stretched upward for days as she embraced the space she occupied in the world. She turned toward the car behind her and began to approach the driver with a slow walk probably confusing all those who were onlookers. I always imagined the soundtrack for her looming presence to sound something like "In the Air" by Phil Collins as she took in each second as if charging herself like a solar car. I am sure those behind the unfolding scene were doing their best to assess her mental state while praying for the person inside the car. Now this, of course, was not safe behavior for my cousin who could have been facing a weapon inside the other car, but I guess that's what made it all the more badass; the not knowing if eminent danger waited for her only a few short strides away.

The lady inside the car refused to roll down her window when my cousin asked her in a tone dripping with honey to roll it down so she could have a conversation with her. My cousin asked again as the honking behind the two cars began to create a symphony of disdain for the entire, childish event taking place. Some cars began to whisk past the ladies on the opposite side unable to wait around for the outcome. My cousin knocked softly again and added a misleading, "Excuse me, ma'am," to the request which seemed to work because the occupant slowly cranked the window latch with extreme caution. Shanda began to ask the woman seated in the car why she had begun honking her horn at her although she knew full well she was not going to accept any justification the lady would give. As the woman began to explain how she felt my cousin had not been paying attention to the changing of the light and needed some nudging to get going, all Shanda heard in her brain was the woman saying she was an idiot who lacked the intellectual capacity to do something as simple take her foot off a pedal in an automatic drive car. As the woman continued to give her explanation, the one thing she was missing was the apology which might have saved her from what was going to happen next, but it is not certain if that would have worked anyway. Everyone in my family believed my cousin had decided the woman's fate by the time she had put the car in park.

In one sweeping motion, as the woman was in mid-sentence, Shanda reached her large, powerful arms into the car and her hands found themselves gripping the front of the lady's shirt. Before the motorist could seek her own safe escape from the clutches of my cousin who had now taken on the persona of a human pit bull, Shanda had pulled half her body out of the car window. As the story goes, my cousin was not able to get the woman's full body out of the car window because of the safely fastened seatbelt across her lap and chest. The woman screamed relentlessly which brought out good Samaritans who continued to try their best to urge my cousin to let the woman go. However, Shanda had a death grip on the woman and as she continued to verbally chastise the woman who was "playing games" with her, and she had no plans of releasing her hold. Tug after tug, and light change after light change, the blaring lights from a cop car was the only thing to end the altercation. After spending a few hours in jail for rude and disturbing behavior, Shanda contacted my mother to pick her up. While pleading her case with my mother explaining the things which had prompted her behavior, my mother provided one clarifying explanation for her actions; she didn't steal it.

Similar to the story of my cousin, I found myself learning my friends experienced similar struggles in their own families. One of my close friends, Rebecca, was faced with a similar situation where her family elected to handle their disagreements with pointless yelling with no, real resolution. The argument between her aunts stemmed from something as simple as a JC Penny bill her aunt had created using her grandmother's account. Apparently, her aunt had missed some payments and the family Christmas dinner, despite its importance to the foundation of the family, seemed like the appropriate place to address how trifling her aunt had been. As they continued to go back and forth slinging hurtful insults they had held inside for many years, one thing was clear, their toxic ways of communication had been woven into the fibers of their family and it would take each of the other family members taking the time to create an entirely new pattern to cut from for them to change the way it had always been. I found perfect logic to that approach and realized my family would have to go down the same path if we would ever heal hurts of the past.

When I had my daughter, I was faced with the fact she would be exposed to the same behaviors of my "loving" family if I did not set the proper stage for her. Although having a relationship with my family was vitally important to me given the fact I had been detached from most of my family due to arguments and misunderstandings, I didn't want her to take on the same mindset and challenges with communication my family had coined as a family character trait. Now, don't get me wrong, no family is perfect but as long as there is love somewhere in the middle, all gaps can be closed. If anyone pretends their families are perfect, they are sorely misguided as EVERY family has its own challenges. Those challenges build a stronger unit and make us who we are.

I made a tough decision to work very hard to give her something I had never been taught, a proper way to handle anger and disagreements with others. I realized for this to work, I would have to teach it early, and even expose her to other families who seemed to have perfected themselves in that area until the lessons were so deep-rooted, it would stick. I never wanted her to be blind to her roots or to be punished for things she knew not of so I wanted her to have a real understanding of family and why it was so important. I wanted her to learn from all of our mistakes and to be better because of lessons learned and stripes earned.

The first few years of her life, I painted her life with flowers and love teaching her how to handle tough situations with the help of Disney who created a world of vivid colors and fantastic characters. Mops danced around kitchen which were already clean and roses bloomed in the most impossible elements. Mice sang gentle hymns in the morning while fairy godmothers whispered blessings of prosperity each evening. In each of her encounters with Disney and its wide array of characters and their inner and external conflicts, she learned at the end of the two hours of plot development, the universal theme that it all works out in the end. As she began to interact more and more with children outside of our little bubble of bliss, she tried her best to hang on to the things she had been taught often finding herself on the short end of the stick. I would force her to share with others and watch them selfishly refuse to allow her to play with their things. I would watch her find her safe place in solitude electing to play with the one person who understood her willingness to be the ultimate friend; herself. I wondered if I had done the right thing by keeping the feisty, tough, rough, blunt, aggressive influence away from her and if I needed to give her a dose of the dangerous juice that would stop people from taking her kindness for weakness.

I recall occasions when I was a walking, talking contradiction forcing her to be nice to those who were not nice to her, but fussing at her when I felt she was being a "punk" for allowing them to treat her any way they decided would make her inferior to them. It was amazing to me how children, even when only four or five years old, had already taken on such predominate personalities and I had to think, did I set my daughter is for a good life, or was she destined to have her heart broken over and over again at the hands of my instruction?

Although I don't have a real answer for this area right now, I am realizing I have not done my part to drive home the proper way to handle things. I understand I will be an ongoing construction site and each of us will have to be willing to revisit the personal blueprints of our lives if we are to ever master the most appropriate ways to interact with others especially when we feel disrespected or attacked. I will have put my hammer to the nails many times to build what I have considered to be a strong, healthy foundation. I will have to continue to try my best to set a good example for my daughter by walking her through the times I have walked away from unhealthy situations and my error when I elected to engage in conflict.

Embarrassingly enough, I have been the first one at the microphone and sang my own song of the "angry black woman" to a crowded auditorium. I have found myself spewing venomous poison at those I love all in the name of being "right." I have done many things I have regretted even though my intentions were good and perhaps my point was valid, but because I failed in the area of delivery, I was in an immediate no-win situation. My daughter watched me bark my own frustrations through Android phones as I turned around to face her and caution her to handle things in the opposite way than I had. In many ways, I have charged her to be a better person than me knowing full well the task before her is great.

As I set the stage for her, she is also setting the stage for me. Our stage is one where we have to learn the importance of the antagonist and the protagonist in each play. She and I need to learn how to respect the opposition for what it is. Opposition is necessary, driving force to teach us how to see things beyond our own freeze frame. Realizing both are necessary provides us with respect for the process and encourages us to function as rational human beings. If all the world's a stage, I want our stage to be set side by side with interchangeable sets realizing she and I will both continue to change our delivery of the roles sent to our dressing rooms. The effectiveness of our execution will depend on our exposure to the world.

If I am charged with providing the parameters of her "box," I will make sure her box is full of variety of encounters to serve as her instructions. I will make sure her blueprint is constructed in pencil so she can always make changes. In the definition of a blueprint, it refers to it as the negative to the original and if this is true, I want her to be able to alter my original design at all times so she always has room to make her own decision. I have come to the conclusion that our lives are not a dress rehearsal. When it's time for our curtain calls, I want to know we performed on the biggest stages to raved reviews with everyone giving us a standing ovation for the wonderful way we allowed our stage to set us up for greatness.

chapter 12

"Make Traditions"

"So, I have learned, traditions are only valuable if they become that thing we can depend on to bring stability to our lives. Traditions should only be introduced if everyone is committed to following through with them despite the bumps and bruises of life." - C. Frazier

Chapter Twelve
Make traditions

Family traditions counter alienation and confusion. They help us define who we are; they provide something steady, reliable and safe in a confusing world.
-Susan Liberman

I hate social media during the holidays. I try my best to close out each application but find myself sneaking back and forth between Facebook and Instragram almost like Pookie in New Jack City. Minus the ashy lips and the reference to the milk in the breasts of his fellow cast mates, I could easily find myself in his shoes during his rehabilitation process off his controlled substance. I mean, "it just be calling me, man," he proclaimed in one the commonly repeated phrases from the film demonstrating the power of addiction. Similar to Pookie, I found myself needing hit after hit of profile picks to the point I began to fear for the survival of my brain cells. It's almost as if I become a glutton for punishment because I continue to scroll my timelines watching the families of the friends connected through reflections and pictures share their interpretation of family traditions. As I bounce from house to house on most holidays, it is bittersweet to see that some families require time set apart each year. I think the most memorable holiday I spent away from my own family was the Thanksgiving I joined my friends for a seafood Thanksgiving.

In my early years when my family was all intact, I remember Thanksgiving was one of my favorite holidays. My mother and sisters would spend much of the days leading up to the holiday grocery shopping for menu items. Although our menu never changed, what we loved most was the fact mom reserved certain dishes specifically for the holiday. No matter how much we begged, my mom would not make her infamous cornbread dressing on any other occasion. As icing on the cake, my mother always kept cranberry sauce on the side just for me to properly top off my favorite side dish. My mom would give us all a job and although my job always included some sort of cleaning duty, it was remarkable to watch it all come together.

My mom would prep the meal by peeling sweet potatoes, baking cornbread, seasoning the turkey and shucking the corn off the cob. The smells in the house the night before Thanksgiving were disrespectful because my mom would torture us with opportunities to lick the spoon or bowl. She would save my dad's favorite Millionaire Pie for last and she always allowed me to eat the last of the whipped cream so I always had something to look forward to. By the morning of the big dinner, my dreams the previous two nights had included a montage of Charlie Brown specials and Butterball commercials. The warmth of the meal simmering on the stove created an atmosphere of comfort and family and it was the best feeling on Earth. Although my mother would have sacrificed sleep operating on maybe a half an hour of nodding while watching VHS movies, she got up early Thanksgiving morning and prepared a full breakfast of eggs, bacon, grits and biscuits for my family. She would wake us and we already knew our routine of brushing teeth and washing faces. We were allowed to stay in pajamas because we would transfer our bodies from our beds to the couches where we would watch the Macy's Thanksgiving parades for the rest of the morning. My dad would have already been up and out in the wee hours of the morning playing a few matches of tennis with his buddies. By the time he would return home, we would all be dying of starvation because mom would not let us touch a morsel until my dad made it to the head of the table.

I think what I loved most was having my dad pass the stack of toast around the table. Because I was the youngest, I always got the stack last but little did my family know, it was perfect for me because the ones cooked first were always cooked perfectly with plenty of delicious butter. We would sit over bowls of his oatmeal with his famous secret ingredient…raisins. He seemed to be proud of his creative addition and I figured he must be the best daddy in the world to give us such a great treat. Life didn't get any better than listening my dad inhale his food and the females in the family make appropriate small talk. The conversation topics always seemed to be over my head but I just liked to be around these people. I liked to hear them breathe and see them smile at one another. Every now and then, they would remember I was there but for the most part, I was always a fascinated spectator. They were my world and as long as we were together, I felt nothing would ever happen to destroy what had been built. Over breakfast, the smiles were genuine; no one cared about past arguments or miscommunications. All that mattered was love.

After breakfast, and this didn't make much sense to me until I got older, my parents would require my sisters and me to get completely dressed. I mean, hair, shoes and all. We would have to all be ready before anyone could sit at the table. My dad, of course, would be the first one dressed and I could smell his cologne as a smoke signal letting us know time was winding up. It never took me long to catch up to my dad because my mom always seemed to sneak in my bedroom and lay out for me exactly what she wanted me to wear for the day. I understood at that stage in my life, I had no say so, no opinion, no substitution; my only option was to comply. It was that simple.

We would finally arrive at the dinner table with the spread perfectly displayed in front of stomachs who weren't quite as big as our eyes but one thing was for sure, my mom was a miracle worker. I never fooled myself into thinking my family was rich but my mom sure had a way of presenting things as if we were royalty. Each of us would take a seat as assigned upon my dad's cue and we would begin by grabbing hands around the table. It was something about the connectedness of our family at that moment which I will never forget. From fingertip to fingertip, from heart to heart, from dream to dream was the future and legacy of my family. Each touch passed the torch from one generation to another. Even as a young girl, I knew this was an important rite of passage and the fact I was included made me special.

Then, my father would pray. Man, he would pray. His prayer covered us in a blanket of patriarchal protection from any hurt, harm or danger. He thanked God for everything from shelter to being "clothed in our right minds" as each phrase was stamped in its stanza with a "and for that, we are thankful." I remember wishing he would hurry it along but now that I am older, I am glad he tarried right there for a while. He would praise God for his power, his provision and his promises and if I had known any better at the time, I would have taken off running right there. The tears would stream down my mother's face as she stood with my father as our strong towers. As the steam continued to escape each covered dish, my parents allowed their gratitude for family to evacuate their spirits. He prayed blessings of abundance for each of us and our future generations and finally concluded with a "forever and ever, Amen."

We would sit quietly for a few minutes as they continued to allow their praises to flow from their lips and we would just allow it to fall on the moles of our heads. For some reason, the food seemed to taste better after it had been blessed like that. Although our capacity to consume lasted only about fifteen minutes, we basted in each other for about an hour. There was nothing like my family. Immediately after assisting my mother in washing the dishes and packing the food into individual containers which would be our serving bowls for the next week as we struggled to be creative in how we repeated each entree to make it interesting, we would pile into a car and begin a long day of visiting our family around town.

With each stop, I would have to go over and over my family tree with explanations of how each one of us were related. I would be asked to guess the names of adults who always seemed to remember when I was only as tall as their knees. I could never seemed to earn points on family trivia but I loved knowing these people cared enough about me to ask questions of my future such as my academic performance, my friends and what sports I liked to play. I felt important to these people and I knew they wanted me to be the best I could be. My parents always seemed to be close enough to be in earshot of my responses. I know they wanted to make sure I had been properly trained to respond with the respectful, "yes, ma'am" or "no, sir." It had been a practice in my home so it always flowed out naturally. I was proud I could make them proud. When it was all over, I remember sitting sandwiched between my older sisters knowing I could lean on either one of them with my exhaustion and they would just let me. I was the baby, the one they would was protect and, watching the back of my parents' heads in the front of the car, I knew with both of them leading us as a team, we would always be headed in the right direction.

After the divorce, my traditions went out of the window. We no longer sat down together. We all seemed to go our separate ways from year to year. Although my mother would try her best to recreate our meal, the food was never the same for me again. The hand holding was missing, the connection was gone, and the love was drastically different. I felt more alone at Thanksgiving than ever before and I just wanted the day to be over. We stopped making our rounds with the family and instead opted to lay around the house. I don't think any of us would have known what to say, anyway. When I got to college and I had the option of where I would want to go for the holidays. I didn't go to my mom's house because I didn't want my dad to feel I had chosen one of the other and vice versa so I didn't go home at all. After all, there was no home to go to anymore.

Each year, I alternated going home with my college roommates sitting at foreign tables where they never passed the bread to me last yet first because I was a guest. They never prayed right and they never had my dad's favorite pie for dessert. But, at least they were together under one roof. I smiled and tried my best to blend in over games of spades and no one seemed to notice me after a while. I felt as if I was just an ornament hanging from the drapes and I began to enjoy the fact I was becoming acclimated to my new life.

That one year, as I sat in front of plates and plates of crawfish, crab, corn and potatoes, I wondered if my friend's family had any idea what holiday we should have been celebrating. Each of her family members were exactly where they had always been doing what they had been taught to do. As each pot was drawn from the row of propane filled apparatuses, the family members hurried for their portion so they could rest in front of the television. There was no prayer, no shared interest…it was just every man for himself. This was not my family…but, it was theirs and that was all they cared about.

As an adult with a daughter, establishing traditions is a challenge from year to year. I haven't been able to recreate that family structure which formed my foundation as a young child. I guess, in a way, I don't want to give her something I can't guarantee will be there from year to year. Although I got to the point I could always guarantee her a tree filled with presents, I never wanted the material things to be the focus. Sadly, I felt it was the only thing I could give her as I never found myself in a relationship during the holidays. She and I would often wait on her dad, grandmother or aunt to come over to fill the room with some sense of family.

Finally, I began to accept the fact that I had done all I could do to simulate a family but my act was up and I elected to send her to her father's family for holiday dinners because I knew they could give her something I couldn't unless I traveled home to Louisiana. I know how important that feeling is and although I missed it, I never wanted to keep it from her. Life is kind of funny like that. Sometimes you have to be real about what you can and can't do realizing it does not make you weak but instead, makes you unselfish. When you can sacrifice your own emotions to invest in the emotions of those you love, you are an adult.

So, I have learned, traditions are only valuable if they become that thing we can depend on to bring stability to our lives. Traditions should only be introduced if everyone is committed to following through with them despite the bumps and bruises of life. One tradition I can give my little girl is to make sure we will have the time for me to cover our family in prayer. Although fragmented and scattered, my prayers are big enough to stretch my umbrella over each of our heads and that is my tradition.

chapter 13

"Never Give Up On Love"

"He hurt me. I had allowed myself to be hurt. After reacting in anger towards him and his female "friend" I had to think about why I had allowed him to pull me out of my character and the answer was simple; I was in love and he had told me he loved me, too. But, if that was true, it no longer felt that way." -C. Frazier

Chapter Thirteen
Never give up on love

It is the color of light,
The shape of sound high in the evergreens
It lies suspended in hills,
A blue line in a red sky.
I am looking at sound.
I am hearing the brightness
Of high bluffs and almond trees
I am tasting the wilderness
of lakes, rivers, and streams
Caught in an angle of song.
I am remembering water
That glows in the dawn
The motion tumbled in earth
Life hidden in mounds.
I am dancing a bright beam of light
I am remembering love.

The first person I ever loved outside of my family was a little boy at my school named Milton Parker. The crazy thing about the situation was that he and I had not spoken one word to each other, but in my mind, he and I had been married several times over. He and I found ourselves seated next to each other in my third grade class with Ms. Salter. I remember smelling him one day when he sat down from the pencil sharpener and he smelled like pumpkins. At first, I wasn't sure if it was a smell I loved or one that would make me sick but after seeing him smile after the first mispronounced name, I knew it would grow on me.

Milton had a funny way of showing me he loved me. He would get up to throw away his paper and would grab my trash off the end of my desk without having to be prompted. During lunch, he would point at my cake and when I didn't move quickly to defend it, he would swipe if and inhale it as if I had made it from a special recipe just for him. During recess, he would always seem to kick the ball right at my head and he would fall out laughing oh so considerately like only he could do. Yes, our love was unique and real.

He wasn't planned. You aren't even looking for him. He wasn't a part of the plan. You haven't thought this through. He was all wrong. You aren't ready, anyway. He's not interested. He isn't ready. You can't be hurt again. He will hurt you. You can't handle this. You will fall in love.

When I met Brandon, there was nothing funny, strange or even extraordinary about our introduction. He and I weren't as coy as Milton and I had been demonstrating my growing interest in the opposite sex. In fact, it seemed as if we had met several times over through a mutual friend who had told me his life story over a few conversations. I must admit, he was presented to be a really great person who just needed someone to talk to. As it was explained to me, it was important he and I meet because it was believed I could be someone positive in his life. The request seemed easy enough as I have a love for people and I was intrigued by his background story so I was felt no hesitation. From the onset, I should have known things would not end well for me knowing full well I was only brought to his attention for what I could bring to his life. He had never, in fact asked to meet me so it was almost as if I was to be forced on him. However, I was in a place in my life where I needed to know I work through my own issues by helping someone else. For some reason, I was going to be his Dr. Phil.

When we met, things were comfortable as if I had known him for years. We shared similar interests and I wanted to do what I had been asked to do from the beginning; I wanted to make sure I showed myself friendly in hopes he would take me up on my offer to extend an honest hand of friendship. He seemed a bit standoffish with everyone else, but with me, it seemed easy for him to open up. In the days to come, he began to hang out with my friends and me at some events for my birthday week and he seemed calm but still a bit reserved. I did my best to ensure he felt comfortable and after a while, I learned it was just his way to remain within his comfort zone and I was cool with it.

After a night of bowling, he and I found ourselves sandwiched between friends at the Waffle House joking over runny eggs and patty melts all in an effort to get to know each other better. The conversation was easy and fun. I could talk to him for hours. And talk for hours we did. After bumming a ride home from Brandon and his best friend, he let me into the details of the tragedy which had occurred in his life a few months prior to our introduction. His story was unbelievable and to have him before me still standing made me look at him in a different light. I had been shown his bright smile for days and for the first time, he allowed me to see his darkness. I understood his darkness oh too well and I became intrigued by the idea of helping him to come out of it as I had.

We talked well into the morning. I felt like he needed it. I felt like he needed to tell the story over and over again. Perhaps it was still so unfathomable to him he had to continue to share the tale as if to ask if it had really happened. I fought back tears knowing he didn't need anyone to pity him, instead, I hoped he would connect to my genuine concern for him as he struggled to move forward with a life which had been turned upside down. After that night, he became a part of my daily routine. He and I talked for hours about everything and sometimes about nothing. It felt good to know he wanted to hear my voice on the other side of the phone and I was happy to hear how his days were going. For some reason, I was drawn to him more and more and found happiness in him with each passing day. Our jokes were hilarious and our conversations meaningful, whether it was about football or diarrhea, it didn't matter, he was growing on me and fast.

I don't know the exact day or time when I began to look at him differently but it was almost as if it had snuck up on me like a well-mixed drink. All I remember is sitting with him in a lobby of a hotel waiting to hang out with a friend and suddenly feeling like a little school girl. I cared about what I was wearing and whether or not my hair was on point. Prior to that, I hadn't given much of a damn if I was in sweats or a bandana from working out because he was the homie. When those girly things began to change the way I looked at myself with him, I knew I was in trouble. In the next few weeks, the frequency of our interactions increased as I would see him every day and if we weren't together, we spent our time on the phone. He made me laugh. I mean, no one had been able to make me laugh like him. I felt carefree with him. Somehow, I felt more important to him than I had to anyone else I had met in years. I felt like it mattered to him that I be there and I loved that feeling.

The more time we spent together, the more I realized I had begun to neglect the rest of my life. I loved spending time with him and his friends and after a time, his family. His mother was the sweetest thing on Earth and meeting the important people in his life only made him more important to me. Now, don't get me wrong, prior to meeting Brandon, my life had been pretty great as my friends and I had established a pretty strong connection. We had plans each weekend to learn our city and our little family had become my norm. However, Brandon was something different. He brought out a side of my emotions I had not been comfortable with in years. He was special to me and although it cost me time with my buddies, I felt it was time well spent.

After months of what I considered to be really cool interactions between he and I our "relationship" took an unexpected turn at a picnic. Although I had chosen to arrive with my friends and hang out with them, when he and I talked, he asked me to come to where he was and of course, with him was where I wanted to be. When I arrived, he seemed a bit different electing to be far less affectionate than he had been only the day before but I didn't let it shake me; we were, however, at a picnic. After a few swigs of alcohol provided by my buddies to give me that little bit of liquid courage and some more than friendly interaction between he and another female in front of me and my friends, all I could think about was how big of a fool I had been to give my heart to this person who easily spit on it because he could. It was kind of funny because I had felt free to be fun and stress free with him and here I was turning into the crazy chick in the club throwing drinks.

He hurt me. I had allowed myself to be hurt. After reacting in anger towards his female "friend" I had to think about why I had allowed him to pull me out of my character and the answer was simple; I was in love and he had told me he loved me, too. But, if that was true, it no longer felt that way.

It's funny how things always seem so cool until the "L" word rears its ugly head. Our "relationship" had been so perfect until we decided to mess it all up by allowing our hearts to get involved. After leaving the picnic with swollen eyes hidden by dark shades, I blamed myself for allowing myself to do what I said I would not do again for a while. I had allowed my walls to come down and now, I was prepared to walk away for good. I realized then he didn't love me as I hoped he had and I felt like I had been hit by a truck. Maybe he said it because he felt he needed to but there was nothing about his actions that day that led me to believe he even liked me let alone loved me. Of course, we had to talk after this situation and the first thing he did was to tell me that I had been an embarrassment to him and how I had overreacted. What I prayed for was to have him start by assessing my feelings knowing very well how much I cared. I needed him to think about what it must have felt like for me to be discarded in such an insensitive way but he let me down; he simply didn't care like I did and maybe he never would. What happened to us? What is my fault? Why didn't he love me?

Everything in me told me to walk away quickly and to accept what I already knew but my damn heart. My heart replayed our conversations, his smile, my joy, our laughs, our families, our trust and I just wasn't ready to give all of it up. We tried to go back to how things were before but something was always missing. True, each day I was there for him as he continued to push through his difficult time, but it no longer felt the same when we talked but, oddly enough, his touch was still the same so it calmed me down and I pressed on. After all, I loved Brandon and I thought maybe we could get back to where we had started.

In the next few months, I felt him slipping away. We didn't argue, we didn't fall out, he just started to slip away. I wanted him to pull off the Band-Aid, but instead, he tortured me slowly tearing down what I thought we had built by acting like it never happened or worse, that it never should have. He broke me. I had nothing left. I finally did what he seemed to be unable to do, I opened my hand and let my bird fly away. Sadly enough, and though I prayed for it, my bird would never return as he had been. That beautiful creature I had learned to love so passionately, so freely, so innocently would never look the same to me again or drink the same water for his nourishment. He had accepted my love freely, but when the cost got too high, he had returned it and demanded a refund. I had allowed him a full refund and I was left with nothing; just like always.

At the age of 35, my relationship with Brandon taught me a valuable lesson about love. I realized that no matter what it looks like, I believe in love and once it has been found, shouldn't be easily abandoned. Although I held on longer than most to my love for Brandon, I never regretted allowing myself to love. I believed my heart was safe with him and all signs pointed to the green light on my decision. When it was all said and done, I struggled with whether or not we could preserve what we had built from the beginning; the friendship. However, how can you really have a friendship if there is no reciprocity? If that person does not see you, what can you expect? I expected love in return. I expected protection and at the very least, I expected to be handled with care. What are you left with once it is all over and you wonder why you allowed yourself to stay so long?

Men are unforgiving when they are hurt. My girlfriends and I often joke about men and how they react to hurt and rejection. If a man is hurt by a woman, it throws his feelings into a typhoon of turmoil and he often allows the actions of one woman to determine how he will act with the next ten women he meets. A hurt man can leave a body count of tormented women from coast to coast for years without much regard for those he destroys. Women, however, are expected to continue to believe in love despite being on the DOA list in many wars fought for love. True to those expectations, even in the wake of my failed relationship with Brandon and an unrequited love, I refuse to give up on love. If I give up on the possibility of love, I have given up on the Cinderella story fed to me like sweet gummy bears forcing me to crave it over and over again as validation of my existence as a woman. It might be sad or even unrealistic but I believe when my prince finds me, I would have finally arrived at the pinnacle of womanhood having found a love that's true and uniquely mine.

I was upset with Brandon for quite some time for leading me down a path he only planned to leave me on fighting my way back to familiar territory but I have to be honest when I say I loved the process of falling in love and learned I could love again. For a time, I thought my fear of being hurt had turned me off to the idea of love, but Brandon taught me to be courageous and trust my heart. Even if it doesn't work out in my favor, I know my heart has just gone through a little workout and it is getting stronger and stronger with each training session.

chapter 14

"Do Your Own Research"

"Finally, one brave voice spoke up above the cloud of impending doom and responded, "Ladies like about everything. I mean, where do I begin?" Almost as if someone had opened the gate to the bullfighting ring, each lady began to interject her own line of defense seeing the need to paint a picture of themselves as the virginal depiction of perfection for any sane man to call his wife." -C. Frazier

Chapter Fourteen
Do your own research

An expert is one who knows more and more about less and less until he knows absolutely everything about nothing.
— **Nicholas Murray Butler**

"Why do women lie so much?" When words trickled from the lips of the assigned narrator for a festive game of 20 questions, I almost felt the air sucked out of the room. The men sat motionless careful not to lock eyes with any of the women in the room all of whom were searching to find the author of the question on the table. Each of them postured themselves like a little boy who knew he had touched his mother's purse and forgot to put her makeup pouch back in its original location. Each woman clearly began to search within their own library of lethal lies and found themselves to be faultless on every hand and silently demanded the culprit to show himself immediately and face his public stoning.

The commentator asked the question of the group again when Camille broke the silence like a hammer against church-stained glass by asking, "So what, exactly, do you all think we lie about?" Again, the neck swirls and eye rolls continued. The question seemed so simple but its implication was much more far-reaching than anyone could have imagined. In my own mind, I thought of my own relationship woes which often accompanied some sort of fallacy which had been fed to me by my mask-marauding Prince Charming all in hopes of getting into my bag of cookies. Although my eyes instinctively began to drift behind my eyelid, I fought off the eye-rolling reaching in an effort to remain more cultured than my female counterparts. I wanted to hear the answers to the question and I had already drafted my own set of creative comebacks for each possible response.

Finally, one brave voice spoke up above the cloud of impending doom and responded, "Ladies lie about everything. I mean, where do I begin?" Almost as if someone had opened the gate to the bullfighting ring, each lady began to interject her own line of defense seeing the need to paint a picture of themselves as the virginal depiction of perfection for any sane man to call his wife. The commentator quickly began to bang on the table and demand quiet in the room. Each of the men had been sitting in their military bunker hidden safely from the scud missiles flying overhead. The commentator asked for clarity from the male-spokesman and as he began to speak, it all made sense and each woman in attendance was being prepared to take a class in "Real Woman 101."

"Ladies, let's keep it all the way real for once," he began in a calm and reassuring tone. "How many of you can honestly say you are 100 % truthful on any day of the week? Almost each one of you in this room is wearing someone else's hair on either your head or your eyes and I'll bet if I jerk up some of these dresses, I will find some sort of wrap sucking you all in," Jeremy spewed with his own tone of triumph as if he had pricked our favorite balloons and was watching them slowly seep their contents into the atmosphere. I definitely kept my lips together while still popping Aleve in response to the throbbing of my scalp which was stretched to its limits under my new 27-inch Malaysian weave. I also thought of thirty ways I would slit his throat if he dared to jerk up my dress with my new waist trainer sawing me in half. As we listened to Jeremy continue to rip us a new one for parading like princesses without a true reflective mirror, we had to admit, there was a bit of truth in his conversation.

I had always assumed what men wanted, based on the prototype of the women who seemed to be earning the coveted title of wife in my age bracket, were the women we all secretly tried to emulate. 90% of the women had "snatched" waists, eyelashes and wore heels so high they must have invented a mighty, effective ankle-stabilizing exercise regimen. They seemed able to maneuver in all settings with confidence while maintaining a level of submission to the men whose arms they held onto with a girlish innocence. Although many of us would have never admitted it in an open forum, each of us had secretly memorized these women and tried to integrate as many of their practices into our own behaviors slowly enough to appear a natural progression. I had abandoned my natural locks and began to invest hundreds of dollars in expensive hair to ensure I could always look the part when I was called upon to frequent a classy place with my professional friends. I began wearing painful heels to even the most casual events to make sure I maintained a lady-like demeanor while balancing an approachable aurora to invite men to open conversation.

After sitting in the room with my friends answering such intimate questions, I learned most women have the game all wrong believing many fallacies taught to us by one certain type of relationship. Each of us had been chipping away at our personal, unique petals trying hard to look like every other flower in the garden and had done ourselves a huge disservice by devaluing all the things that made us priceless. I vowed then and there to stop allowing my behaviors to be controlled by my countless "wine and whine" sessions with my girlfriends and instead, I would do the research for myself to make sure I was headed in the right direction toward ultimate happiness.

My first study became my friend Kenny who seemed to want the women in his life to be given accurate information so they could make the best informed decisions for themselves. After years and years of riding on the manipulative male motorcycle pulverizing every woman in his path, he had finally hit a major speed bump in his life which forced him to evaluate his contribution to his outcome. In his quest for understanding, he found the euphoric fountain of truth which he had decided to share with the women in his life in hopes it would be his redemptive measure on his journey back to the straight and narrow. Had Kenny and I met any earlier than my thirties, I would have written him off as a male chauvinistic butthole because his truth was brutal. The first two times I thought I was ready to engage him in real conversation, I was drained of all confidence feeling as if all the hurts I had experienced had been at my own naïve hand. Finally, after probably a year of dancing around a much needed conversation, I accepted the challenge to be stripped naked so I could finally be clothed in reality.

What I found interesting was the simplicity of men. Oftentimes, they are not as hard to figure out as women have believed. According to Kenny, the wants and needs of a man are simple; a man wants to be needed, respected and taken care of. He wants to be appreciated verbally even for the things perceived to be his "role." Men want to always have the same package he bought off the shelf so he needs his woman to continue to keep herself up as their comfort level increases. What does that mean? A man does not want to pick up a woman off the shelf who has a super fit body with an award-winning personality only to get her home, break open the package and see rotten contents. Men want us to be a gift that keeps on giving; be that showroom piece they picked up but continue to re-gift yourself. With time, men should continue to unwrap us, layer by layer, only to find our contents continue to increase in value.

As I did my research on the practices of most women in my circle, I noticed each of us made similar mistakes. We often unwrapped our own packages and much too soon for a man's interest to peak. We would devalue ourselves in our conversation which dripped with sexual innuendo and we found comfort in belittling ourselves afraid our men of choice would not be able to handle our "realness" or our "strength." For the most part, none of us could exclaim that no man wanted us because what we continued to serve was a lukewarm T.V. dinner doused in kerosene.

When Steve Harvey betrayed the "guy code" by publishing his award-winning novel, "Think Like A Man," he provided women with valuable research needed for most modern-day women to make smarter decisions. In the book turned Blockbuster movie, women were encouraged to be the most honest version of themselves, and to encourage men to be the most authentic version they could present to a woman. Although many men felt Steve had ruined some sacred fountain of fornication which would now be tainted by our talons, one thing was clear, if we take the time to do our research on ourselves and the men we date, we just might make a better decision.

When dating a man with a child or multiple children, research is imperative. When I had my daughter, I found myself shying away from dating men who weren't parents because they never seemed to understand how my daily schedule was set up. If a person does not have children, they won't understand why they don't come first in your scheduling process. Dating such people will have you dropping your child off at your best friend's house at midnight so you can meet your beau at a lounge for Tantalizing Tuesday knowing doggone well you have to get the baby up early for school. There are a few very important questions to ask a man with children to fully assess if he is worth your time.

When is the last time you spent time with your son/daughter?

A man who stutters over the question of when he last saw his child is not involved in his child's life. Any man who can go weeks and months at a time without seeing his child might not be the perfect father for your child.

How do you and your child's mother get along?

If a man begins to curse on instinct when the mother of his child is mentioned, run for the hills. A man who has not found a way to be the "head" of his situation, even in a failed relationship that resulted in the birth of a child, he will bring some baggage into the relationship. If he still hates his "baby mama," she still occupies too much room in his emotional wallet. If she can still ruin his day with one text message, you need to give him additional time to get his business under control.

Are you sure you should spend all that money on this trip? Isn't your son playing football?

If he does not go into the ways in which he has maneuvered his finances to fund his son's extracurricular dues as well as your weekend getaway, be cautious. No man should put the needs of his child above an excursion with you. If you have a man who opts to take you to play miniature golf instead of Miami so his daughter can cheer, that man is a keeper because he will always have his priorities in order.

Of course, there are a million questions one can ask of their potential significant other to qualify the potentiality of success in their relationship, but we have to take the time to ask the difficult questions not fearing the response. At this stage in my life, I have to ask the questions geared toward a forever-type of love. However, I don't penalize a man for telling me his truth. I accept it and move on...or, in this case, I chose to stay.

It is important as an adult to ask the right questions and not to be afraid of the responses. Oftentimes, we don't want to do the research because we know what we find could and should change the way we move. When we know the truth, we are responsible for the information. It seems more comfortable to maneuver in dark, naïve silence but wonder why the wool is pulled over our eyes. At this stage in my life, I am ready to know the gospel truth about everyone I am dealing with. That way, when I make a decision to stay and play or run away, I know I am protecting me first.

chapter 15

"Don't Be Afraid to Tell People You Love and Value Them"

"The bad thing is, the only time I ever felt bad about this was when people told me I should. I never considered my father to be insensitive or callous but instead, it was just his way. It wasn't until I was told my father had never loved me because he had not painted me with his praise nor blanketed me with his blinding love declarations. I always thought my dad was pretty damn cool."

–C. Frazier

Chapter Fifteen
Don't be afraid to tell people that you love and value them

I dreamt we walked together along the shore. We made satisfying small talk and laughed. This morning I found sand in my shoe and a seashell in my pocket. Was I only dreaming?
— **Maya Angelou**

One of the funniest movies I have ever seen is called "Wedding Crashers." I can't even remember how I lucked up on the movie but once I sat down to view it, I knew it would always been included in my entertainment library. Amongst all of the various comical skits played out in the movie, I found myself most interested in the fun poked at the family structure. Whether it was the blunt grandmother who outed her grandson during the family dinner, or the flirtatious wife whose husband had forgotten the importance of noticing the changes she had made to beautify herself or even the sisters whose underlying jealousy for one another lured them into a false sense of sisterhood and security, each symbolic relationship revealed one astounding fact, all of our families are screwed up.

During one of the earlier exchanges between one of the main characters in the opening exposition of the movie found Jeremy being invited by one of his female coworkers to enter into a voluntary agreement to be fixed up with one of her friends. As he explained his reasoning as to why he had no interest in her offer, he detailed the awkwardness of the hugs and how they were often the most uncomfortable part of the entire exchange. As I thought about it and this, the 15th lesson of 35, I reflected on what a hug means and how we can use them to express our value for one another or the implication of withholding our affections.

My father always made sure to give the "ass out" hug with this really clammy arm that would beat you in the middle of your shoulder blade and I often wondered why he would even hug at all. His embrace would never exceed about five seconds and it was almost as if he had taken one giant leap for mankind each time he made it through one of his required demonstrations of affection. When he saw you leaning in for your hug, he would take in an awkward breath and prepare for you to invade his personal space. I remember watching my dad many times to determine if he was trying to send me a message by withholding real, thoughtful and purposeful hugs but, as I watched him with other family members and friends, I realized the thought of hugging and public displays of affection was my Superman's kryptonite. Much like Superman, I am sure he felt himself subjected to genetic mutations each time he was required to love on others through physical contact.

Perhaps even more rare was hearing the words, "I love you" from my dad. I think, even at 35, I can count on two hands how many times my dad has actually pieced those words together to form that validating phrase. He would linger on the phone with his goodbyes but never to give me that thing I desired; the final declaration of his undying admiration for me coupled with a parental pride that would bring clarity to my world. The bad thing is, the only time I ever felt bad about this was when people told me I should. I never considered my father to be insensitive or callous but instead, it was just his way. It wasn't until I was told my father had never loved me because he had not painted me with his praise nor blanketed me with his blinding love declarations. I always thought my dad was pretty damn cool.

So, when I evaluate the entire concept of valuing someone, I feel value is determined in many different ways. It sounds simplistic but when I think of placing value on someone or something, I relate it to how I did pricing for my cupcakes when I ventured to start my own dessert catering company. I would often underprice my product because of the cost of materials. The fact that the flour had been on sale, sugar was never expensive, eggs came with a coupon and the other ingredients were easy to find at each and every supermarket with no problem, I didn't see the point of charging $2.00 for each of my treats. It took my friend from Brooklyn, NY to teach me how to price my desserts after he sat with me one night and watched me put together and order for a client. As he and I argued about what I charged for a dozen, they had to remind me of several things:

1. The cost of the products might not have been much, but I had to drive to the store to purchase them.

2. Even though some of the items were on coupon, I still had to drive to the store and purchase the Sunday paper to get the coupon, research the stores where the sale would occur and match the coupon with the proper brand.
3. I would have to turn on my oven which would immediately increase the cost of gas and electric in the house.
4. After completing the cupcakes, I would have to cool them in a freezer specifically purchased for the desserts.
5. While the cooling was occurring, I would have to clean and bleach the entire kitchen to make sure all of the sweet products had been cleared.
6. I would have to individually ice each cupcake and package them in a specialized box.

When I reviewed the process, it made sense to place more value on the product because of what I had to sacrifice to provide it to my client. While I would not provide the details of my process to my client, it was understood that they could expect a certain personal touch because the product was not coming from a store bakery. If I had a conversation with my cupcakes and the ones from a store, my cupcakes would be able to stand up and proclaim my love for them because I had shown them what they were worth to me. I never left them alone during the process and I had taken the time to ensure each one of them made it safely to their destination. True, my motivation was to make sure they were perfect so I wouldn't have to do them over again and so I could secure future orders, to them, they knew they meant a lot to me based on how I treated them.

The same was true for my father; although I could not recall him verbally giving me the words that seem to define love, I always knew he loved me through his actions. So, I guess you can say I learned to communicate my love and affections for another much as I had been taught by my father. I often felt as long as I showed my appreciation through my action, what was understood wouldn't need to be said. After all, in many cases, anyone could say the words and it would never amount to a hill of beans if they never backed it up in a way I could find it clearly shown.

When thinking back to my first "relationship" with a guy I will just call Jay, I think I fell in love with him the first day we met. I was invited to one of those good ol' sweaty Louisiana parties at a local hotel and I remember walking in the door dancing. The air what thick with Pear Glace and Cool Water as everyone was putting their best pelvic thrusts on the floor in hopes it would excite someone to fornication by the end of the night. After working the room in search of the lucky man who would have the honor and privilege of pressing his manhood up again my rump shaker for the remainder of the night, I ran into my friend, Bryan, who would make the introduction that would set me up for a rollercoaster of life lessons.

As we exchanged youthful pleasantries which included nothing more than the correction of the pronunciations of our real names, we spent the remainder of the night simulating sexual positions as if we were auditioning for soft porn. Perhaps if I hadn't been such a shameless tease, he actually would have been able to cash that check at the end of the night, but he simply had to settle for me slipping out during the final song of the night which, by design, was supposed to be the final four minutes to seal your deals. I felt I had shown him he had captured my attention by the way I ignored everyone else in the room and had made the ultimate commitment; I had allowed him to be the only one to hunch me all night. In the days to follow, the dreaded dance began. Each night I entertained a waltz of worry regarding what my beau would do to find me given the fact I had not left my phone number as opposed to the Cinderella glass slipper. However, I had left one important piece of me behind, Bryan, and I was sure my boy would play his role properly.

True to form, when my phone rang and the deep voice on the end of line began his rehearsed script, I knew my friend had been a noteworthy wingman. We talked for what seemed like hours about things we felt monumental and Earth-shattering at that time. You know, things like the best basketball player, the defense the Saints should run during the season and who had the better fries, McDonalds or Burger King. It wasn't too long after that we met at the number one date spot for youngsters; the mall.

Now, you have to understand what a huge move this was for both of us. In a small, Louisiana town much like the one I called home during my high school years, the mall symbolizes a majestic mecca for every person despite age, race, creed and religious belief. Every Saturday was the day in which all area residents and visitors would descend upon the collection of retail stores in hopes of catching deals they had missed the weekend before. Much like the adults who frequented local zydeco dancehalls, for teenagers, the mall's purpose was to serve as a safe and secure meeting place for potential lovers. For the two of us, to select the mall as our meeting place meant we had made a decision to make a bold declaration to the world. Walking through the mall together meant the formal announcement of our courtship and each of us seemed ready to take the plunge. We had even gone so far as to color coordinate our wardrobe; this was serious! He liked orange and a weird powder blue. Thankfully, my job at the GAP had us ready to take the city by the balls all in the name of love.

As the mall doors swung open with me and my new cutie intertwined by our fingers, the world seemed to stand still as the cool Cajun breeze glided us over the threshold. This day would be the deciding factor of our relationship. Would we be able to survive a few hours of lunch, arcade, window shopping and chance encounters? After about six hours of walking every square inch of the mall several times over, I had never been so sure of anything in my life. He and I had done the impossible; we had passed each test set before us and we were now safe to attach the label of boyfriend and girlfriend.

During our "relationship" I viewed love as that freeing feeling I could share with Jay because I felt he and I had a mutual respect for the evolution of our emotions. He cared about the things that made me feel beautiful and I lived to do the things that made him feel invincible. Love was the natural reaction. I don't think it mattered to me he had not said the words after months of dating and even after sharing our bodies on several secret occasions. I could tell he loved and valued me because of the way his friends treated me. He had clearly taught them about me and they worked hard to paint him in the best light possible by always reassuring me my name dripped from his lips frequently in their day to day interactions. He had even given me a secret beeper code so I would know he was thinking of me. Each time my hip vibrated with assurance of his feelings, I was in heaven. What a lucky girl I was!

I can't say anything went wrong in our relationship other than the fact I allowed my girlfriends to crawl into my cranium. They demanded I have him declare his love for me openly and publically or else our relationship was nothing more than a glorified playdate between children. I had never needed this before and why I felt I needed it so urgently, I still don't understand, but I began to question the authenticity of his feelings. "If you love me, why can't you say it?" I would ask. After watching his reluctance to comply, I began to feel as if I had lost my value with him. I needed him to prove to my jealous, judgmental, nosey, lonely, pathetic "friends" what we had was real and when he refused, I began to devise my escape plan. Six months later, I packed into my mother's car and left my hometown for college, leaving him and his tight lips behind sure I had done the right thing for me. I honestly never looked back feeling I had make the only choice I could make for a person who had no real confidence in our relationship and its future.

Now, at 35, I have learned several things. If, based on your definition, someone in your life is showing you love through actions and deeds, it is not always necessary to have them say those specific words. Anyone can combine as set of syllables and call them words, but without real emotions, feelings and genuine concerns somewhere in the mix, they are mere words. Over my life, I have had many people tell me they love me and turn around and withhold the deeds I needed to make me feel valued in their lives.

In Dr. Gary Chapman's award-winning book, "The Five Love Languages," he outlined the way we communicate our emotions by five categories. 1. Words of Affirmation 2. Quality Time 3. Receiving Gifts 4. Acts of Service and 5. Physical Touch. Sadly enough, Jay had been speaking his own love language but I had not translated it properly. Even my father had been speaking his own language of love but it looked nothing like mine so I could not make the connection. The truth is, until we discover the love languages of those we love, we will always assume love is fleeting when it is right under our noses.

If I had to change the title of this life lesson, I would change it to say, "Don't be afraid to SHOW people that you love and value them." I would also caution others not to require the other party in their relationships, whether romantic or not, to reciprocate their feelings in only one way. Allow that person to speak their love language in their own way and, trust me, you will be able to interpret it clearly. That way, you both will be all the better because your lenses of love will be clear on both sides. Wipe off your loop and the brilliance of your gem will shine through with great clarity.

chapter 16

"Surround yourself with people who make you better by telling you the truth"

"I was proud to say I had a group of friends who would automatically check the heels of my shoe for toilet paper before we would exit the restroom after one of our partner trips to check our faces. The same friends would respectfully remind me to suck my stomach in if I had gotten too relaxed, purchase shoes which would properly accentuate the perfect pair of jeans or share deodorant with me at the gym if I had been moving too hastily.

Real friends." -C. Frazier

Chapter Sixteen
Surround yourself with people who make you better by telling you the truth

Surround yourself with people who make you happy. People who make you laugh, who help you when you're in need. People who genuinely care. They are the ones worth keeping in your life. Everyone else is just passing through.
-Karl Marx

Growing up I lived in a very nice neighborhood. My parents were the first ones to move away from the more impoverished area of their small town to surround my sisters and me with a different caliber of people. We lived in an area called Dixie Lane and it was an area of homes heavily populated with either elderly, well-to-do white people or a new generation of black people wanting to expose their families to more. My next door neighbors Phil and Faye were the nicest people I had ever met and my first real encounter with white people. After years of walking in their house without knocking, I no longer saw them as a color, yet as family.

Their youngest son, Brent, was my real friend. Everyone called him "Booty" and we did everything together when our parents would make us go outside and play. He stayed with me when my dad made me stay outside until I stopped giving up on learning to ride a bike and he stuck up for me when other kids in the neighborhood called me chicken. Perhaps the one thing which solidified our friendship was when he had to help me stand up to the neighborhood bully.

I always wanted to be liked by the people around me. My sisters were a lot older than I and never really wanted to be bothered with doing the things I liked to do so my friends were very necessary. Booty was my buddy and having him to count on to ride bikes, make mud pies and fish in the ditches with was my world. One day, we decided to go on the back streets of our neighborhood. I don't think either of us would have ventured into that unfamiliar territory without one another because we simply had not been properly introduced to the parents of the kids who lived back there. On this day, we had no fears but just wanted to do something different. Much like on our street, the kids on the back street were huddled up in the middle of the street on their respective bikes. As Booty and I rode up, the kids looked back at us as if we had infringed upon some private mafia meeting. We didn't say much as we just circled around each other about ten feet from the other pack. Suddenly, three of the kids broke away and came over to us. After they questioned us about what school we went to and what street we lived on, we got the invite to come over to the group. It was almost as if we had been properly frisked for weapons and finally cleared to approach the head honcho.

The boy who was at the center of the group had clearly earned his position. No one spoke until he gave them the permission and no one moved unless he knew where they were going. It was funny in a way because no one was really his friend but they respected his position. All of us sat around talking about absolutely nothing until someone brought up that boys were better bike riders than girls. I knew Booty had taught me everything from jumping ditches to popping wheelies so without even thinking, I began to challenge Caesar. After a few minutes of exchanging verbal jabs, he said, "That's why you are the color of dog crap." I had never been so insulted in my life and each of the other kids stood in disbelief, even the other black ones. Without even thinking about it, I ran my bike into the front wheels of his not realizing his head what down toward the handlebars. Upon impact, his eye had been struck by the handlebar and blood began to drip from a small cut above his brow.

Instantaneously, Booty looked at me and said, "Let's get outta here!" We pedaled hard and fast looking back occasionally to see the other kids hot on our trails. Although Booty was a much faster rider who had stood up on the bike to maximize his pedal stroke, he continued to look back for me yelling, "Come on!" when he felt I had fallen too far behind. As we approached our street, it seemed as if our chasers had gained momentum and were only a few houses behind us. We make a sharp left onto our street and only eight houses stood between safety and what we assumed would be inevitable death. I pedaled faster than I ever had before and noticed my father's car in my driveway. My Superman was home and he would protect me. All I had to do was to get to my yard.

I could hear the herd behind me and as I skid into my yard with Booty breaking off into his, I allowed my bike to hit the wall and I erupted from my bike and began to knock on my front door for my family to come out. My mom opened the laundry door; she must have been in the kitchen and not in the living room, and I had never been so excited to see her in my life. Safely shielded by her tall frame, I looked back to see my bounty hunters circling in front of my house like vultures. I hoped Booty made it in okay but more importantly, I was sure I had saved my own life. As I ignored my mother fussing about crashing my bike into the house, I knew one thing was for sure, it was not over.

I didn't have to worry about the kids bothering me at school because they were middle school students and I was in the 5th grade. Booty and I spoke about the near death experience briefly before breakfast and as he fussed at me for going too far, he also assured me he would not let the boy hurt me. Despite my faith in Booty's loyalty, I did not believe he could fight off the Backstreet Bastards. So, that day I decided I would never go outside again. I never told anyone in my house what happened but I felt if I took up reading, my parents would be none the wiser about me hanging out in the house more.

For about three months, I elected to stay indoors. A few times, some of the Backyard Bastards would ride down my street and look toward my house. I would sometimes hear them calling my name but there was no way I was falling for that trick. Then one day, Booty had some friends from school over to play with the Slip-N-Slide in the backyard and my dad came in my bedroom and told me to put on my swimsuit and come outside. He and Booty's dad, Phil, were sitting outside on under the deck drinking a beer. I knew if my dad was outside, I would be safe and I had been cooped up in the house for months so I was super excited.

I played for hours as if I was a little bull finally allowed out of my constraints. Everything, for that one day, was back to normal. Then Phil said, "Well I'm glad she's finally coming back outside. It's time she stopped hiding from that kid that lives back there." My dad looked as if he had been asked the Daily Double on Jeopardy and the question involved molecular gastronomy. As my dad asked Phil to elaborate, my face dropped knowing I had just embarrassed my entire family. My dad ended the conversation abruptly saying it was past time for dinner and as he ushered me into the house, he assured Booty I would be outside again the following day. I was mortified.

Over dinner, I was lectured for over an hour by every member of the family about being a chicken and running from people. I knew I had no choice in the matter any longer; I would be forced outside each day until I faced my fear. My dad even forbade me to play in front of my house, instead he wanted me to venture away from the comfort of our property line so I would have no one there to handle my business for me. I hated my entire family after dinner and I believed each one of them would be to blame for the bloody result of my last stance. As the night drew to a close I was waiting on my mom to come in and tell me I didn't have to listen to my dad but, for once, the two of them were on the same page.

The next day, the school day seemed to fly by for the first time and I found myself on the bus. As the kids around me played, laughed and joked with each other, it was almost as if they were taunting me. The bus pulled up at the stop only a few houses from my driveway and I waited to be the last one off the big, yellow bird on wheels. I looked around all the sides of the bus looking for possible assailants but the coast seemed clear. "Come on," Booty comforted and I knew I would not be alone as my parents had designed. As promised, my sisters had been given strict instructions to have me to take off my school clothes, check my homework, give me a snack and force me back outside. I pretended my Mathematics worksheet was giving me problems but my sister only allotted me five additional minutes to complete. After picking over my snack of fruit and a sandwich, I was shoved out into the wild to fend for myself.

It had been months since I had been on my bike but my old friend was just as sturdy as ever. She and I rode back and forth down the street but not too far from my driveway and soon, Booty emerged from his house to hang out with me. As we slowly feel back into our routine of jumping ditches, I was lured into a false sense of security as a "lookout" had been sent to report I was finally back on the streets. Within minutes, the Backstreet Bastards were at the end of our street headed my way. My heart began to pound so loud in my ears that if I had a piano, I could make a hit record. It was time for me to face the music and I was afraid.

As I sat immobile on my bike, just as the top guy was within earshot, Booty parked his bike in front of mine. He looked back at me with no fear in his eyes and I wondered just how far he would go to protect me. "So, you've been up in the house," said my arch nemesis. I uttered no response. "I've been looking for you," he continued, "and now it's time for you to pay for what you did to my eye." I got off my bike and parked on the side of the street. If I was going to get beat up, I didn't want my bike to be damaged. I didn't move far from Booty but I was ready to accept what was to come.

Then, Booty said, "Look, she's sorry for what she did. She didn't mean for you to get hurt. Can she just say she is sorry will you leave her alone?" Everyone sat around as if they were pondering his proposal. He turned to me and said, "You should apologize because what you did hurt somebody. Say you are sorry," he instructed. I apologized as he had told me to. Truth be told, I wanted to say I was sorry because I felt bad about the whole thing.

Surprisingly enough, the head honcho said, "That's cool but she still has to prove she can jump ditches because I don't believe her." For the rest of the week, we all made it a point to meet up so I could demonstrate over and over again what Booty had taught me. Who would have thought; something my friend taught me had gotten my out of a boiling pot of water. I learned to keep people around me who could teach me things I would find valuable, tell me when I was wrong, but never leave me to go through tough situations alone.

My girls and I were hanging out at a little swanky lounge in Atlanta one Friday night in an upscale part of town. We decided to abandon our usual $5 mixed drink spots and traded our flip flops for more flirty stilettos. We felt super fancy to the point we even paid for valet as opposed to risking one hair being out of place before we made our grand entrance. My ladies and I had a different type of swag to us that night; not unapproachable but not inviting any Tomfoolery, either. We flashed our licenses as if they were black cards and stepped past the bouncers with one smooth, gliding set of steps. It was official, we were feeling ourselves.

I looked around at my team and I was pretty proud of us. No sooner than we had selected our special area to come in for a landing did we find ourselves staring down a group of ladies vying for the same VIP section.

Each of the ladies in my crew, probably unaware, began to size each of the women up. While we browsed each woman with the side eye, we noticed the two who seemed to be running the show had both selected very racy garments showing off figures who hadn't seen a complex carb in years. It was obvious they had either dressed in close proximity of one another or visited the same makeup artist because they clearly loved rouge blush, but for the most part, we had to appreciate the time and attention they paid to themselves. The other two women in the group, however, seemed like a watered-down version of the pack leaders wearing dresses which didn't seem to be their styles based on the frequent pulling and tugging but they weren't far off from the group goal of fabulousity. However, the girl sandwiched between the group was the one who seemed to hold our gaze a lot longer than her counterparts.

Almost as if she had been planted as some sort of alien lifeform among princesses, the ladies had one inclusion to the group who stood out like a sore thumb. The round and awkward shaped woman stuffed into a tawdry imitation of the popular BodyCon dresses made popular by the women who prided themselves in juicing six days a week, stood among the trees and tried not be hidden by their shade. Her hair was extremely dry refusing the lay naturally around the frame of her face. Her makeup had clearly been done during the ride to the club which must have including hitting every pothole which failed to be reported to the city for immediate repair. Her eyebrows had entirely too much concealer below the makeshift arch and her foundation looked as if it had been done by the first eliminated queen on RuPaul's Drag Race. Her face had not been highlighted but yet had been illuminated to imply she was completely out of her league. Her lack of confidence would be cleverly hidden by the fact she could dance and the numerous shots of Patron she would consume during the first thirty minutes of their arrival would show us why she had been chosen to run with such a crew.

As the liquor began to flow through her body, she began to run through the dance steps from "Rhythm Nation" down to the final breakdown in the routine. Her friends, the self-proclaimed super models, looked on as she warmed up to the music booming from every inch of the room. As she began to allow her body to be engulfed by the pulsating base, their section came alive with onlookers. Although she was giving it the best she had, the spectators were not laughing with her, but yet at her as she had clearly forgotten the area in which she and her friends had chosen to venture into on this night. Her friends watched as she became the clown of the party dropping it low to the ground providing all patrons with peeks at her panties and one thing was clear to me, not one of these girls with her were her friends.

At the Waffle House a few hours later over a perfectly prepared All Star breakfast, my friends and I reflected on the definition. I was proud to say I had a group of friends who would automatically check the heels of my shoe for toilet paper before we would exit the restroom after one of our partner trips to check our faces. The same friends would respectfully remind me to suck my stomach in if I had gotten too relaxed, purchase shoes which would properly accentuate the perfect pair of jeans or share deodorant with me at the gym if I had been moving too hastily. Real friends. We carefully analyzed all of the things the other team of ladies had done incorrectly for their less than fabulous friend and realized she had not one friend in the bunch.

Before leaving the house or mutually agreed upon meeting spot, each of the women should have been subjected to a head to toe and front to back check. Had this been done, her makeup would have been reapplied properly. If they were not sure how to correct it on their own, one resourceful person in the party would have googled the appropriate makeup tutorial and each of them would have taken a section; eyes, cheeks, lips, foundation. Additionally, no one in their right mind would have allowed her to wear an outfit not flattering to her figure.

Perhaps one of the most uncomfortable but eye opening conversations I have ever had took place between my best friend, Olivia and I. As we prepared to attend a mutual friend's party, I had put on a few pounds based on my newfound love and appreciation for fries with cheese, bacon and ranch dressing and my body could no longer hide my indiscretions. I searched high and low for a dress designed to hide my trouble area and draw attention to my lovely, shapely legs. Surprisingly enough, Ross Dress for Less had become my friend and I found the perfect aborigine ensemble cleverly accentuated by a new pair of shoes purchased from an online vendor who finally sent me my merchandise without having to contact China. I thought I was looking pretty darn spiffy. Then, in walks my friend as I was putting the final touches on my lipstick. She seemed to be in great spirits when she first came into the house even singing a little song as she climbed the stairs to my bedroom. However, after I poked out to say hello, the tune dissipated and there was a weird silence in the room. She fiddled with her curls in the vanity for a few minutes and then draped herself around the side of my doorway. After exchanging small comments about nothing, she finally took a long breath and said, "So, I want you to wear something else."

I swung around to face her with an, "I know you didn't" roll of my neck coupled with a smack of my lips. I asked, "What's wrong with what I have on now?" Although I asked, I think I already knew the problem. I could only imagine the dialogue taking place in her brain as she struggled with a polite way to tell me my ass was fat and I looked like I was in my second trimester, but I watched my friend struggle to do the most important thing in any relationship, tell me the truth. She must have been in this position more than one time in the past and clearly it had not worked out in her favor because she had her new approach down to a science. She began comforting me with compliments on my hair and my lovely jewelry but as she approached the apex of her argument for a wardrobe change, it was clear she was aware she would be putting the depth and breadth of our friendship to the ultimate test.

"This dress isn't flattering to your figure," she began, "It draws too much attention to your midsection." The bomb had officially been dropped and the shrapnel from its impact continued to bounce off the wall of the bathroom and boomerang back to slap me in the face over and over again. I immediately began to smooth out the stomach area of my dress knowing exactly what she was referencing. She must have sensed my evacuating self-esteem because she immediately sprang into action making a mad dash to my closet. As I stood in my mirror, no longer wanting to look at myself, I could hear the shuffling of hangers as she frantically searched for a purchase previously made with my bad eating choices in mind. When she returned to the bathroom, it was almost as if she had a golden ticket in hand. "This one is going to kill 'em," she said and I actually believed her. Once I had slipped on the dress, her eyes lit up and I knew in that moment, this girl was truly my friend.

There was a picture that showed up on my Facebook timeline one day of a lion surrounded by other lions. The message was clear, you are who you surround yourself with and those you elect to have in your company serve critical purposes in your life. Each person you allow in your space should understand what you need from them and agree to uphold that purpose in your life. Often, our company is that thing that either propels us or stifles us. So many times, I have learned it is okay to change my circle as I continue to evolve, but my circle must be reflective of my goals in life.

When I first realized the challenges and strains of being a single mother in a big city like Atlanta, I found my circle included a lot of mothers I deemed successful in the area of balancing motherhood and professional pursuits. I found myself leaning on them to learn the tricks of the trade regarding how to properly care for a baby and still reach for goals I had set for myself prior to bringing a life into the world. In my weakest moments, they were my foundations. From them, I learned everything from proper burping techniques, to ways to soothe colic and even the cure for constipation for my daughter and myself. During that season of my life, I had no desire to associate myself with women who frequented area happy hours because my happiest hour occurred during 6:30 and 7:30 when I had just gotten up from my nap but could count on my daughter remaining in hers so I could have a few minutes to myself. I had nothing against these women; I'm sure from time to time, I envied their lives. But, my life had taken a turn and I had to make sure all those on my route wanted to see me win and would be able to help me to be a great mother.

A few years after I had gotten the swing of motherhood, my circle changed again as I began to focus more on my career. I spent long evenings on the phone with colleagues who were in pursuit of, or had obtained, the degree I was seeking in my field. What meant the most to me was hearing them discuss how much more in love with the profession they had fallen as they ventured deeper and deeper into the educational pedagogy of our practice. Our conversations were stimulating and like-minded; we all seemed to want the same thing and we all had creative ideas as to how we would arrive at our goals. They all inspired me to dream again. I had stopped dreaming about my own goals replacing them with goals I had set for my daughter. I felt as if I could make it all work because they loved all of my ideas and believed I could do exactly what I had put before them.

The fact of the matter is, if you ever want to grow and to be the best you can be in life, you have to surround yourself with people who not only tell you the truth about themselves, but about you as well. If you find yourself surrounded by a robotic group of "yes" men who see you struggling and uphold you in your foolishness, you are doomed for failure. When your circle can share their downfalls, shortcoming and successes with you in a safe space where everyone has the goal of learning and growing, you have found a circle worth keeping. When you can seek truth and honesty from those you elect to allow in your safe space and accept their perception without getting sensitive and falling out with them for ten years, you will be on the way to being your best self.

chapter 17

"Learn when to speak vs. when to listen"

"As I got older, I found some of my most effective friendships involved individuals who knew when to uphold me in my foolishness by allowing me to talk their ears off until I had removed the poisonous stinger lodged in my flesh. Sometimes, they never offered their own perspective or advice knowing I would jump at their approval of my erratic behaviors but instead allowed me to arrive at my own conclusions reminding me to remember to always acting from a place of maturity." –C. Frazier

Chapter Seventeen
Learn when to speak vs. when to listen

> Most people do not listen with the intent to understand; they listen with the intent to reply.
> — **Stephen R. Covey**

Listening to my friends in my twenties was pretty simple. Most of our problems surrounded our confusion regarding the mixed messages sent by the random guys we were dating or we spent time discussing the practicality of fashion trends and hair products. In fact, when we would ride in the car together, we would put on concerts assigning lead parts to each other and laughing at the end of the song. Our real life conversations would last all of fifteen minutes, then we had the rest of the ride to talk about absolutely nothing. So, one could imagine how impossible it was for me to switch gears the night one of my closest friends really wanted to "talk."

I couldn't have been more than 21 at the time having just graduated from college and preparing to relocate to Atlanta when my friends of a few years asked me to meet her at a local restaurant to hang out. I jumped in the car and headed her way looking forward to another night of pointless convos. We started out talking about guys and all that jazz when she shifted her questioning by asking, "What do you think about me and Drew getting back together?" There was an excitement in her voice when she asked the question. Looking back at it now, I can say I hadn't seen her excited about much since she and Drew called it quits. For months, she sulked around us while trying to jump back out into the dating scene. Each weekend, we forced her from the comfort of her own home and dumped her on dancefloors with random men clearly not looking for the promise of forever. Unfortunately for Drew he had "torn his drawers" with each of us and had no advocates on his behalf.

Drew had committed the oh-so-common infraction of going away to the beach with some of his buddies from college. He presented the trip as a way for the boys to reconnect over some beer and boarding and my friend was not reluctant to encourage him to have a great time. Their relationship had been solid from the beginning and each of us was secretly jealous of the bond they shared. When she told us about the trip, we didn't think anything of it and even began to plan a girl's weekend to mirror. It wasn't until we found out from a phone call things were not exactly as they seemed and our boy Drew had signed his own death warrant before he got back home.

As we were hanging out over lunch after pedicures, one of the girls in our group got a phone call from one of her friends who had some interesting questions about Drew. They beat around the bush a bit in the beginning, but as the conversation took its turn, my friend showed obvious discomfort as she relocated to the sidewalk in front of the restaurant. We speculated what might be going on but she wasn't crying so we weren't too concerned by whatever news she was receiving. When she returned to the table, no one spoke hoping she would be forthcoming. After a few moments, I asked if she was okay and she said she was upset. We followed her gaze hoping her eyes didn't fall on us almost like on A League of Their Own when the messenger came to the locker room to deliver the devastating news that one of the women was now a widow. When her head turned toward Drew's girlfriend, inside, all of us took a deep breath relieved we wouldn't have to kill anyone that night. When she started the story, we knew it was not going to end well.

She started by making sure we all remembered who the girl was who placed the call. I recalled meeting her in passing but she was no one I would know off hand. Many of us had come to a vague identification of the female but wanted her to get down to spilling the tea. In hindsight, I think she spent a lot of time trying to see if we could remember her because she felt it would give us some sort of foundation for the validity of her eyewitness report. She went on to say the young lady called her from the "boys trip" reporting every detail of what was going on. We had our very own spy accidentally planted in the middle of the event! A mole, a rat, an informant labeled our new best friend and she was detailed and concise in her descriptions. She shared that she and some friends had been invited by one of Drew's buddies to accompany them for the weekend under the pretense it would be one big relaxing getaway from the city. She and her five friends traveled to the beach only to find five gentlemen at the beach house they would share. That night, they enjoyed each other's company and after a visit from Jack Daniel's, things had gotten "interesting."

I am sure any onlooker could see the wheels turning in each of our heads as we painted the most disgusting pictures possible of what Drew and his buddies were doing with their weekend roommates. Drew's girlfriend immediately popped her purse on the table, coincidentally one she had received as a gift commemorating her anniversary with Drew, and began fiddling on the inside. As the cell phone that had been tucked safely in her bag made a grand appearance, we immediately pleaded with her to hear the rest of the story before contacting him. The look on her face told our orator she was on borrowed time so she would have to get to the point and quick!

According to the story, Drew had been recognized from an engagement party he and his girlfriend had attended at the Atlanta Botanical Garden. The pictures they had taken in the Cascades Garden seemed ready to serve as engagement photos for the two of them giving her a glimpse into what her life could be. The bride-to-be was the sister of the reporter proving once again it's a small world after all. She couldn't report much regarding Drew's behavior because she had become involved with one of his friends, but she commented feeling very uncomfortable with his exchanges knowing he was involved with someone and had been for quite some time.

And there it was.

The anger had turned to tears and she began to spew out her displeasure in his actions. It was almost as if a geyser had finally erupted and there was no clear ending in sight. Each of us listened to her ranting and raving with little effort to interject. I believe we all felt a sense of betrayal and now hated Drew for ruining all of our fairytales. I don't think we had enough evidence of wrongdoing to condemn him for treason, but there we were, burning him at the stake. First, we took in the information somberly, then it started. We started giving that advice each scorned friend gives compounding the situation with their past experiences with men and their cheating. Each girl seated at the roundtable took their turns sharing their sob stories with a strength they never had when dealing with their own situations. Suddenly, each of them had become their own matrimonial Marvel character shooting weapons of destruction at Drew's relationship until it combusted all over the restaurant. Drew's girlfriend had been silenced by our personal interjections. She was soaking it all in. After we had successfully transferred our own hurts on to her, we instructed her to place the call we all wanted to be present to enjoy. Each of us had already given her pieces of the script we wanted her to perform and it was time for the lights to come on and the cameras to roll. We had decided he was going to suffer on behalf of each man we had been hurt by and his demise would be a message to all men of what could happen if they ever tried us again!

The call began with a normal, casual greeting. It was clear to us she was luring him into her web and was ready to trap him in her sticky silk created by her spinnerets lying just beneath her words. The poor, unsuspecting fly had flown just a little too close and was now being prepared to satisfy her hunger by exposing his conceivable wrongdoings. As she began to question him extensively about his weekend, he began to struggle against the fine silk threading she had used as adhesive. As she sensed his struggle, she began to travel down the path of non-stick webbing created as a cleaver path for her to get close enough to her prey to watch him become his own demise. After he folded under cross examination, one thing was clear; the damage had been done, the trust had been broken and the awareness of those in their inner circle had deemed the relationship irreconcilable.

To our knowledge, she cut Drew off cold turkey almost like an addiction to nicotine however, there was no patch she could slap on her shoulder to ease the cravings. We knew it had been hard for her, we knew she wanted to take him back and, most importantly, we knew he probably had not done half the things we had constructed in our heads. Instead of us listening with an ear to hear and heal, we listened with the purpose of destroying and devouring. Nothing about our responses was indicative of our ability to listen. Had we been listening, we would have known how much Drew meant to her, how much their relationship had cultivated and refined her as a woman and we would have encouraged her to approach the situation with caution and not a jack hammer. I think we all learned a valuable lesson; we learned to determine if our friends need us to listen or to speak.

As I got older, I found some of my most effective friendships involved individuals who knew when to uphold me in my foolishness by allowing me to talk their ears off until I had removed the poisonous stinger lodged in my flesh. Sometimes, they never offered their own perspective or advice knowing I would jump at their approval of my erratic behaviors but instead allowed me to arrive at my own conclusions reminding me to remember to always act from a place of maturity. I began to look for more friends who possessed this ability as opposed to my "ride or die" chicks who would drive the getaway car and keep me amped up the entire ride to commit my crime. As I got older, it required less to act out of impulse, yet wanted to learn to restrain my emotions and learn to harness my frustration.

I remember getting a call from my daughter's father one day as I was preparing to join my friends for a day of fun. He had agreed to babysit for the day and give me a much needed and much deserved break from the monotony of motherhood. I was SO excited to have some adult fun I could hardly contain myself. I was almost out of the door when he sent me a text informing me he planned to expose my daughter to a situation I had asked him to shield her from. He had gone back on our deal and was presenting his plan to me as if I had no choice in the matter. Almost immediately, I began to take off my cute sundress to exchange it for some Jordan's, tank top and a ponytail. I had endured just about all I was going to take from him and as I jumped in my car to head to his parent's house, I had one friend in the car with me ready to ride out.

During the ride, she sat silently on the passenger side probably completely oblivious to this side of me which I had learned to keep cleverly hidden from my adult friends. I called my sister who encouraged me to follow my plan of kicking his butt given the fact I had made my stance on the situation very clear. Even my mother gave me her permission to address the situation in the fashion I felt best. I had all the validation I needed. Apparently, my trusty sidekick had been texting one of my more level-headed friends because my phone began to ring. She asked roundabout questions but I could tell she already knew what was going on. I vented to her through a shower of obscenities screaming my anger and my relentless attempt to work with him as a co-parent and how he continued to spit in my face. She remained calm, allowed me my time and when I was done, she calmly told me to breathe and tell her what kicking his butt would solve. I went all around the question knowing the answer but I needed to do this; I had to.

By the time I drove up to his parent's house, I was still frustrated but I was no longer seeing red, Instead, I was only seeing blue spots. I didn't feel I would pull his head off his shoulders in one snatch; instead, I thought I would reconsider his punishment and only kick his kneecap backward. Much better option. My home girl riding shotgun entered the house with me, began to play with the kids and entertain his father so I asked to see him outside. As he slowly sauntered toward the front door, I found myself growing more and more upset at the leisure way in which he was approaching the situation. I felt he was moving at a snail's pace almost as if he had nowhere to be and nothing to do except waste more of my time. In the thirty seconds he took to walk the twenty steps from the dining room to the front door, I was so ready to break his arm off and hit him with it. Although he got an earful, I was able to save myself from earning a ticket to trial for assault because I had been surrounded by friends who knew what I needed to hear and when I needed to hear it. I heard their advice and their concern and by the time I was to react, their influence had embedded itself into my brain enough for me to make a smarter decision.

I remember working with a kindergartener one Monday morning as we racked our brains trying to figure out why he had been tearing up the classroom. I received a call to my own 8th grade classroom asking me to intervene with the student because I had been viewed as the toughest teacher in the building when it came to discipline. I made sure my students were covered, working diligently on their assignment and I put on my "mean lady" hat ready to go to war.

I could hear our young student before I actually saw him. The crashing sound of instructional materials ricocheted down the hallway and reverberated in each corner of the hall. I was actually a little excited to show I was the right woman for the job; the only one they could and should call on in their time of trouble. As I approached the door of the classroom, other members of our administrative team were already assembled near the door and I was informed the boy's mother had already been called to come and pick him up. Discussions of removing him from the school had already gone forth and his jacket had already been summoned. Before going in, I listened to everyone explain the various research-based strategies to curve his behavior and how they had gone left. I wondered what they expected me to do or if I was being set up for failure.

After putting all the information together, I opened the door to the classroom which had been evacuated by everyone other than the young boy who seemed to be having an adult-sized meltdown. He was throwing everything he could reach and crying uncontrollably in between. I stood watching him and instead of viewing him as a criminal in the making, I saw his hurt and allowed his tantrum to speak to me. It was obvious he was very hurt by something and could not seem to find the words to express his feelings. I moved quietly into the room and closed the door behind me. One thing was for sure, I was either going to solve his problem or create one for myself.

The young man turned to look at me. For a moment, the look in his eye gave off the vibe of fear more than anger. Perhaps he had heard of me and felt I was coming in to rough him up a bit, but in that moment, he stood still and our showdown was underway. I noticed he had been going to town on the teacher's bulletin board so I began to search for her stapler. When I found it, I went to the board and began to put the letters back on with great precision. The boy stood quietly watching me. He seemed confused and although I wasn't yet sure what I was hoping to accomplish, I continued to work toward putting the room back together again.

After the board was done, I started standing the chairs back up and placing them under the miniature-sized tables. I started singing a song as I worked and I never acknowledged the young man still standing motionless in the middle of the room. When the tables were all set again, I looked around for the Lysol wipes. I found them near the sink and pulled two of the towels from the hole at the top of the cylinder. I decided this was the time to address my young onlooker. I walked over to him and offered the Lysol wipe. He did not move nor try to get the wipe out of my hand so I put it on the table. I took my wipe and began to clean the table in large circles. I saw the boy move a few steps toward the table inch by inch until he was standing before the wipe. He allowed his fingers to walk toward the wipe until he had it in his hands. He started wiping the table and I began to sing a little louder. Before I realized it, he and I had put the entire room back together.

I stood at the front of the room and said, "Now, that's better. Come on, let's take a break." I walked to the door and offered him my hand. He now skipped over to me, took my hand and we walked out of the classroom toward the front office. I was sure we had been working for about 30 minutes and his mother should have been on the campus but I had only calmed him down. I wanted to find out what had set him off and I didn't want anyone else to give me that information because I felt it would be more meaningful if it came from him. I wasn't sure if he could articulate his feelings to me but it felt it was worth a shot. After all, he had already done enough to earn a few days of a vacation with a nice invoice coming to his parents. I wanted to understand where he was coming from and if I could somehow find a way to get some answers to our questions.

I found some bottled water and sat down on the floor near the copy machines. My new friend sat next to me and I helped him to open his water. I finally asked him, "Can you tell me why you made the room so dirty?" He looked at me and began to cry again. I scooped him up and put him in my lap. I held him for a few moments and asked him again. He said, in his own way, that he hated school. When I asked him why, he said it was because he wanted to be with his mom but he had to come to school. Now, this was normal but for it to set him off in such a dramatic way was still a bit foreign to me.

His mother was escorted to where he and I were sitting. When I saw her face, I could see the worry. I invited her to sit on the floor with us and I passed him from my lap to hers. After she calmed him down again, I asked him to go into the restroom and to wash his face. He complied and I took a moment to share with his mother the events of the day. She explained how the two of them has escaped a domestic violence situation only a few days before and how the boy had seen her beaten at the hands of his father. The boy had been injured trying to defend his mother. She said my decision to have him clean the room with me was smart because he had often helped her clean up the house after her husband had thrown her around the house. We now knew what we needed to know to help the young man all because we had listened and not spoken.

At 35, I have learned as someone's friend or casual companion, you have a responsibility to learn what they need from you and when it's appropriate to give it to them. In order for us to come to this much of this information, we have to know when we just need to be a presence and not a voice. It's natural for you to be protective of your friend and find yourself just as upset about some of the situations they encounter as they are, however, you have to know when your opinion will only fuel the fire. If the goal is to help each other be the best person we can be, each of us will have to take on the job of reminding them of what's most important. Sometimes, what's most valuable is not where they have been, but where you know they are trying to go. True, you can't shield them from their storms but you can be there with a cup of tea and a towel when they make it inside to dry off.

chapter 18

"Be Consistent"

"As an adult, the consistency of a friendship must not be taken lightly on either side. When a friend shows you consistent care and concern, it is taxing on them. When you agree to be receiving of it, you are making a commitment on your part to be open to it and to reciprocate it whenever you can.." -C. Frazier

Chapter Eighteen
Be consistent

Small disciplines repeated with consistency every day lead to great achievements gained slowly over time.

— John C. Maxwell

I hate funny acting people. You know exactly who I am referring to when I say that because we have all experienced wishy washy people who pretend to be our friends in private but who pull a Judas routine on us when in the company of others. I think the Real Housewives of Atlanta have brought a whole new meaning to the phrase by behaving as two-faced monsters attacking the very ideal of true friendship. Although it made for great television for many seasons, I wondered if they were giving us a silent approval to be inconsistent as friends.

One of the funniest episodes of the show made popular by NeNe Leakes, her friend Cynthia Bailey was ridiculed for constructing a friendship contract. The contract called for NeNe to understand Cynthia's needs as a friend and to clearly articulate what would be needed for their friendship to be defined as a successful relationship. For the most part, Cynthia's concern was of NeNe's "flip flopping" behavior which showed NeNe loving on Cynthia one minute, and bashing her and her marriage the next. Cynthia, oftentimes, had been cautioned by others to be mindful of NeNe's behavior however, Cynthia elected to support her friendship and address the immediate concerns in a calm and comedic manner. While the friendship contract seemed silly to the rest of the housewives and most reality television addicts, Cynthia was on to something; as long as friends could remain consistent, the friendship could survive.

A true friend will bring your fat butt a honey bun. I knew Camille was my friend because she became my own personal caped crusader during my fourth grade school year. If you want to know what a real friend looks like, you can consult any dictionary and see a picture of Camille who could easily serve as the poster child for friendship. What had Camille done to make her such a remarkable friend whose name should be etched in the Guinness Book of World Records? Camille had, single-handedly, smuggled over 250 iced honey buns for me and escaped prosecution undetected. This might not seem like a big deal to you, but I know the skill it required for her to serve such a purpose and she will always be one of my childhood heroes for her tenacity and innovation.

It was no secret I had a weight problem much of my life. My problem was simple. I loved sweets and French fries! My mother, however, was tired of my father making reference to my growing waistline through his subtle hints suggesting she was not paying enough attention to my diet. Although she was a masterful, Cajun culinary artist, my father expected her to figure out how to create the same delicious menu which had been the source of my fat deposits and modify it to get some of the unwanted and unattractive pounds off my stomach. I took advantage of the fact it would take my mom a long time to figure out how to substitute heavy cream and cheese for a healthier diversion and began to construct a plan to combat the changes I knew were coming. Little did I know, but Camille would serve as the perfect Thelma to my Louise.

As my mother began to work harder to monitor my food intake, my life slowly became a hell of healthy snacks and portion control. My allocated daily food amount was barely enough to nourish a toddler yet I was expected to chew slowly and savor each bite. I decided I was not going to take such abuse lying down so one day, I decided to take matters into my own hand and allow school to serve as my official ground zero as it was the only place my parents could not implement dietary restrictions with any real supervision. Camille, who was in full support of rebellious behavior, volunteered to smuggle some forbidden contraband into the walls of the schoolhouse for my pleasure. Her rationale was that by providing me with those things I would need to survive such as sweets and pastries, she would be supporting a healthy life for me at home. As long as I was stuffed with sugar, I would be a more pleasant daughter and would be more reasonable with my oppressors.

Each morning, Camille would meet me in between the library and the gymnasium cleverly hidden by iron trash cans decorated with red and white tiger paws. We would exchange pleasantries until we secured the perimeter and completed the handoff. I would give her a heart-filled hug and send her to class with an assurance that she was the bomb.com! After our meeting, I would scurry my chubby tail to the restroom near the Art class which was always the cleanest one, and in the stall closest to the back, I would remove my treat from my bag, sit on the toilet and take delicate bites of my Big Texas.

Now, if anyone claims to be a true, authentic Southerner, they are familiar with a Big Texas. A Big Texas is a cinnamon roll packed into a small wrapper concealing 460 calories per dessert. It is not uncommon to eat a Big Texas out of the wrapper, but if you want to take things to a whole new level, you can take the bun out of the wrapper and zap it in the microwave for about 10 seconds to prompt the melting of the icing. What you will have at the end of that process will be a delicious ooey, gooey pile of sinful delight. During my special, secluded moments with my daily Big Texas treats, I didn't mind having to scrape most of the icing off the wrapper given the fact it had been tucked into Camille's Jansport backpack. The only thing I cared about was blowing my entire diet and doing things my way.

Most months, Camille continued to surprise me with everything from Cheetos to peanut M&M's and my mother could not figure out for the life of her why my scale continued to tip on the larger side. I would simply shrug my shoulders when asked why I had not been dropping any weight knowing darn well it would be impossible for me to make any changes with my hidden secret blowing my daily calorie count out of the water. I felt badly for my mother knowing she would have to come up with a creative explanation for my father who would now be annoyed at their inability to change my physique. Although I wasn't happy about what she would endure, I took it all in stride.

Then, one day it happened...I showed up for my daily meeting with Camille and she wasn't there! For the first few minutes, I didn't panic knowing she had to ride the bus to school. Instead, I leaned against the wall and waited patiently for her to arrive with my special delivery. After what seemed like forever, I realized she was cutting into my private time so I began to drag myself to class. As my first period class dragged on into oblivion, I was worried about Camille. This was not like her at all. I hoped she was okay and that my treats would arrive unblemished. I could not wait for her to meet me in the hallway armed with an apology for ruining my morning but as I looked down the hallway, I could not find her. What happened to my friend?

Camille showed up around lunch time and I was elated to see her lined up to get her pizza. I wondered why she had not come to my P.E. class which was right by the cafeteria but I was not going to cry about it. I was just happy she was okay and I couldn't wait to return to our regularly scheduled program. I moved closer to her however, as I neared, she looked at me, turned and walked in another direction. I was sure she had not seen me; perhaps she had been blinded by the shining glare of the metal milk cooler. I excused her error and continued to advance toward her. She seemed to increase her speed and finally slowed at a table decorated in pink, denim and sparkles everywhere. Camille was sitting with some other girls from our class and I noticed there was no room for me.

I wasn't sure what was happening but I didn't want to bring attention to the situation. I turned slowly and began to walk toward the door. I glanced back to catch Camille's face only to see her engrossed in conversation which included frequent hair tosses and clapping hands. I was totally confused but I exited without dialogue or explanation.

For the rest of the day, Camille ignored my very existence. She walked right past me as she hurried to catch up with the new group of girls who seemed to grab her attention. I noticed she seemed quite comfortable with her new team and she was perfectly happy being their Minions. As she scurried to fall in step with their uniform movements, she no longer looked like my precious Camille who valued the importance of the priceless Big Texas. What happened to my friend?

Camille continued her new song and dance for weeks to follow. I grew accustomed to looking her way only to have her turn away or, even worse, not look in my direction at all. I no longer expected my daily fix from her as she seemed to forget I had ever existed. While I was clearly angry about her decision to abandon me in my time of need, part of me was happy she had found a home with girls she could enjoy in the open hallways of our school as opposed to the secrecy of our holes. I was happy she would not have to nurse their habits or deceive their parents. My friend had found...friends with benefits.

One day, as I rushed to my class as if the world was still spinning on it normal, unpredictable axis, a familiar voice cut through the educational fog. The voice seemed calm, yet uncomfortable. I turned to see Camille standing about ten yards from me. I should have been happy to see her, happy to have her acknowledge my presence again but, instead, I was instantly furious. How dare she speak to me as if she had not disowned me like a rag doll? Although the weeks of our ridiculous dance found me feeling more empty than I had ever felt before, inside of me was a decent amount of pride and I was not going to let her get away with disowning me. I wanted her to understand that although I was a physical mess with a ton of crap going on in my family during that time, I was still deserving of a friendship. She needed to understand the fact that although I might have viewed myself as trash, she had to always see my treasure. Weird, huh?

Camille elected to take the denial approach to a possible reconciliation. She never admitted she had ever stopped talking to me suggesting it was my fault because I appeared to be so busy. She believed our time apart had been beneficial for both of us so we could focus on the cure for tuberculosis or whatever pressing bit of information we needed to be focused on. I simply looked at her with a "shut up, trick" look on my face hoping she would realize I knew she had been blowing smoke up my butt. I began to hope we could go back to being best buds. To tell the absolute truth, I missed her. I just needed to know she would never subject me to such a crazy phase in our friendship again. Just as I had begun to embrace the idea of our friendship again and was prepared to welcome it with a hug, Camille's new buddies appeared in the hallway. Now, this was the time for Camille to prove to me she was my true friend and no matter what, we would always survive the funnels of friendship. Camille, however, turned toward the opposite wall, became oddly fascinated with her watch and walked away to catch up with her team. I watched her walk away...and never look back. It was then I knew, the honeymoon was truly over.

I didn't know what a consistent friend looked like until my mother passed away suddenly. So many things happened in such a short amount of time for me and my family. It seemed like days would drag across a burning desert filled with ash only to repeat itself with each day. Although most days immediately following her passing found me wearing the same, long black sundress, it was not the consistency of my wardrobe that I could count on. The one thing I began to set my clock to was the phone calls I would receive from my best friend.

No one teaches you how to be there for someone when they lose someone as precious as a mother. It doesn't matter how many times you have been there when a friend needed a sober driver or how many times you held their hand through a breakup. When the unimaginable happens in their lives, you are forced to evaluate their importance in your life and you in theirs. It is at that time you have to decide if you are truly in the relationship for the long haul understanding that once you offer yourself as a crutch, you might forever serve as that saving grace. To be someone's saving grace means you have signed a contract with that person to be a walking representation of the redeeming grace of God. That is a huge undertaking and one to never be taken lightly.

I learned a lot from my best friend during the first month after my tragedy. I learned that a real friend takes on your pain as if it is their own and they work very hard to try to ease that pain on a daily basis. No matter if it is a card, a text, a kind word, a hug, a dinner, a surprise party or even a scream session, they make sure you know you are not alone. I can't say it takes the pain away, because it absolutely does not, but I can say that it makes it bearable to know that it is recognized as a crippling handicap you must now learn to handle.

As an adult, the consistency of a friendship must not be taken lightly on either side. When a friend shows you consistent care and concern, it is taxing on them. When you agree to be receiving of it, you are making a commitment on your part to be open to it and to reciprocate it whenever you can. I now know how to be there for a friend, for my best friend has taught me how to survive through the love of a friend who won't leave me; no matter what.

chapter 19

"Proximity does not define importance"

"I developed an understanding that just because friends were no longer a short drive away, as long as two hearts were on the same page at the same time, that was just as good as being in the same space and time." -C. Frazier

Chapter Nineteen
Proximity does not define importance

The scariest thing about distance is that you don't know whether they'll miss you or forget you.
— Nicholas Sparks

My first year in my Master's program, my professors threw a bunch of resources my way knowing as a new educator, I would need an arsenal of good ideas to meet the needs of my kids. I combed through articles and articles each night preparing for class quickly learning how to qualify the things I could use and the things I simply needed to have some type of awareness of. In one of my classes designed to curtain behavior concerns, I learned all about utilizing proximity partners. The basis of the idea is that when working on a task, if the student gets hung up, they are allowed to work with the other kids who are within their reach. In other trainings, this method is designed to increase student support and to prompt social interaction in situations where students might otherwise work alone and potentially suffer in silence if they have not grasped the concept.

The first time I introduced the concept in my classroom, I used it as a way to keep down the noise level in the classroom as it set boundaries in the room and taught the kids that the only people important to their immediate success were the ones seated closest to them. Prior to putting this idea in place as a strategy, the kids elected to sit with their friends creating a classroom party on a daily basis. The kids who sat near each other often lived in the same neighborhoods and, therefore, knew each other well and shared experiences and encounters over the years. While I felt the kids should have been able to handle sitting with their friends knowing full well the academic requirements necessary to pass my class, my kids lacked maturity and discipline so it was time for me to intervene and put proximity partners into heavy rotation. After explaining the parameters in great detail, I began to see a shift in the class structure after the first two assignments were graded.

Slowly, the kids began to swap seats to sit with other kids in the class who seemed to be performing better than they were faring in the course. I started shortening the class time in which the assignments were due which kept the kids ever more focused and many of the students realized they were not going to make it without the support of the person the closest to them almost to the extent the rest of the kids in the class did not matter to their success for those 90 minutes.

When I completed my 9th grade year, I faced the harsh reality I would have to move away from the city I had called home for only about 8 years. Yet, again, my mother's job was uprooting me and forcing me to start my life all over again. Although I had been through it before, it was different this time because the girls I had become the closest with for four years had become my proximity partners. We did everything together including dressing alike and taking classes together. On the weekends during our 6th-8th grade years, we found ourselves together hanging out and high school had been no different. Now, I was expected to be the last one welcomed into the group and now, I would be the first one out. It was unfair to me on so many levels as we had challenged each other to be excellent students bragging on straight A's like others would brag on notes from boys. I didn't know how I was supposed to last without them. We had become a clique, and indestructible sisterhood with bonds visible to any onlooker. We were truly joined at the hip.

The day I left to make the move, I remember immediately deciding I was going to hate my mother for years to come. There was no way I was going to let a day go by where she wouldn't feel uncomfortable dealing with me because she had taken my support system from me and I had no choice in the matter. As the mile markers continued to pass me by hour after hour, I could no longer turn around and see anything familiar to me and I realized my friends weren't going to be at arm's length. I was again going to be on my own in a new place expected to still do great things.

Arriving in the new city was no exciting moment for me. The air stank with unfamiliar accents and the slow pace of the cars coupled with the ancient cityscape made me sick to my stomach. I hated it and I hadn't even unpacked one suitcase. My mother seemed proud of the apartment she had selected for us giving me a room far away from hers to allow me some privacy. I was, to say the least, unfazed by all of it and went into the room and shut the door tight. I left all of my things in the car that night hoping during the night I would grow the balls to jack her car keys and steal the car. My destination would be clear; I would be going back home. I lay awake all night listening to my mom talking to random people on the phone soliciting their advice on how to deal with me knowing I had razor blades in my glare waiting to cut her in half.

In the weeks to come, it was time for me to get prepared to start my 10th grade year at a new school. I was mortified knowing it would never be the same for me being around the kids at my new high school. I finally snuck on the phone late one night and called one of my friends from home; the one I had first met who made me feel like I had real friends. When the phone rang the first two times, I was afraid she had already forgotten about me and I would never talk to her again. I wondered if it was best for me to rip off the Band-Aid and accept the fact I no longer had them as my proximity partners. Suddenly, she was there. The voice was just as I had remembered it all those years. Immediately, hearing Carmen's voice brought out the tears I had refused to give my mom and this God-awful city. I said I would not let the change in locale break me by bringing me to tears but I couldn't lie to Carmen. I was afraid, angry, discouraged and destroyed by this new situation in my life and I felt my proximity partner was the thing I needed to bring balance to my being.

When she realized it was me on the other line, she just took a deep breath and told me she was happy I called. I continued to cry as I struggled for the words to tell her so she could understand all the thoughts I was feeling on the inside. She seemed to know how I was feeling already because she began to answer the questions I couldn't seem to bubble in on my mental answer sheet. She told me how proud she was of me because she knew I wasn't going to let my grades fall. She promised me I was going to make friends easily and she and the crew would find a way to come and visit me. I believed every word she said and although I couldn't stop the tears, my heart was becoming steadier inside my hollow chest.

I began to choke my way through my anger towards my mom and she immediately cut me off. Carmen reminded me of the importance of having a mother in my life by explaining to me where she felt she would be if she didn't have her mother with her each day. I listened to her as she wrote her personal ode to her mother through the phone and I was envious, as I had always been, of the outpouring of love she always seemed to have for her mother. She made me promise I wouldn't quit and I would keep college on my mind. I began to dry my eyes and I promised my friend I would keep my end of the bargain. We promised we would be together again our first year of college and I knew she would be there. I wanted to meet her there. I couldn't promise I would like it, but I promised her I would try my absolute best to stay connected to them and what we had learned as proximity partners.

Through the years, I struggled being away from the ones I considered to be my real friends. No one ever seemed to "get" me at my new school and I always felt like an outsider. I felt no matter what, everyone was always looking for ways to remind me I was a visitor and I never tried to conform to their way of doing things. When things felt lonely, I never rubbed elbows with the students at my school like I had with my friends from home. Instead, I ran up my phone bill calling them every chance I got hoping to feel connected to them from four hours away. I missed them and I felt like their lives were going on without me and I was not happy.

Phone call after phone call, I tried very hard to stay attached to my friends and they always reached back to pick up my broken heart. Each time we spoke, they glued my life back together enough for me to get back on stable footing so I could endure the daily struggle to try to make new friends. I realized my proximity partners would always be hours and hours away but their love and support always seemed to fly down the highway ignoring all stop signs and speed traps. Their love would wrap me up at night to help me get through the days and years that followed.

I continued to move a lot going from one college to another. When I finally settled in Atlanta, I found a lot of my close friends spread all over the South. Although many of them I could not seem to coordinate time to see them, I always knew a phone call was just as binding and an impromptu trip would be. In many ways, I felt closer to friends in Texas than I did with women I had met in Georgia. I developed an understanding that just because friends were no longer a short drive away, as long as two hearts were on the same page at the same time, that was just as good as being in the same space and time. Thanks to what I learned from my friends a long time ago, I believe in the long distance relationship and the possibility that no matter the nature of the relationship, as long as there is a true bond, proximity does not determine importance.

chapter 20

"Embrace your differences"

"Both of my pinky toes are adorned with sexy little nails who had a conversation one day and decided to turn black on the same day at the same time." -C. Frazier

Chapter Twenty
Embrace your differences

It is not our differences that divide us. It is our inability to recognize, accept, and celebrate those differences.
— **Audre Lorde**

Both of my pinky toes are adorned with sexy little nails who had a conversation one day and decided to turn black on the same day at the same time. I couldn't quite pinpoint the day it actually happened, but one morning while rushing to turn off my squealing cell phone resting on my night stand alerting me to 6:50 a.m., the nail on the right foot decided to shake hands with the bottom corner of my bedframe. Needless to say, I grabbed the toe tightly to ward off the mind numbing pain threatening to skyrocket through my foot up through every vital nerve of my body until it crawled out of my pores in the form of hot tears down my cheeks. As I rested on my bed for the few seconds required to allow the pain to subside, I glanced down at my toe prepared to find it dangling by a thread after the abuse it had just taken, but it stood tall and steadfast. However, as it looked back at me, it no longer had its angelic, cream coat peering from the top of my foot. Instead, it now wore a frown of dark brown never to leave as a reminder of just how much the little guy had taken over the years. I figured, that old soldier had marched, and for his trouble, the least I could do was to be forced to wear dark colored polish to hide his war wounds.

I figured I should be embarrassed by my newest deformity being it was sure to draw negative attention to my clumsy nature. I found myself looking for shoes to cleverly conceal my odd new identifying mark sure someone would have something slick to say about my frustrated friend. Sooner than later, I decided it was time to suck it up and allow the world to learn I was not perfect as the Georgia heat began to force us all into less and less clothing. It was important for me to stay as cool as possible which meant I could no longer hide behind Nike and Reebok if I was going to survive the summer. Old Navy had been my best friend with its annual flip flop sale giving each shopper a chance to purchase shoes for $1.00. I had purchased ten different colors to match each tank top and short set for the heated days to come. As I stepped out, prepared to brave the world and its judgmental eyes, I had subscribed myself to the looming questions sure to come about my baby toes. I was careful to remember the importance of a positive approach. I was definitely cautious of the professional "ribbers" who considered it an art to break people down if they dared engage in a tit for tat slinging of insults.

My first stop was to my friend's house as we had a date at a local park party. As we performed our usual "pregaming routine" of drinking a few shots of whatever remained from her last house party where a bottle had been the cost of admission and enjoying a flashback session with the classic record, 400 Degreez, I tried my best to bring up my toe in hopes she would provide me with my first encounter with public scrutiny. After several attempts to all but put my feet in her mouth, I finally asked, "Girl, how does my toe look?" As she looked closer and closer at my toe, she examined it from all sides and replied, "If you hadn't said anything, I would have never noticed." She then went on to take me on a tour of her plethora of weird and unusual distinguishing marks as if to ease my mind of being ashamed of my appendage.

After our human Venn diagram was complete, we sat together with nothing else to expose about our physical imperfections as we had addressed everything from hangnails to hemorrhoids. One thing was clear to me; if we ever doubted the validity of our friendship, it had now undergone its final test of authenticity for we had revealed what we considered to be the worse about one another and laughed at how ashamed we had been about each one of the war wounds we had earned. It was apparent that what we considered to be the things that would provide others with a platform to push us away, we had used them as the glue to hold us together for we had learned to embrace those things that made us different for in those things, we had found our commonalities.

Now, my encounter with my witty friend, Kirsten, did not go so well. After bravely revealing my toe to her after receiving a more supportive response from the bestie, I was met with a much more critical response. She began to compare my toe to everything from sweet Gherkin to a Christmas pickle forcing my toes back behind the leather of my Adidas. I realized that, on the flip side, everyone will not be as sensitive to your insecurities so before you reveal them to others, you better have skin thick as leather. After Kirsten had brought herself to tears wiping them away with a trembling hand, I wanted to shove my toe dead in the back of her throat. Instead, I did my best to join in on the laugh at my own expense realizing I had just given her permanent permission to laugh at my pain.

I was sure I was going to regret it because this particular friend had a talent for saving things in her memory bank and withdrawing them at the perfect time to make you the ass of any joke. She would slide your imperfections into her "examples" required to prove her points showing us we were all subject to being the butt of her witticisms at any time. If we had been smart, we would have put her butt on the stage at Uptown Comedy Corner and made some real money.

When I was eleven, I began my middle school career at Tarver Middle School. I had moved to Shreveport, Louisiana with my mother as her job with BellSouth had demanded her relocation. We left my family behind, including my father, and found ourselves two hours north of my hometown of Alexandria. I was only eight at the time but it was clear I had no say so in the matter. After finishing my fourth and fifth grade year at Island Elementary School, I was happy to move across town off Pines Road to attend TMS. Once again, I found myself as the new girl at school as most of my classmates had attended Turner for years in its adjoining elementary school. I sat in most of my classes trying to learn the ropes at a new school with sports, music programs and new classes whose location I could not seem to find without the assistance of teachers hanging from the classroom door frames.

One day, as I sat in my Math class trying my best to ignore the most beautiful boy I had ever seen in my life, I felt a tap on my shoulder with a pencil. I turned to see the face of a skinny girl with pink-rimmed glasses smiling at me. "You dropped this," she said. I looked at her face and it seemed like I had known her forever. I thanked her and turned back in my seat trying my best to make sense of the numbers on the page in front of me. I noticed she was writing feverishly behind my head and the slow pace of my pencil indicated I would need to do something different if I was going to do well in my class. I took out a sheet of paper and wrote a quick note to the buddy on my back simply asking, "Do you understand number seven? Can you help me?"

I turned around in my seat and put the note on the corner of her desk as not to disturb her flow. She immediately looked up with the same gentle look in her eyes and opened the note without losing my face. She read the note and nodded her head. She raised her hand high in the air and I sat confused as she waited patiently to speak to the teacher grading at her desk blocking the examples of the problems we were working. It took forever for the teacher to acknowledge the elevated arm in the air as she forbade us from yelling out in her classroom. Finally, she pried her eyes from her assessment and said, "Yes, Carmen?" Carmen went on to ask the teacher if she could work with me on the problems. Although I was embarrassed the entire class now knew I was struggling in Math, I would be more embarrassed if my mother came up to the school to show out on me if I didn't do well in the class so I was willing to endure the uncomfortable feeling of being called out in front of my peers for the greater good. The teacher agreed to allow us to work together and immediately after she had rendered her decision, hands began to creep their way into the air as my colleagues realized they, too, needed some help. Carmen began to help me with my Math and after we had completed the assignment with proficiency, we began to prepare for appreciation from our peers who were now tucked safely away in their tutoring sessions.

Carmen and I worked very well together and it was clear Math was one of her strong suits. She eased me through the problems and explained it in a way it seemed as if I had known the process for years. She seemed more proud of me than she was of herself and as the class ended and we were instructed to submit our work to the teacher's red, wire crate. We both knew we had A's coming our way. For the first time since moving to the area, I felt a bit more comfortable seeing I could find ways to experience success in my new surroundings. Carmen, who seemed more focused than any other kid in any of my classes, had done more for me than she could have imagined.

After class, amidst the sounds of screeching tennis shoes and idle chit chat, Carmen extended an invitation for me to join her in the cafeteria. I knew I had to check into my fourth period class before going to lunch so she and I agreed to meet up later near the Fruitopia machine. I was excited at the opportunity to have actual conversation during my lunch period as I had be sitting in silos by the ping pong tables drinking milk from a carton in hopes no one would notice the fact I had no friends. I subscribed to watching random boys and a hollow, plastic ball dancing across a table while convincing myself it was worth my time. I would find myself hit by their balls every now and then but at least I was confident I was alive through the jarring of the unsuspecting assault. The option of discussing anything other than table tennis was an exciting change and I found myself ducking and dodging the other kids in the hallways to fulfil my attendance duty prior to joining Carmen for our lunch date.

During lunch, I met several other friends who seemed to be the same as Carmen. They were nice, helpful, and quiet and a bit more mature than the other girls in had met. They seemed fascinated to hear more about my life in my previous city. They were enthralled by my annual visits to Christmas festivals and large fairs with my family and I felt important. I shared I could sing which required me to put on a mini concert at the table which normally would have shamed me. With them, I felt I could do no wrong and after my rendition of a popular song, their reassuring smiles showed me I was the missing piece to their puzzle. Each of them was interested in something else; Carmen enjoyed orchestra as did Rhonda while Lesha loved basketball. I decided I would try both things to see if I could enjoy them as well.

After a few months of learning each other, one thing was clear; each of us was needed to complete our circle. There was room for everyone to have input given the fact each of us was having our own experiences separate and apart from the group. No one could give a report on the orchestra except for those of us who took the class. No one could make fun of the pep squad because four of us found ourselves on the team. No one could bad mouth girls' basketball because we had a buddy suiting up each week. It felt good to know the circle seemed complete once I entered as the final piece to the puzzle.

As an adult, I had to learn to keep my circle small after some unfortunate attempts to run with a big crowd. Now, don't get me wrong, nothing is erroneous about having a large group of people to have in your social circle. In fact, I encourage everyone to keep a team of about twenty people who will stand hand and hand with you and gladly accept the consequences of a drunk and disorderly conduct violation all in the name of your 35th birthday party. However, there has to be a clear boundary between that group and those who you will expect to show up for your child's awards day ceremony.

Now, prior to arriving at such a realization, I made a ton of mistakes. I shared my shortcomings and insecurities with those who would make it the focus of subliminal shots on social media outlets. I watched people who had weaseled their ways into my space, take the nuggets of truth I fed them with great openness and regurgitate the contents all over those who desired to see me fail. I had spent a lot of time trying to fit in with everyone else by showing them all of the ways we were actually the same, but when it was said and done, what I found was that all they were looking for were the things that made us different which they would use against me.

As adults we have to learn it is not always a good thing to fit in so snugly with every group we encounter. Yes, you should always be prepared to function in various settings, but what makes you uniquely you will be the contributions you bring to the conversation. If your swan song is identical to everyone else, you are simply a clanging symbol. To embrace the differences of others, you must start by embracing your own personal differences. Once you are comfortable with your ugly toe or your tendency to be the overly protective designated driver who tends to ruin reckless nights of fun with your adult, professional counterparts, you will understand that you are just...different. In embracing that reality, you will value what you bring to the group knowing it is the piece that will complete any puzzle. Without you and that awkward thing you bring to the table, the world will be devoid of the final piece to make it complete. Be different, look for friends who are different and get out there in the world and enjoy some different experiences.

chapter 21

"Reciprocity"

"Although nights were lonely, most of the time spent in solitude was arguably one of the best decisions I made for my personal growth."

–C. Frazier

Chapter Twenty One
Reciprocity

The tiger will never lie down with the lamb; he acknowledges no pact that is not reciprocal. The lamb must learn to run with the tigers.
— **Angela Carter**

I remember my 7th grade middle school Math teacher quite well because she always sat at her desk eating sour pickles from the jar as we worked tirelessly on her assignments. The smell of the juice was often nauseating due to its expert paring with vanilla flavored coffee but each of us were forced to endure it as we were merely human calculators stapled to creaking desks. Day after day she introduced Mathematical concepts I couldn't help but to wonder when they would ever be used in my daily life, however, what I needed more than anything was the "A" in her course to keep my parents in my pocket, or better yet, my greedy hands in theirs. So that morning when she came in to introduce reciprocal fractions, I paid close attention to the instruction.

The concept was quite simplistic. All one needed was a clear understanding of the numerator and denominator. If you understood that the numerator was the number of parts and the denominator was the number of parts it could be divided into, you would be able to find the reciprocal. The only step that would remain would be to flip them on top of each other. I couldn't quite understand why my classmates could not seem to master the concept but I found myself being summoned by many of my counterparts needing help completing the worksheet we had been provided. As I weaved through each group, I wondered why the teacher was still tucked away behind her desk snacking away but I did my job as the top of my class and I worked to build my learning community. Now that I think about it, that pickled cucumber eating lady owes me some dividends for doing her job!

I heard the term reciprocity again during freshman week in college during an introductory panel session where we were assigned the topic of relationships. Undoubtedly, the upperclassmen and deans were concerned with our newfound freedom and how it would lend to some pretty childish decisions of a sexual nature so the line of questioning was designed to probe our brains about our relationship experience. One overzealous girl from Houston, who would later serve as one of my roommates, braved the topic and shared her definition of a relationship as a reciprocity. The room began to buzz with her new vocabulary lesson but what she said next as her explanation was what I found most profound.

She mentioned how she had watched her parents share roles in her house with the father showing his love for the wife by working a lucrative job and performing a daily "honey do" list with an appreciation for his contribution to the family structure. The mother, on the other hand, demonstrated her love for her husband by having a career of her own which allowed her to make financial contributions to the family's bottom line while providing him and his children with a nurturing home. The great detail by which she explained the structure of her family was cute but the reciprocity piece needed a little more work. So, as if she realized she had not tied her example to her word choice, she brought it all together by assuring us that in some cases, her mom's job was that thing that held the family together and at any given time, the importance of her father's role was irreplaceable. What seemed most obvious was the fact the children had been taught the value in both jobs so at any time, for their family to work, either could flip the other.

Many people will argue to the point of physical contact as to whether or not a man and a woman can have a platonic relationship. For some strange reason, people believe if a penis and vagina are in close proximity to each other, they have no choice but to play a nasty game of "just the tip." Even as a young adult, this could be argued as true because high school guys were notorious for seeking new and creative ways to talk girls out of their panties. Yes, the girl could be someone they had sat next to in class since they were in preschool, but when they got a taste of the sexual nectar withheld from them until they were old enough to grab a sip of it behind the backs of their caretakers, every girl with a box became fair game.

After many years of sexual encounters with members of the opposite sex, one would assume the edge would be taken away. It would seem probable to have a man and a woman operating in close quarters without the presence of temptation ever looming overhead. For some reason, many believed this could never happen despite being professional trained in our fields, paying bills and even starting families, we all seemed to lack the discipline to cultivate real relationships with members of the opposite sex. When my male best friend and I publically presented ourselves to the world, we quickly learned everyone around us had not gotten to the point they could be around the genitalia of others without being tempted to touch.

In this case, I did not realize how much I needed a man in my life and in what capacity. I had grown accustomed to doing most things for myself as a single mother. Outside of calking a sink or repairing the siding on my house, I had learned to do most things on my own. When I made the decision to be abstinent, I felt I had finally rid myself of the crippling need for a man in my life. Although nights were lonely, most of the time spent in solitude was arguably one of the best decisions I made for my personal growth.

When Marvin and I met, it was by mistake. I was teaching an indoor cycling class and he was a member of the class. He was very cordial introducing himself as one of the veteran members of the course I was now taking over. He made sure I understood the previous practices of the former instructor so I would not be blindsided by the backlash I would receive for making changes to the routine. He, however, vowed to stay with me if I would remain committed to the job. At that moment, we made our first, real vow to one another and I felt I could trust him.

Over the months to follow, we began to walk out to the parking lot together. Now, I think his motive for making sure I made it to my car safely was to ensure I was not going to quit after the prediction had come to fruition. He watched me endure much controversy from other class members who were not as welcoming of change and he could tell the continuous challenges to my talent was taking its toll on me. During our walk to the car, we would act out silly parodies showing us we had a lot in common. He was easy to talk to and the more we laughed outside of class, the more I looked forward to continuing with the class despite its challenges.

I planned my 33rd birthday celebration a few weeks after Marvin and I met however, I felt I had known him for years so he received an invitation. He agreed to attend one of the events with his girlfriend and when they showed up, I knew we had reached a milestone in our relationship. The fact he had convinced his girlfriend to attend the birthday party of a female friend she had never met showed me he must have been sharing some information about our bond outside of my knowledge. I was honored to have him to share in my special moment and I was sure I had made a lifelong friend.

In the fall, his relationship with his girlfriend had taken a turn for the worse and he found himself back on the market and severely scarred after their civil war. Although he was reluctant to discuss the details of the break up, I found him hanging out more and more at my house. We grew accustomed to hanging out after class and I got the point I could count on a taste tester each night as I worked in the kitchen to recreate some of my mom's best dishes.

Sometimes, we would talk for hours and other times we wouldn't say anything at all. The first few weeks of him coming over, he would ease out around 3 in the morning but after that, we would wake up on the couch gripped by the pain coming from our limbs that had been locked in impossible positions for hours. I would lay my head in his lap and sleep better than I had slept in years. It was a comfort in knowing he was there to handle any situation should it arise in the middle of the night. Because of his presence, I could rest without worrying about being the man of the house.

One Thursday, after watching a hot and steamy episode of Scandal with our mutual friends, we decided to invite our good friend, Jose Cuervo, to the party. After shooting through several bottles, we found ourselves feeling a bit...friendly. As various combinations of people began enjoying a good, old-fashioned "make out" session, he and I locked eyes and made an understood pact we would NOT engage in such behaviors. Our mutual feeling was we did not want to cloud our relationship with condensation of confusion caused by the crossing of forbidden lines.

What made our relationship so special was each of us brought a piece of the reciprocity equation to the table. He was the security I needed. I had given up on believing men could be dependable, consistent and strong unless they felt they had to in order to coerce you into sex. He had given up on good women feeling we were all liars, cheaters and deceivers who posed one way at the onset of the relationship only to flip the script at the end. I didn't want him to look at me and see those qualities and I am sure he felt the same. He forced me to see myself through the male lens and I urged him to believe in us again.

When my mother passed away, there was no question in my mind he would be right there to hold my hand as he had many nights on my couch while watching the ESPN highlights. When he arrived in support, I could finally breathe knowing my comforter had come; a special gift from God had appeared to help me through my storm. As we stood over my mother's casket together, his hand never trembled and his heart grieved openly for my loss. I knew in the days and months to come, he would forever give me that thing I would need and I would work hard to give him back all that he would need to be the best "him" he could be.

Yes, it is possible for a man and a woman to be strictly platonic when each of them feels in the gaps presented by life's challenges. When you need power and he needs truth, it is important to be that special thing for one another. I believe he came into my life to flip my beliefs on its head. It is my hope to have hundreds more relationships like ours to be that flip I know I need.

FINANCE

chapter 22

"Save Your Money"

"Saving money is not only about the conservation of funds for the infamous "rainy day," yet it is more about the discipline it takes to think ahead towards future opportunities. Being frugal today can make you well-traveled tomorrow."

−C. Frazier

Chapter Twenty Two
Save your money

Soon gotten, soon spent; ill gotten, ill spent.
— John Heywood

My decision to purchase my first home was actually a way for me to save a lot of money. Many people view home ownership as a tremendous strain on the pocket and I am sure it can be if it is done incorrectly. When I approached my father with my plan to purchase a home after noticing how my apartment complex had changed over the years I had called it home, my father was slow to respond. When he finally engaged me in conversation he told me, "I won't believe you are serious until you have at least $10,000 saved in the bank.

At first, I was VERY upset with my father for requesting what I thought to be a totally unfair amount for any struggling teacher and I rolled my eyes at him assuming he was making a mockery of the money he knew I would never make. I looked at my budget over and over again realizing I had little less than $200 left after my bills, I was confident my dad had set me up for the ookie-doke. In my mind, if he was not going to help me to get my house by imparting his financial wisdom, I was not going to ever get a house. Simply put, I did not make big moves without my dad's permission and blessing.

One night as I was returning home from my late night graduate class, I found myself packing my daughter up a steep flight of apartment stairs. Huffing and puffing up each step, I resented the fact that I did not have my own home with soft stairs or a living room on the first level where I could leave the doggone carrier. As I continued upward, a man startled me from behind. "Hey, you need some help with that?"

Now, knowing I had elected to live in Decatur, GA for its affordable rent and its distance to and from my job, I was not oblivious to the fact that I was not in the safest of neighborhoods. However, due to the rigorous screening process when I contracted to rent at this particular property, I was sure only the up and coming professionals would be accepted as tenants so I was comfortable. However, during the two years to follow my first lease, I noticed more and more of my professional neighbors moving away for new jobs, bigger houses or marriages and they were being replaced with individuals who must have been able to correctly fill out the application. The property began to show signs of a clear decline and I was desperate to get out. Now, having an unidentified man approaching me in the late evening…in Decatur…with no gun…and no man, I was ready to pee in my pants.

As I turned to the man, I was sure he could read the message in my eyes which told him he had "better leave me alone" with a mixture of "I will scratch your eyes out if you try to touch me or my child." Although I thought my message was clear, he missed the message because he began to advance up the stairs in my direction. I did my best to stay calm and assured him my boyfriend was in the house waiting on us. What he said next is the reason why I am in my house today.

"I know you don't have no man up there. It's just you and yo baby. We watch you when you come home. I think you need some help since you work and go to school all late and s*$@. I can help you."

I stayed calm on the outside but as urine began to drip slowly down my legs, I was sure I was going to have to kill this man in front of my child. I was confident he was planning to rape me as if it was a matter of conquest for him. I took in the air and a little bit of courage and thanked him for his concern. I began to speak to my daughter who was fast asleep. I prayed she wouldn't wake up as I climbed the final three stairs.

"Let me get that door for you," he said reaching toward me. I guess he was reaching for my keys which my dumb behind has left in the side of the diaper bag. I realized I was going to have to put my daughter on the ground in front of the door in order to flip the diaper bag around to get my keys. I was never so upset with myself for not doing what I knew I was supposed to do; always have my car keys in my hand.

I ignored him and in one swift motion, opened the door to the apartment, flung my daughter over the threshold and slid through the door locking it behind. Once safely behind the door and its protective locks, I sat on the floor next to my daughter and cried. Sitting there with my school books, my diaper bag and my little baby, I felt helpless and unable to protect my cub. It was at that moment I was confident I would do whatever it was going to take to get out of that place.

Saving the $10,000 was no easy feat for me. I had to cut a lot of corners in terms of my leisure activities and I opted for the full refund check awarded for my tuition. I didn't like having to extend myself through student loans but if it was for my daughter, I was willing to take to hit for her to get the yard with the picket fence. After about 5 months of literally pinching pennies and a combination of student loan refunds and my income tax return, I had the money I needed to approach my father again with the idea of homeownership. Three months later, I was packing my U-Haul and headed to my first home.

Almost immediately, I learned why my father has required me to save the $10,000. Between moving costs, deposits for utilities, blinds, carpet cleaning and all of the other things that come with homeownership, the dent in my savings was obvious within the first three months. When you move from an apartment to a house, there is a natural increase in the amount of the bills you will pay. I went from paying a power bill in a two-bedroom apartment that was no more than $140 per month to cooling a two-story house totaling $156 on average. Now, this seemed reasonable…until the gas bill was added to the equation. Adding an additional $141 to the budget, the new expenses I had not planned for began to chip away at the monthly income. It took over six months for me stabilize the bills and thanks to the nest egg my father had mandated, I was able to survive the switch.

For most Americans, saving money is not as impossible as we all think. In fact, during my research for this chapter, I learned about six new ways I can save more money this year. For starters, I LOVE coffee and Chai teas. When I added up how much I was spending in a month's time, it was well over $100.00. The first thing I changed was my approach to my guilty pleasure. I purchased a Keurig and it cut my annual cost down over $1,000.

When going to the movies, instead of spending $40.00 for a show, decided to go during the matinee when prices were much cheaper. Instead of treats at their overpriced concession stand, I smuggled candy and sodas past the unsuspecting teenage ticket-tearer for only $3.00 as opposed to the $12.00 I would spend at the counter. Instead of waiting to purchase the things I needed when they ran out, I would look at my top 10 most used items and when shopping, search for sales. Sometimes I would purchase toilet paper although I had over half of the originally purchased rolls remaining just because the grocery store was running a sale. I found if I worked in front of my budget instead of in response to it, I would never shop out of desperation. Small changes to my normal routine had me racking up the extra money and never running out of my household essentials. I was proud of myself for trying to develop better financial habits. Although I had not managed to master ways to pay of my debt, I was freeing up more money to enable myself some wiggle room to address my financial dangles.

As I got older and began to befriend other women who wanted to work toward financial freedom. I found each of us searching for ways to save a buck and even hosted "girl's nights" cleverly disguise as think tanks for ways to save more. I tried the large jars like my dad had kept but we never seemed to make it all the way to the end of year "roll it up" party. I once saw my dad roll over $600 in coins! If my dad proved to be nothing else over my years idolizing him as one of the most intelligent men I ever met, he was patient. He rushed to no decisions and would sleep on all financial moves carefully marking his moves with precision. He always reminded me that the real savings came with waiting. I, unfortunately, did not have the gene of financial responsibility passed to me so I was going to have to learn.

I learned that the gift of online shopping was often left unwrapped. When online shopping, there are almost always the same deals offered in the stores if not less. I found I saved money when shopping online because I was not walking around a mall looking for additional items discovered during my window shopping and I did not spend extra money eating in the food court. By shopping online, I had an opportunity to think through my purchase after spending so much time typing in my credit card information. Oftentimes, I would change my mind before hitting the checkout button as opposed to being in the store line with a cashier giving my card a quick swipe before I had a chance to change my mind. In many ways, by eliminating my traditional Saturday routine, I was saving myself hundreds of dollars.

There are over 100 ways to save money but almost all of them encourage you to pay yourself first. We are advised to set a biweekly savings goal and take that money off the top of your budget. That way, before you begin spending money on frivolous things, you are assured to have money set aside to take care of yourself. In addition, I found the most effective way to save the most money was to record the amount of money in my account the day before my direct deposit hit and deposit that money into my savings. Yes, it meant living from check to check, but it also meant writing a check to your own account.

Having money in a savings account is not only about the conservation of funds for the infamous "rainy day," yet it is more about the discipline it takes to think ahead towards future opportunities. Being frugal today can make you well-traveled tomorrow. When you discipline your spending to make room for your savings, you allow yourself room to do the things you always felt impossible. Take a vacation, schedule a massage or even splurge on an expensive gift to yourself. Why not? It's the least you can do for the amazing job you have done preparing yourself for greater later.

chapter 23

"Invest in You"

"Student loans are the devil! It's amazing how we all probably knew they were a bad idea from the beginning and anyone who has ever taken the time to read a Promissory Note in its entirety knows just how much of a scam they are."

−C. Frazier

Chapter Twenty Three
Invest in you

There is no such thing as disappointment for those who continue to cherish the selflessness of which is born the noblest inner self. There is no such thing as failure for those who invest in the potentialities of the Ideal of the Soul.
-Ameen Rihani

Student loans are the devil! It's amazing how we all probably knew they were a bad idea from the beginning and anyone who has ever taken the time to read a Promissory Note in its entirety knows just how much of a scam they are. I think I realized they were a bad idea the first time I got a refund check from school. While everyone else looked forward to the thousands of dollars being handed out like government cheese, I was not so jazzed. Usually, those who were excited only wanted the money so they could plan for the big parties which always seemed to take place after the first disbursement date. Maybe I was lame, but I always felt it was a bad idea but a necessary evil for those less fortunate Americans who had not come from families able to put aside thousands of dollars for a college education.

Each time I looked at the disbursement amount, I felt like someone was setting me up for a big fall while all of the other kids treated it like lottery winnings. Perhaps the most horrible joke I have ever heard came from one of the financial aid counselors at my first university. While each of us realized we were paying three times the amount of tuition we would pay in a state school, each of us presumed the prestige associated with the private school umbrella was worth the cost of admission. After signing my Promissory Note which should have been an illegal document as there was no way any of us had the mental capacity to understand the terms of the contract, she commented, "May your college memories last as long as your student loans."

Year after year as the time continued to roll around for us to decide if we wanted to sign yet another Promissory Note, I had to have a long, purposeful conversation with myself. I realized I was working hard in school and performing well in all of my classes never making below an

A on average, but I had to continue to remind myself of the tens of thousands of dollars I had taken out to pay for my education. I made an annual commitment to myself to perform at the top of my class so I would have a chance to earn the right amount of money to afford my student loan repayments. So, although I made it a point to attend each and every one of the refund check block parties, I wondered if everyone had made the same deal with themselves to do their absolute best for each of us had chosen to make an investment in ourselves.

When you ask most individuals what it means to invest in themselves, 90% of them will mention something regarding a financial investment in a project or product they felt would yield them an even greater financial gain. Many individuals also invest in properties and land hoping to have an opportunity to earn more money. They cling to hopes of creating a better life for themselves. However, many ignore the fact there are many ways for each of us to invest in ourselves which include investing in our health, our creativity and cultural experiences. In many cases, when we invest in only things for financial gains, we run the risk of feeling as if we are a failure if our business plans don't work out the way we planned. Now, if we spend time investing in other ways to make ourselves better, we put ourselves in a win-win situation.

When I turned 29, I looked in the mirror and stood 86 pounds overweight. For years I had blamed it on baby weight but with a four-year old running around the house, that dog would no longer hunt. I looked old, felt tired and wondered what it would feel like if I made some healthier decisions toward losing weight and getting healthy again. My first day in the gym a year prior had left me feeling defeated and discouraged as I realized I had a lot of work to do. I had enjoyed being able to eat all the time and still manager to lose weight so having to change my entire lifestyle and still be unable to see any real results for months was not something I was ready to accept. I went back to my unhealthy habits therefore almost immediately allowing my self-esteem to find a home in the bottom of the toilet. I hated looking at myself so I didn't and just keep moving on with life.

The day I decided to change things for good, I was ready to put in the work and I knew I would be able to sustain for the long haul. The day before, I had been at the local park with my daughter and I was teaching her how to ride her new bike. I had purchased all of the protective pads and a cute little Minnie Mouse helmet to make sure we minimized the number of scrapes and scratches she could get if she fell. We were ready to brave the park. Her first few tries were very rocky with her trying to figure out how to go forward instead of backward. Once she mastered it, however, she was unstoppable, literally.

During one of her peddling sessions, she got overly excited and the bike took off down a hill. At the bottom of the hill, there was a sharp turn to the left. I knew she could not handle it on her own and as she began to travel faster and faster down the hill, I lost my grip on her seat and found myself sprinting behind the bike. I saw my baby getting further and further from my reach and as I looked ahead to her reality, I knew I couldn't catch her. I screamed out for the entire park to hear. I desperately needed someone to help me grab a hold of my daughter and my terror was obvious. Everyone seemed to have delayed reaction because by the time they got in motion, she had already zoomed by.

As she drew closer and closer to the turn, I could hear her calling for me and I was yelling and running as fast as I could behind her. I was giving it all I had but I had to accept the fact I wasn't going to make it. As my mind drifted to all the things that could happen to her, I felt as if all the air had left my body and I braced myself for the worse. Almost in the blink of an eye, a man came out of nowhere and sprinted across the grass. He grabbed my daughter in just enough time for her bike to go crashing into the turn and I fell to my knees feeling the worse I had ever felt in my life. As he returned my daughter to me, I just cried with my hand buried in my hands. He must have understood my tears as he placed her in front of me and eased my mind reassuring me my daughter was okay. When I finally looked up into his face, no words were necessary. He simply said, "You're welcome." It was then and there I decided to invest in my health so no one else would have to be there to catch my daughter.

There was not one day that was easy for me as I tried my best to change my life. I often went to bed feeling hungry and I had to research every bite before it went into my mouth to make sure I wasn't undoing all of my hard work. I had to sit with water at social events because of the calories in alcoholic beverages and I often ordered dry salads to prevent myself from making bad food choices. Workouts were brutal as my knees had developed aches from the weight and pressure over the years. Many mornings, to get out of bed was a chore and sitting down was its own adventure. However, when the first ten came off, I became addicted and after the first forty, it was even more of a push to complete the goal of 86 pounds.

In the months to come, I hit many walls and wanted to give up on the rigorous routines I had integrated into my life. It was impossible for me to balance my life. The strenuous mandate of my workouts presented a hard mental fight each day. For over a year, I fought the good fight but after the results continued to come, I felt I could slack off and enjoy life a bit. Slowly, the pounds began to come back and before long, my hard work was drifting from my reach much like my daughter had during the getaway bike ride. Although I had become a cycle instructor to bring accountability back to the table, I began to resent the fact I would always have to be in a gym eating inedible food just to maintain. I started to tell myself it was too hard, much like I had concluded the first time around when I had quit. I don't know if it was the thought of my daughter seeing me fail or the realization I would continue to hide from myself in each reflecting mirror for the rest of my life, but somewhere inside, I decided to fight. The competitor in me, and the judgmental eyes of those around me, forced me back into focus and I was determined to get things back on track again.

Making an investment in yourself can extend to investing in your creativity. I have always loved to write. I am sure I have thrown away some Pulitzer Prize material chalking it up to doodles on lonely lines of leisure simply electing to speak through my pen. Investing time in taking Creative Writing courses for adults and teaching young adults provided me with growth in terms of my writing and its ability to reach multiple crowds. I learned to write with passion and freedom which elevated my senses and gave me the confidence to share my world with others. Learning to embrace my love for painting, singing, stepping and baking awakened a deeper connection between my soul and the universe as my investment prompted me to reach deeper and expand wider than ever before.

Investing in my culture helped me to search for ways to connect more to the musical side of myself. My love for various genres of music found me in hole in the wall showcases listening to artists belting out notes under red lights. I sat on the lawns in the cool of Southern evenings with friends over picnic lunches allowing myself to be blanketed in the silky tones of male singers and acoustic guitars. With each experience, I found myself being cleaned from the inside out by allowing my heart to be massaged by songs of lost love and a hope in the possibility of happiness in another. With each lovely encounter came a deafening song of passion and life continued to renew itself for my ears had become a conduit to my road toward personal redemption.

As I work my way into the next segment of my life, I will buckle down again for the investment in my health which will cost me dearly. I will pay the price in sweat and pain to reach my apex knowing each day I put in the work is one day I will have a return on my investment. I will continue to write until my pen runs dry, sit in those cypher session and sing along until my soul is filled. Shoot, I might even go back to school and finish the doctorate although student loans will have to make a grand entrance in my life again. However, whatever I decide to do, I will do it with tenacity for if my investment is in me, I deserve my best!

chapter 24

"Be Cheap"

"My love for saving money did not stop there. Once I felt the rush of a good, free spree in a store, I looked for ways to save more money in different areas. I began to search for free dining opportunities, discounts on clothing and free entertainment all over the city. Surprisingly, there were places with deals on a daily basis if we only took the time to search."

—C. Frazier

Chapter Twenty Four
Be cheap

My parents always said that knowledge was the best gift they could give me, probably because they were too cheap to buy me Christmas or Birthday presents.
— **Jarod Kintz**

Can you imagine a safe place like Wal-Mart turning into a war zone? Well, no one could have prepared me for the events that took place on a cool and crisp fall day last October. In fact, the day was pretty routine; my daughter and I had just settled in from a long day of school and work and we prepared for a dinner of grilled chicken and vegetables. No sooner had I prepared the chicken for grilling did I notice that I was missing one important ingredient; the vegetables. I reluctantly prepared myself to pack up my daughter and take a trip to the one place I dreaded more than the gynecologist office for my annual exam; Wal- Mart.

My daughter was not too happy about having to go to the store in the middle of her favorite episode of iCarly! She pouted as she buttoned up her new pink and cream striped peacoat. Ignoring her whines and pleads, I continued to prepare myself for the trip. With a few steps, we buckled ourselves into my car and headed out of the driveway toward Wal-Mart. I could never seem to convince myself to spend the extra ten to fifteen dollars to go to a smaller, cleaner, more professional franchise rationalizing the hundreds of dollars I was saving each year by opting for Sam Walton's ingenious idea. So, there I was again, sealing my fate with each turn of my Honda Civic. I was headed to Wally World.

As usual, Wal-Mart presented a sea of scurrying adults hoping to escape the cash register under $100.00. The sound of coins coming out of the change dispenser and the swipes of debit cards let me know that I had a huge task ahead of me. I would attempt to ONLY purchase the vegetables I had come for without diverting my attention to additional frivolous purchases. As I walked down the aisles, the smell of the freshly baked bread and cookies began to annoy me. The chocolate and vanilla circles of goodness wafted through my nostrils and taunted me to make the left at the bananas and take a few for dessert. It didn't help that my daughter was asking for everything her eyes could behold. "Mom, can I please have some silly bands? Mom, can I please have an Oreo snack? Mom, can I ...." She begged. I began to fear that I wouldn't be unable to escape Wal-Mart's grasps without scar or blemish.

Once the vegetables had been retrieved, I remembered that we were running a little low on milk and that would pose a problem for my morning oatmeal. Therefore, I turned toward the milk aisle to grab a quick gallon of 2% milk. As I turned the corner, my first impression was that everything was normal, however, as I neared the milk, I quickly realized that things were about to take a turn for the worse.

"I thought I told you to stay away from my son!" screamed on woman standing near the yogurt and cookie dough. She was a small lady with short red hair that had been dyed in her kitchen sink. I wondered which YouTube channel she had subscribed to for I planned to report it to that imaginary entity which threatens to deactivate social media accounts. She seemed to be normally very quiet from her docile wardrobe and the uncomfortable way her lips curled over her teeth but her temper was definitely flaring during this exchange. As she engaged her adversary, her rising temperature shook her entire body as she convulsed with fury. She had managed to put a cart between her and her attacker but judging by the size of the opponent, she would need more than that.

"This is Wal-Mart, lady. I did not come here looking for your son!" replied the second party to the argument. She had a bad wig that was cocked to the side resembling an eye patch and she did not seem to have a mirror in her house based on her ensemble. She was all in the other lady's face and definitely letting everyone in the store know that she was not going to back down from anyone. I guess I should have fancied myself too sophisticated for such a performance but I have to admit, at that time, I was not above enjoying the front row seat. I felt it was the least Wal-Mart could do for forcing me to come to this dreaded place. I fumbled with various creamers knowing coffee was not at all a part of my daily menu.

The ladies continued to go back and forth with each other while the sound of their voices began to cut like a knife. Onlookers began to sheepishly slow down to sneak a peek. They were so loud they probably woke up each of the chicks in the egg cartons. The anger on their faces was like looking in the face of a deranged soldier. I wanted to help in the situation but the ladies looked like two pigs fighting for the last hull on the farm so I decided to mind my own business. To my amazement, everyone simply continued shopping as if they could not hear the ladies arguing. I decided to do the same. I figured, if after the five minutes that had elapsed with not one fist flying, the best we would get from this display would be some cleverly devised combinations of insults.

I turned my cart toward the front of the store and left the two tyrants to their embarrassing display. As I got my total, $6.37, I smiled a bit realizing that I had done the impossible, I had escaped Wal-Mart's grasp with minimal damaged. As I went for the door, I saw three police officers headed toward the back of the store. "Let's hurry up and arrest these two so we can get back to the game," said the tallest cop with a grin. I was happy to be headed home and vowed to go to Publix and avoid such cheap behavior in the future.

Now, for me to feel better about abandoning Old Faithful, I would have to construct a plan to benefit my pockets in the process. In comes the wonderful idea of extreme couponing. Although I had been taught to loathe the elderly women who would add an additional ten minutes to their shopping trip matching their slips of paper to each nonperishable item parading down the conveyer belt, when I entered my 30's coupons became a mathematical geniuses best kept secret. The high I got leaving a store after outsmarting all of the cashiers hoping for Employee of the Month by refusing to accept my clipped blessings was indescribable.

I was introduced to coupons by one of my good friends, Valencia, who seemed like a quiet, little kitten based on her soft spoken tone and her small frame. Little did I know, she was a store's worse nightmare. Her goal was always to leave a store with items that were now free or with a credit for money she would be owed in the future. On our first stopping trip, I was amazed to see how her mathematics skills worked through the folds of her brain. She knew the exact order to place items on the conveyor belt to ensure it was scanned in the correct sequence. She knew how many she could purchase to offset the number of coupons better than most cashiers and as she would leave the store, she would leave faces of bewilderment in her dust.

Couponing did not come natural for me. I was always nervous to attempt the process fearing the cashier vying for Employee of the Month. All dedicated couponers have found themselves up against that one cashier who didn't want to see the items leave the store without adequate payment feeling they would get a bonus on their check by holding us to the required limit. Although I was nervous my first few times, Valencia walked with me through each transaction and celebrated me when I was tucked safely in my car with my items resting in the trunk.

As a part of the couponing family, it became a daily hustle to outrun the deals before they "died." A dead deal could occur within seconds as stores found themselves being raped all over the country before pulling the coupon down or the items off the shelf. Before I realized it, my garage became its own store stocked with paper products and cleaning agents to the point of addiction. I had found a new passion for savings and it consumed all of my extra time.

My love for saving money did not stop there. Once I felt the rush of a good, free spree in a store, I looked for ways to save more money in different areas. I began to search for free dining opportunities, discounts on clothing and free entertainment all over the city. Surprisingly, there were places with deals on a daily basis if we only took the time to search.

As an adult, there is nothing wrong with being financially responsible. Why spend all of your money on things you can get for free if you would just carve out time and PLAN? While couponing was once a sign of financial struggle, it is now evidence of proper planning. When we can make more sound decisions with our finances, we can experience total freedom. There is nothing wrong with buying the medicine without the label. Did you read the active ingredients? Aren't they the same? Why not spend $1.00 less and purchase a sandwich? We have to take more time out of our day and invest the time in making better decisions regarding our finances. Most companies make billions of dollars doing the things for us we are too lazy to do for ourselves.

After reading this chapter, take a moment and look for interesting ways you can do the same things but on a tighter budget. Restrict your spending by tracking your habits. Use your debit card ledger and add up the trips to Starbucks. When you tend to spend $25.00 per week for your favorite coffee drink, consider purchasing a Keurig and make life easier. When examining your habits, look for ways you can make smarter purchases even if it means having to get up a little earlier or staying up a little later.

Although my favorite coffee drink did not taste quite the same when I made it at home, the money I saved allowed me to treat myself to an entire breakfast with my coffee drink on the weekend. When it boiled down to it, my attempt to cut corners was costing me BIG and it was time to get some discipline. I wish I could say this lesson has some sort of new and creative spin on an oldie but goodie but the message is quite classic. Stop being lazy and be CREATIVE!

chapter 25

"Leave Work at Work"

"So, I received the fact that my life's balancing act was now dependent on my ability to come up with a plan to replace the time I had spent making love at night to my students' essays with time for me to find a man to take the place of my writing assignments."

−C. Frazier

Chapter Twenty Five
Leave work at work

Too much work is bad, too much fun is bad. Find that balance in your life, live smart. Live good.
-Jc Caylen

I never remembered my mother or father bringing home their work. Now, true, they worked in telecommunications and would probably struggle packing up cable lines and converter boxes, but I don't recall them ever coming into the house with briefcases, papers, files or anything suggesting they planned to do any work when they got home. What was funny to me was they always taught us something completely different. My parents always insisted we brought home all of our books whether we had homework or not for there was always something we could be reviewing from previous lessons or we should be reading ahead in anticipation of the lessons to come. In their minds, work never stopped so I never understood why they never seemed to live their own teachings.

Night after night, even without the prompting of a teacher's lesson plans or instructional direction, my parents would insist each of us devote time to get better at our jobs which was to go to school. As for my parents, however, I never seemed to see them doing the same for themselves. Of course, we were forbidden from ever asking the question insinuating we felt we were on the same level as our parents, so we just had to add that question to the bank of inquiries we would only have answered when we were adults. In many cases, I wondered how my parents would ever have the time to review the things they had encountered during their work day as they began a completely separate set of duties when they walked in the door of our house.

My dad would come through the door and survey the land making sure the house was functioning much like a factory with all of us working on our assigned tasks with diligence until we were released for dinner. Once he had ensured all things were in order, he would complete the things on his "honey do" list therefore solidifying himself as the man of the house. By the time he was done with his tasks, if my mom was working according to schedule after her usual homework checks and room inspections, his dinner would be simmering beneath clear-topped back Teflon pots. If we all were on point, we would have to stop reading or calculating the products of our mathematics problems to come up for air so we could eat. After all, we could not be done with homework until our parents felt we had absorbed all the information our brains could soak up for the evening. We had to be very careful not to waste a millimeter of space in our heads where we could store another balanced chemical equation.

Each day, the monotony of our days did not lend too much room for fun and frolic but it was our denotation of the word normal. On those special occasions when we would be allowed to sit together and watch the Cosby Show or a Saints football game, it was special to us as nothing would interfere with our time together. We could enjoy our moments together knowing everything was in order around the house and even our choral breathing seemed perfect in those moments. I learned very early from my parents the importance of leaving work at work to perform the jobs at home and to prevent interference with the few moments of family time each day allows.

As a young professional, it became important for me to work beyond the work day if I was ever going to be the best at my job. Oftentimes, I had so much on my plate at work, I could not cram it into an eight hour day. It was very important for me to stay a few steps ahead of others if I was ever going to be at the top of the food chain. I would come home, after leaving my daughter at the daycare until the allotted time of 6 p.m. before I would be charged a late fee, and immediately complete my tasks of cooking, bathing and playing for a window of 45 minutes in which I would mentally record any changes in her body or behaviors so I would not miss anything. Once I rocked her to sleep singing songs from Luther Vandross into the folds of her neck, I would continue my work into the wee hours of the morning. I would wake up early to prepare our bags for the day and begin the process all over again on a maximum of five hours of sleep each night.

Heading into work, one thing was for sure, I was never unprepared for a meeting, never behind a deadline and always ready to accept new opportunities to grow as a leader. I stood steadfast in my belief that I would and could balance it all without needing much time for rejuvenation. In many respects, I felt I had learned to do the impossible; I was balancing parenting and career with ease and I had to pat myself on the back.

As the years wore on and I began to resent my dedication to my job as a professional and a single mother, I had to take a moment to review what was missing from my life. When I sat down with my life calendar, I took inventory of the things taking up my time. I found work, family, school and…nothing. There was one gaping hole in my life and possibly the reason for my recent frustration with the direction my life had taken. I had left off a very important part of my life which was the need for a personal life. Nowhere in my day had I allotted time to be with myself, with friends or even a significant other. If I was going to have true balance in my life, I was going to have to sit down with my life and put a big, red "X" on something that had defined my existence.

I had the hardest time balancing my own personal equation finding each area of my life important to my being. I considered what my life would be like if I "X'ed" out school, but I realized the pursuit of higher education would then be an unattainable goal. If I was going to be better, I would have to hold fast to my goals of higher education or I would be shut out of the opportunities I had dreamed of before having my daughter. Having certain degrees under my belt would help me set a great tone for her life by showing her, through example, the possibilities of excellence despite challenges in life or extenuating circumstances. So, I made the decision not to eliminate the area of school in my life.

Next came the area of family which included my time devoted to being a great mother. It was very important to me to be the best I could be in the area of motherhood. I realized my interactions with my daughter were non-negotiable for many obvious reasons so it could not be compromised for any reason. So that only left work. Oddly enough, I could not see myself giving up the extra time at work given the fact I needed to extend myself past the work day or I would forever be behind the eight ball. So, I accepted the fact that my life's balancing act was not dependent on my ability to come up with a plan to replace the time I had spent making love at night to my students' essays with time for me to find a man. He would have to take the place of my writing assignments and grade me on my ability to be a suitable mate and his ideal Ruth.

The first step was to evaluate what had caused me to run out of time during the work day. I began to pay attention to time I had wasted on idol activities. In the morning, I spent a lot of time chatting with my co-workers in their rooms or in the hallway as we waited for the kids to come down the hallway. In my first week of combing through my schedule, I calculated I was losing about 40 minutes a day simply socializing with my teammates about nothing. Now, I realized it would cost me some valuable bonding time with my work buddies but cutting out that time and using it to grade papers would save me almost 200 minutes a week. After further analysis, I calculated during my class time when my kids were instructed to read independently, I had spent that time reading my own book. Now, while I loved to read, I would have to sacrifice those 10 minutes of reading plus the 7 minutes I would allot for them to give me a brief summary on what they had read and use that time to grade or work on my school assignments which would give me back 17 minutes per day or even 85 minutes per week.

After learning better ways to assess my students other than essays, I also found myself being able to give them more immediate feedback to guide their revision process. Instead of focusing on an entire paper, I learned to focus on thesis statements and engaging openings found in the introductory paragraphs. My second step involved allowing them to submit one expertly written body paragraph as opposed to five to determine if the format had been followed. I had cut out having thirty papers to read four nights out of the week eliminating the additional three hours I would spend grading. Adding three hours each night back into my weekly bank gave me 12 hours which left plenty of time for me to enjoy having a life again. Now, the only problem was, I had forgotten how to have a life.

It is so important for us not to lose ourselves in our jobs because that is time we have taken away from enjoying the fruits of our labor. I became a better professional when I was forced to research better ways to be more efficient at my job. When I began to research more time effective pedagogy, my product and that of my students increased therefore building ME in the process. When I added my lost time back into my bank, I found myself right back in the routine of engaging experiences as

I now had time for plays and movies and games and shopping and bike riding and working out and seminars and REST.

I learned from my parents the importance of leaving the work at work to have time to build and restore on a daily basis. As I enter into this next phase of my life, I will continue to shave more and more time off of my day to make time to do things like write books and love my daughter. At the end of the day, when the work is no more, all I will have will be the slide show I will replay in my mind of the life and I refuse to let pass me by.

chapter 26

"Find the job you want and plan to have it"

"As life began to unfold for me, much like the episodes of the Cosby Show, it was never quite like the popular sitcom. Instead of having parents who always seemed to make it home in time to handle all of their kids' growing pains with the perfect advice, I had parents who were doing their best to be in a better place than the generation before."

–C. Frazier

Chapter Twenty Six
Find the job you want and plan to have it

Work to become, not to acquire.

— **Elbert Hubbard**

At an early age, my dream job was to be an attorney like Claire Huxtable on The Cosby Show. I figured, this woman must have the life being able to balance a family and a career; something most of the women around me complained about on a daily basis. Thursday after Thursday, I watched Claire move perfectly about her day with a healthy, luxurious bounce to her shoulder-length hair. Her makeup always seemed perfectly done and her slight heel was the perfect ending to her knee length skirts. For some odd reason, most of the show centered itself around the father, Cliff. However, it was when Claire was called on to contribute to the moral lessons reaffirmed during each hour-long glimpse into the life of the All-American family, the role of the African-American mother took on a whole new meaning. When my mom would turn the show off and send me to prepare for bed, it was back to life as usual with everyone complaining about their daily sacrifices for the family. Man, I couldn't wait to be an attorney like Claire.

As life began to unfold for me, much like the episodes of the Cosby Show, it was never quite like the popular sitcom. Instead of having parents who always seemed to make it home in time to handle all of their kids' growing pains with the perfect advice, I had parents who were doing their best to be in a better place than the generation before. With such lofty ambitions, there wasn't much time for a troubled teenage girl and her issues as I got older. So, with Claire in mind, I began to do some research on her profession. I prided myself in learning all I could about the field of law and prominent women with a similar background to my own who could teach me, through their biographies, how to be the next Claire Huxtable.

Once I had my research implanted in my brain, I began to focus more and more on both my studies and my ability to debate. I must have been a pain to deal with because everything became a platform to prepare myself for my future occupation. I argued just because I could and always tried to rebut any situation just to see if I could persuade others to agree with me. Truth is, it became my identity; I was the one you hated to see coming because you knew I would always have to interject a perspective often differing and overly passionate. My life had been decided and I was moving full speed ahead.

Closer to my college days, things began to take a turn as I faced the reality of passion versus possibility. After studying various criminal case such as Ted Bundy, Ian Brady and even OJ Simpson, one thing became clear to me, although these individuals had committed heinous crimes seemingly punishable by death, each of them had rights. It was amazing to me how each defense attorney worked tirelessly to argue the rights of the individuals. They protected their clients from the judicial system and how it was designed to protect the law-abiding citizen despite their clear disregard for human life. I was sickened by the realization that each attorney would face a time when the law would be and could be twisted and turned to protect those who would seek to harm other and destroy families. It was one Saturday at the local collegiate library that I changed my mind about being an attorney and thus deciding to abandon my dream of being an attorney.

During my first two years in college, I wasn't one hundred percent sure I was ready to call it quits so I majored in Pre-Law but found myself spending much of my time in the Arts. I had always loved to sing and found myself to be pretty good at it. After joining my college's choir, I lost myself in musical and written expression learning through the college experience just how freeing it was to express myself in various ways. Attending a Historically Black College and University provided me with a stage to embrace the staples of my culture and learn the importance of using my voice as a weapon. My classes provided space and comfort for me to argue controversial points and to have my analytical skills be praised by upperclassmen during programs hosted by various campus organizations hoping to prune us for membership. I argued passionately and read books during the week to strengthen my literary spectrum and my cultural diction. During each panel discussion, I began to be looked upon for my views and prided myself in having something profound to share.

Week after week, experience after experience, I began to wonder if there was a future in oration as I began to enjoy providing audiences with long explanations of seemingly simplistic topics. I wondered how many people I could sit in an audience and hold captive with my newfound cultural references. I enjoyed seminars from artists like Nikki Giovanni who passionately presented an entire lecture on the rapper Tupac Shakur inspiring me to read his book, "Holler If You Hear Me," twice. I realized the power of words and the passion involved with delivering them to the point of penetration into the minds of those held captive to their youthful beliefs. Although I was now sure law was not the route for me, I was even more torn as to where I would fit in the professional world.

Fast forwarding a bit, my pastor in Atlanta preached a sermon on the Lion King. When I recognized the award-winning introduction from my countless viewing parties with my young daughter and my fun-loving mother, I joined the congregation in singing the African-inspired tune with a childish naivety. Although many probably missed his symbolic reference finding comfort in the images of well-discipline, wild animals, for someone analytical such as myself, it was an intellectual's paradise. As the correlation between Simba's predestined occupation in life and that of most people my age still fighting for purpose played out with each second of film, the impact was deafening. He began with the opening segment of the movie where Simba was presented to Pride Rock as the next king showing Simba's inability to venture from his path in life. Upon his birth, Simba was placed on his college track and was enrolled in life courses to prepare him to take over the kingdom. Mufasa went through many hands on scenarios often having to save Simba from near death experiences to prepare him for his future occupation. My pastor went on to share with the congregation the error of most American families who allowed their children to decide their career paths during college tours their junior year in high school. He suggested such practices left little time to ensure the young adults were making realistic choices. He suggested taking a more proactive approach to the preparation of each generation. By directing them from an earlier age to their destiny using the adolescent years as a preparatory period, they would be better prepared for their future.

Thinking more on the subject and examining other cultures to plan everything from occupations to spouses for their youth, I realized I was about five years behind where I needed to be to be sure about my future in the world. What a shocking revelation! So, I then decided I had only one choice as to how I could marry my love for reading, debate, literature, oration, learning and the arts into one harmonious relationship but I sure didn't want to travel that route; education.

I cringed at the thought of teaching children like myself who would challenge every lesson plan in search for errors and opportunities to insert their superiority to their instructors. I thought about long nights of grading mediocre assignments much like those submitted time after time from my own high school counterparts who often used the morning breakfast time as their quick fix for completing homework assignments. At 20 years old, I pushed that thought from my mind and had a long talk with my academic advisor realizing it was time to stop wasting time and money. After our long meeting, which seemed to add to my sense of misguided direction, I knew two things for sure: 1) my school could not support my professional goals and 2) I was going to have to take a giant leap and major in Literature.

The next month, I prepared to transfer to another college in hopes the state university would be able to provide more opportunities in my new field. I pondered all the things I would leave behind. I realized I would now be a social security number instead of a member of an elite class of future professionals deeply engrossed in cultural awareness. I would be a number; a test; a degree with no face. It was time to jump in the water and hope I could swim.

Two years later, I walked across the stage with a degree in hand realizing most of those seated on the dais had never met me and wouldn't care about me even five minutes after the commencement of the ceremony. They had confirmed my degree and were sending me in the world thinking I was prepared for success. Three weeks later, I loaded up my car and moved two states away at the age of 21-years-old unsure of what would be waiting for me other than a job at a local hotel checking in guests. I had the degree but no idea what the job would be. I moved up through the ranks rather quickly given my work ethic and dedication to my job description. I knew hotel management was only a paycheck and it would never fulfill me. I was always very honest about that. I looked around at each of my co-workers on a daily basis and we all seemed to be asking ourselves the same question on a daily basis, "What the hell am I doing here?"

Community service helped me to decide my occupation as I became a volunteer in the one place I said I never wanted to be; the middle school classroom. For two years, what began as a simple step team then turned into my passion as I realized I could give all of my talents a home in educational curriculum. I even found the person in the job I wanted. Her name was Lisa Butler and her classroom was run to perfection. I decided

I wanted to learn all I could to be just like her, no, better than her. There was only one thing that stood between me, my newfound passion in life and my plan to further my educational pursuits; my newborn baby.

I began shadowing Lisa during my planning time instead of hanging out in the teacher's lounge talking about the normal gossip. I elected to drink my lunch in the form of a smoothie and camp out in Lisa's classroom. I was a sponge and took in each word as if it was liquid gold. I studied her movements, her mannerisms, and the reaction from the students. She was truly poetry in motion. I loved the control she had over her class and there was one distinct difference between she and I; she never had to raise her voice. Students entered her classroom with an expectation of the challenge which awaited each day. She spoke with confidence in the content and her ability to tie concepts into one another made her a genius of our craft. She created a love for reading by providing her kids with a reading corner equipped with pillows, soft lighting and fuzzy mats. As her kids read, she joined them by reading books about effective leadership. She was perfection in my mind.

One day as I was "glancing" on her desk, I saw her degree from a local university called Mercer. I figured any school producing such educational professionals was the place for me. I never told Lisa I planned to follow in her footsteps but, instead, I began to do my own research on the program. I realized it was going to take a lot of money and time I didn't have to make it through the rigor of the program. In addition to being a single mother with a child on bottles and in diapers, I was still coaching full-time and working as a full-time educator. The way I figured, I would need an additional six hours added to each day just to be able to bathe and sleep. What in the world was I getting myself into?

Once the program began, I watched Linda even harder. She heard I had chosen to attend her alma mater after being "outed" by my principal in a faculty meeting. I expected her to come to me immediately after the meeting with welcoming arms offering those behind the scenes things I needed to know to learn the ropes but instead she said nothing; never acknowledged it at all. I have to admit, I was taken aback but I chalked it up to her underlying understanding that I was coming for her and I had NOTHING to lose. See, there's only one real dangerous person in the world and it's not the person holding the gun, but the one who is staring down the barrel without flinching knowing there was nothing in Heaven or Hell to keep him/her from their destiny. My revolver was my degree and I stood face to face with it with no fear in my heart.

During my matriculation, I decided not to stop at my initial certification but instead elected to remain in the program to earn my master's degree and my Specialist degree as well. With each completed course, I became more and more of an expert. I utilized my extensive and expensive training to impact the learning of my students through my instructional practices. My classroom underwent a huge makeover utilizing all of the research-based strategies to promote student achievement. I played classical music, dimmed the lighting, carefully selected mood enhancing colors, analyzed student data, tutored and enriched tirelessly realizing my classroom was my evidence of excellence. Each day, I made it a point to operate in expertise as I solidified myself as one of the best in my building. Almost as if it was a perfectly executed plan, the administration began to lean on me as one of the stellar classrooms in the building. I began to get invitations to serve in leadership roles because I had shown my dedication to the field and a desire to be on the fast track.

When you get to the point in your life when you are sure about what you want in life and you find the person in that position, my sister's advice is the best I have heard in a while. My sister, Chelle, taught me that the person sitting in my job position is taking my vacations, going on my shopping trips, driving my car and living in my house. That person is the only one who should be my daily motivation. It is not until I am ready to pick up my keys, dust off my passport and move my furniture into my place in life that I will be operating in my purpose. Although imitation is the greatest form of flattery, what is most flattering is when the imitator becomes the illustrator and becomes the template for others to trace. When I decided I wanted to create my own stencil, I learned to appreciate the grind, the sacrifice and the price to be the best. It has been money and time well spent.

chapter 27

"Learn to Say No"

"What do you need to say no to? What do you need to let go? Be honest with yourself and learn to make your life a yes by saying NO!"

–C. Frazier

Chapter Twenty Seven
Learn to say no

When you arrive at a certain level it's very easy to say yes: that is the moment to learn to say no.
-Jose Carreras

I played basketball in middle school and for a time in high school for many reasons I still cannot put into rational thought. For those who don't believe me, I have embarrassing proof that I played on the team and I have the pictures to prove it. During that time, I thought I wanted to be the star player on the team when I saw how much attention they received from the school at pep rallies. It seemed like fun. At the beginning of my seventh grade year, I made the decision to go out for the team. Although I could barely dribble the ball without having to chase it down the court, my name was one of the first announced on the doors of the school. It was kind of hard to believe, especially because it seemed like the coach was totally disgusted with all of us at the end of the four-day audition process.

Coach Brown loved the game of basketball. In fact, I would say he was infatuated with the game much like an unrequited love. We would hear him referencing effective offenses and legendary players in normal conversation with the other teachers all of whom only nodded politely and laughed when he walked away assuming he was ready to go postal at any moment. He had coached the boy's team to multiple championships and was well on his way to making a name for himself as one of the best coaches in the area. For some reason, however, his passion was put to the test when his beloved boys were taken from him and he was assigned the job of coaching the ridiculously pitiful girl's squad. Unknown to those of us excited at the chance to put on the uniform, Coach Brown was in pure D hell.

During the first day of tryouts, Coach Brown had some of the veteran boy players to work out with our neophyte team. They showed us drills we would be expected to execute with great skill and precision. The boys made the "figure eight" drill look like poetry in motion and we all couldn't wait to try it for our coach. We were divided into three rows at one end of the court. The rows were spaced out allowing a lot of ground to cover as we were instructed to take the ball from the person in the middle and have them toss it to the girl running alongside on the right. The girls on the left was to continue to move with the trio as the girl who tossed the ball had to run behind the recipient. The goal was to continue to toss the ball to each other and run behind the person who had thrown it until you made it to the end of the court where one person would have to lay it up, off the backboard, and the drill would continue back down the court. Sounds pretty easy, right?

As expected, we all looked like a H.A.M. (hot ass mess) and the coach just stood motionless on the sidelines probably wondering where the nearest bridge was that he could jump off. By the end of the drill, the coach told us all to line up on the baseline. As the boys demonstrated a basic "suicide," all of us were prepared to crash and burn. We all seemed to survive the first few blows of the whistle but after about five rounds, we finally understood why they were called suicides. It seemed as if each time we ran previous suicide, he would shave off 5 seconds from the next one. So, if the fourth one had a time limit of 30 seconds, the fifth one had a time limit of 25 seconds. The mountain he was setting before us seemed to be getting steeper and steeper to climb and it became a game of will. The coach seemed to get a little excited as our groups continued to make it past the baseline before the time elapsed but it only prompted him to push us harder.

After about eight rounds, we must have finally lost his attention because he quietly left the gym without so much as a word to any of us or his assistant coaches. Each of us looked around at one another as we struggled for breath somewhere in the room. We all loomed secretly waiting for someone to be a leader and end the practice so we all could go home. However, it seemed almost too good to be true that Coach Brown would end the torture chamber without some parting words or a partial benediction. We all just stood around and tried to look strong and tough. It's a good thing we didn't leave because after about three or four minutes, we heard Coach Brown's feet. For some strange reason, it sounded like he had a small army with him. The whistling scuffle of Nikes grew closer and closer to the gym and then it happened... the doors flew open and it was obvious the fun had just begin.

Coach Brown had done the worst thing you could do to a young lady going through puberty and hoping for breasts; he had brought in the boys basketball team. Each of us cringed realizing our hair was a mess and we were all struggling to close our mouths out of sheer exhaustion. Before us, glistening like perfectly basted Christmas hams was each of our crushes. The boys stood tall like Miami palm trees, many of whom continued to wipe their faces with their practice jerseys. My lover boy, in particular, bore the name of Nick and he looked like an Adonis with a bit of white crusted in the corner of his mouth showing his dehydration as his sweat dripped like chocolate sauce on to the wooden floor. I got my second wind. It was clear we all had been through the ringer that day, but we were all expected to find some fresh energy and tackle the next task at hand.

Coach Brown informed us we would be running two additional suicides before the end of our day alongside our male counterparts. The boys quickly embraced their competitive nature as did the more "manly" girls on our team. The rest of us, who stood still trying to figure out why in the world we were still in the room and why our legs had not carried us back to the safety of the locker room, grimaced at the thought of pushing our bodies any further. As we lined up, the final blow was delivered. All of the girls would have to make it past the baseline before the last boy. Now, this might have seemed unfair but the girls had a secret weapon up their sleeves. Little did coach know, but one of the benefits of taking gym class with the boys during the spring semester was the unit on Track and Field. During this academic unit, each of us would take our turn demonstrating our ability to run various distances. We smiled because standing on the line was our weapon of mass destruction; Jerry!

Jerry must have been at least thirty pounds over the limit to be considered obese and he was probably forced to play school sports all year round to help him drop some of his weight. Jerry was the nicest kid in the school with a winning spirit and infectious smile, but there was no way on God's green Earth his nice ass would be able to beat all of us whether we were tired or not. As the whistle blew, Jerry shot out the gate like a cannon and each of us found ourselves already ten seconds behind each of the boys. As the last boy cleared the baseline and over fifteen of our thirty- six girl squad struggled to get close, it was going to be a long afternoon. Coach Brown informed us we would run the suicides until each of us made it in as instructed. After ten attempts, the boys were not letting up electing to pick up the pace. At one point, it was almost comical how much faster than us they were moving.

About twenty minutes into the 18 thousandth suicide, the coach walked over to one of the girls on the baseline who seemed as if she was within an inch of her life and asked, "Are you ready to go home?" Without hesitation she replied, "Yes, sir." Coach Brown spun around like a prima ballerina with his clipboard clutched tightly to his chest and exclaimed, "What? You want to go home? Only losers want to go home before they have won the big game." With that said, he lined us all back on the line and the torture continued for what seemed like hours. Once all of us were laid out against the wall mats forcing our lungs to inflate, Coach Brown walked back up to the same girl and asked the same question, "Are you ready to go home?" Each of us waited with baited breath for her response hoping for the first time in our life that a kid would lie to an adult. Her eyes darted back and forth from the girls she hoped to stand beside in the championship game to the boys who stood ready to run again at the whistle of the coach. He would decide if she went home with nothing more than an tight chest grasping for cleansing air after all this work. She finally whispered, "Yes."

Just was we all expected, coach lined us all up again and began the whistle for more suicides. Now, all of us began to drag our way to the line showing we all were tired, hungry and thirsty. At one point, many of us found ourselves stuck at half court bumping into each other was we tried to get our eyes to focus well enough to direct us toward the home stretch. After about five minutes of running, Coach Brown finally sauntered up to our defending attorney who was charged with getting us off the hook and we prayed this time, she would ignore her pride and become our savior. Coach repeated the question with a passion he had not shown all day hoping she would put us out of our misery. Finally she replied, "No," and just like that, the torture was over. What we learned, after vomiting up everything we had eaten, was we had to learn to say no. Learning this lesson saved each of us and our onlookers some serious hurt.

As I got older, I developed many different talents simply because I always seemed to be bored with the routine of my life. At one point, one could set their watch to my routine and the monotony of it all was driving me up a wall. The first project I took on was personalizing purses and clothing using puff paint. I had a unique way of working the paint like an artist and although it kept me up late at night and didn't make me enough money to be worth the effort, it was tons of fun for me. As that died down, I quickly moved into my next venture of selling weight loss shake mix. I really knew little to nothing of the product but it seemed like a great idea and my up line was confident I could use it as an additional stream of income. I didn't wait to quit that one before another friend encouraged me to become a jewelry consultant. After dropping the weight loss shake mix, in came the big idea. My sister and I would go into the dessert business together.

My sister and I were not trained bakers. Although we hailed from an area known for its decadent cuisine, we had never really prided ourselves on being experts on sweet treats. However, out of a love of the idea of being able to leave some sort of tradition in our family, we took the plunge. In the beginning, we had the most fun trying out new recipe ideas and researching the top dessert caterers in the South via social media. We would spend tons of individual hours watching tutorials on the perfect way to cool down cupcakes or the best buttercream recipe. As we marketed our product for free to our friends, we quickly realized we had a talent and it could lead us somewhere great.

Each of us had natural roles in the process. My sister was the brains with the practical approach and I was the passion with the creativity. My sister looked at the finances while I focused on the fondant. She was all about the long term and I was all about the lemon extract. From the beginning, it was going to be a challenge for her to make me more serious and for me to loosen her up. The orders began to fly in and we found ourselves having to divide up the orders between our two houses. As both of us juggled full time jobs and our new business venture, it was clear we had not prepared for our overnight success.

Our growing popularity began to be a bit of a struggle forcing each of us to sacrifice sleep and personal time so we could meet the needs of our clients. At one point, our difference in approach began to cause my sister and me to choose meringue over the movies and strawberry shortcake over Sunday brunches. My sister made the rational decision to pull herself out of the rat race. I was left to decide what I should do about something I had grown to love. When she asked me if I was going to keep it going, I know I should have probably said no but my answer, fueled by my pride which forced me to accept the possibility that I could do it all on my own, was a powerful yes. There was no way I was going to give up until I was ready to do so and I was far from ready to throw in the Baker's Joy.

One of my clearest memories was the time I received a call from one of my friends asking me to do an emergency order for her daughter's birthday party. Apparently, she had agreed to purchase the child's cake from another baker who pulled out at the last minute sharing she had an unexpected emergency with her own child. As a mother, both I and my new client/friend understood the priorities of a real mom so we knew the possibility of her doing the cake was slim to none. I received the call on a Wednesday night and before I thought about my own personal schedule, I agreed to bail my friend out of her jam. I felt great about my decision until I remembered it was competition season for my daughter's cheerleading team meaning she would have practice each day of the week until 10 p.m. When I received the picture of the cake I was to attempt, I swallowed HARD! To put it simply, the cake was entitled "Bee Sweet" and there would be nothing sweet about it other than the frosting. The cake was a double layered, two-tiered cake with protruding bumblebees made from rice treats and marshmallow fondant. The cake was adorned with alternating yellow, black and white polka dots and a big hive sitting on the top. After thinking through the task at hand, I knew I was in trouble.

For the next two days, I worked to design a schedule that would permit me to function in all capacities. I would need to be a full time employee, a mom, a cheer mom and a baker all at the same time and there was simply not enough hours in the day to ensure I could pull it all off. I began to get on the phone to find out who could assist me by driving my daughter and her teammates to cheer practice. After begging and pleading, I found a friend who could fill in for me with the cult known as "cheer moms." Next, how would I find the time to actually work on the cake which proved to require a lot of details? The only solution was to call in sick to work, but knowing my sick days were few and far between, I struggled with the decision. After coming up with a creative explanation involving a spoiled burrito from a local restaurant and coupling it with the fact that I had not been absent in over six months, it was not a problem to get someone to cover for me.

I spent no less than 14 hours creating a cake I had never attempted in my short-lived baking career. The baking part was far too simple with each layer popping out perfectly from its pan after it had been properly cooled. The buttercream had accepted its yellow tinting effortlessly and all seemed to be going well. Then, it was time to stack the layers. The wooden dowels required to set a strong foundation were difficult to shave to an identical height and the cake continued to lean to the right. There was no way the cake would withstand the scrutiny of other moms at the party so I could not stop until it was perfectly centered and sturdy.

After measuring each side over and over, I was finally able to lay the top cake safely on top of its larger partner on the bottom. After using buttercream to seal in the cracks, it was time to smooth the fondant I had used to cover both cakes prior to the stacking process. The covering process had taken over an hour due to my inexperience with the substance which had become popular thanks to the wonderful competitions on the Food Network channel.

Through the help of over fifty social media tutorials and much intervention from a merciful and generous God, I was able to complete the assignment with great detail. When my daughter finally got home, she and I tackled homework and once she was off to bed, I sat motionless on the side of my bed. I realized when I returned to work the next day, I would have a ton of work to get done and yet another night of cheer practice ahead of me. There was a huge distance between the next 12 hours and a good night's sleep and I was nothing short of exhausted. When I finally delivered the cake to my client and bathed in her praise, I could not wait to make it home where I could nurse my swollen feet from being up for 20 hours trying to make all happen.

It must have been two months later when I received a call from a potential client who had been referred to me by my "Bee Sweet" client saying she had been told I was the perfect person to call for last minute cake creations. Although she shared a similar story of how she had made previous plans for her cake only to have them fall through at the last minute, the movie of my last experience played vividly in my mind. I felt myself reliving my terror all over again. I listened to her compounding concerns about the party and her willingness to spare no expense on the last minute request was very attractive to me. I thought of the bills I had sitting on my counter laughing at my paycheck and as I reached out my hand to hit the "accept" button, my brain connected to my experiences with a violent jerk. No amount of money would persuade me to travel down the road again and I delivered disappointing news to her but freeing news to myself.

In this life, we will encounter many decisions we might feel to be unfair to someone else because it will put them in a bind. However, in this case, I had to consider the fact my damsel in distress could have planned better by selecting a more reputable baker therefore, eliminating her need to search for me. She could have embedded mandatory checkpoints to assist her with identifying areas of concern earlier. Because she had not done her due diligence, I could not take on her personal dilemma at my own expense. Although the money would pay some bills, the impact it would have was not worth coins. I learned that sometimes, we have to have the intelligence to say no if we are going to maintain our own personal sanity. What do you need to say no to? What do you need to let go? Be honest with yourself and learn to make your life a yes by saying NO!

chapter 28

"Be Creative"

"What they soon came to realize, as many successful people do, success does not come without its share of greedy onlookers who feel entitled to your benefits without any respect to your grind."

–C. Frazier

Chapter Twenty Eight
Be creative

You can't wait for inspiration, you have to go after it with a club.
– Jack London

Harlem Nights gives us a lot of lessons regarding finances if we would only take the time to pay attention. I must admit, quite a few lessons that have stayed with me over the years came from Harlem Nights as well as Trading Places. Harlem Nights found Richard Pryor and his business partner, Eddie Murphy, facing a cash flow problems. Their competitor decided to make a play for their thriving nightclub business and they found themselves in an unexpected situation. The duo had been living the high life running a candy shop as a front, an illegal card party in the shadows of a backroom storage room and a lavish dancehall in a classic parlor as the attention-getter. What they soon came to realize, as many successful people do, success does not come without its share of greedy onlookers who feel entitled to your benefits without any respect to your grind.

When the two found themselves facing a decision to give their profits to a money-hungry gangster or leave town, the two elected to opt for a change of venue but not before orchestrating a creative escape. Now, this is the part of the movie I loved; when the two stopped focusing on the injustice of being forced to bow out gracefully, and instead, used their brain power to make a conscious financial decision, the real battle was won and their mighty Goliath fell.

The plan began as a simple bet to be placed on a boxing match but served as a camouflage for the men to pull off an unforgettable robbery under the nose of their adversary. The men assured their employees they would walk away with at least $50,000 each which was a selling point for each of them to agree to face a giant with confidence. Now, I was not sure I would have agreed to participate in a plan that could get me killed so I did a little research regarding the impact of $50,000 in the 1930's. During this time period, a $50,000 payoff is the equivalent of $687,572.67 in 2015 so I immediately understood why such a bold move would rock the very world of their gangster protagonist.

In true debonair fashion, the men, dressed in trench coats and top hats on a daily basis, divulged a plan to get rich creatively using every resource they could muster including the solicitation of sexual talents from the infamous "Sunshine" to guarantee all bases were covered. When it was all said and done, the men were able to secure a financial future, obliterate their obstacles and walk away from an impossible situation with new possibilities to rebuild.

When I was younger, I can honestly say I never worried about money. My parents cleverly presented money as a tremendous burden no one should want and my sisters and I were none the wiser. We never pretended to be interested in how our parents made their money or what it would take to make our house function behind the scene so we always waited patiently for our parents to distribute our piece of the pie each month. The first lesson I learned regarding money was attached to academic performance. During this lesson, I found that exceptional performance could prove lucrative for me. I was enthralled.

Now, the formula was simple; each "A" would be paid out in $5.00 increments, "B" grades would earn $3.00 and "C" grades would bring in a whooping $1.00 payment. My math was simple; the only grades worth my time would be the A's so my father had successfully brainwashed me into being an exceptional student! The first semester as he rolled out his terms, I carefully took notes. In his plan, he would only payout his funds at the end of the marking period. Now, after the first marking period (9 weeks), I realized if I negotiated for a more frequent payout coordinated with the progress reports and not just the report card, I could stand to make 2.5 times more money than his proposed system.

The conversation I intended to have with my father would be a tricky one. My father was not one you could ever slide anything by without extensive questioning. I anticipated having to answer a million and one questions before he would take the idea to his man cave for further review. I would have to decide, then and there, if I was as smart as I hoped I was to get a confirming handshake at the end of it. Now, I would have to stand up to the giant armed with only my own Elementary School formula and a prayer of, "Lord, help me."

The day I scheduled my meeting with my dad, I had to complete the prerequisite course involving the cleaning of my assigned areas or the meeting would be cancelled indefinitely. I was confident my chores had been completed to his standard when I knocked softly on the glass door of his man cave. Now, my dad's man cave had been added onto our home a year or so before I was actually allowed to walk in for any other reason other than to answer the house phone. The room was filled with Cherrywood-colored bricks and a 72-inch television in the center of the room encased by two, bricked bookshelves housing movie cartridges, vintage records and sports memorabilia. The room had a large bar fully stocked with the best scotch and shiny glasses of different shapes and sizes which I had been forbidden to touch. The room was always dark and my dad seemed to sink into the sectional couch hoping to blend into its shadows away from the overwhelming responsibility of fatherhood.

My gentle taps on the window were finally answered and I was granted permission to have a little talk with my man upstairs. As I set the tone for the meeting, I would see he was impressed with my thought process. He nodded his head frequently and stopped me at various points to answer additional questions showing me he was contemplating my request which was more than I could have asked. As I went through the effort associated with each class's workload, I moved effortlessly through each challenge I faced as a scholar and how the monetary incentive (I am sure I did not use such a term) would help me stay focused on college. Now, I had dropped the trigger word...COLLEGE.

Of course, my dad sat motionless for a few minutes breathing in my air without any quick judgement. I anticipated a dismissal with a, "Let me think about it," to follow so I prepared my facial expression to be one of appreciation and not disappointment. As his lips parted, he uttered the most beautiful words I had ever heard, "You got it."

I had done it! I had creatively flipped his idea into one that would more than double in amount and my payment calendar would have me paid out every 4.5 weeks. I felt invincible and I realized I could do the impossible if I took the time to think through my plan with great detail and consideration.

Now, at 35, I can say money is not flowing the way I want it to, but it is flowing. As long as there is movement, there is space and opportunity to see it grow. I have to look at the places where I can turn my everyday interactions into money. For example, I love to work out so I figured out the way to save money in that area was to join the team as an instructor of indoor cycling. This saved me $35.00 per month, paid for my gas and enabled me to enjoy free training sessions. All in all, the decision brought in an additional $200 to my household budget each month. Such creative thinking will be necessary in all future plans if I am to see financial freedom. So, be creative in how you plan your finances. You might just come out on top!

Freedom

chapter 29

"Discipline Your Body"

"One thing is for certain, when you make a decision to discipline your body, you sign up for a neon green sign on your forehead with big, orange blinking letters saying, "I'm trying to live right. Please come and mess it up." Men began to come out of the woodworks when I decided to make my bold choice. Phone numbers I tried to delete always seemed to pop back up when my phone would undergo a reset. Nights seemed to get longer and longer while my bed seemed to get bigger and bigger begging for a male body to fill it. The first few months didn't seem to be so heavy, but after six months, the cravings returned and with a vengeance."

—C. Frazier

Chapter Twenty Nine
Discipline your body

Respect your efforts, respect yourself. Self-respect leads to self-discipline. When you have both firmly under your belt, that's real power.

-Clint Eastwood

After months and months of begging, my parents finally showed up one Monday afternoon with a box that seemed to be having some sort of conversation on the inside. I could tell by the holes which had been poked on every side that what was inside the box would push my parents to the top of "world's best mom and dad" list. As the youngest of three, I always wanted a puppy to play with but my mother was always dead set against it. No matter how good my grades were or how well I completed my weekly chore list, my mom wouldn't bend. Now, as my dad stood with the box in his hand, I knew he must have promised her something pretty expensive for her to have relaxed her decision.

My dad set the box on the kitchen floor and it began to move a bit to the left. I was about to jump out my skin waiting for my mom and dad to finally pop the top on my new toy. Before my dad uncovered my gift, he wanted me to sit down to have a discussion with him and my mom. Both my parents went through a laundry list of do's and don'ts and summed it up with a long lesson about responsibility. Although I nodded my head and offered the respectful responses. As I had been taught, my mind was already on the cute ball of fur only a few feet away. Finally, they allowed me to go to the box with my dad towering over me. I uncovered the box and in the corner was a tan bundle with big brown eyes clearly afraid of its new surroundings. I reached my hand in to pick him up and laid him over my shoulder. I was in love.

For the first few days, I mastered the art of playing with my new puppy. I couldn't wait to get home from school each day so I could play with my baby who I named Chancey. Chancey was my loyal friend who was always excited to see me based on the drop of urine he would leave all over the covered porch when I got home from school. We played for hours and hours chasing each other across my yard and in the adjacent field in front of my parent's house. Even though each passing day deepened my love for Chancey, it was time for me to make good on what I had promised my parents. It was time for me to take on a little less fun and a little more responsibility. It was time for me to work on potty training my lovely puppy and I was in for the ride of my life.

It took weeks for my dad and me to come up with a plan that would finally work for Chancey. We tried a series of combinations including getting up at 5:00 in the morning before school to take him outside. My dad explained we were trying to teach him how to discipline his body. I thought it was quite simple; if he urinated in any area other than the one designated, he would get a swat on his hind legs and we would put his nose in his mess so he could connect his action with our reaction. On the other side of the process, when he would complete the process as directed, we would reward him with a doggie treat we kept in the kitchen cabinet. Chancey knew when he had done something right because the noisy foil holding the treats would prompt him to come in the kitchen and begin to jump around our feet. Although every now and then he would make a little mistake, my dad explained to me that Chancey was working against what his body had taught him to do and that the process to discipline his body was something he would have to continue to do with our support.

My time with Chancey was short-lived because although we could discipline his potty breaks, we couldn't seem to stop him from chewing on the laundry room wall. In fact, it was almost as if he was boring a hole through the sheetrock like he was trying to escape a Turkish prison. Each day I went into the laundry room, I knew his days were numbered. My mother never wanted to play with him anyway but in the final days before Chancey walked the Green Mile, my mom hated to see Chancey coming. We finally arrived at the place we all hoped to avoid. It was the ultimate ultimatum issued to my father by my frustrated other. It was either the dog...or else. So, that day when I got off the bus and my friend was no longer waiting for me under the porch, I knew exactly what had occurred. Chancey was gone all because he had not learned how to fully discipline his body. Because he failed to control himself when it mattered most, he was no longer entitled to his treats or even his home. Chancey was gone.

My decision to be abstinent was a pretty simple decision for me which, in the beginning, required little to no effort to maintain. The fact was, I had been in a series of physical relationships for almost twenty years before I made the ultimate commitment to myself to learn to discipline my body. I had tried abstinence once before after the birth of my daughter.

I often heard of women who would go back to the doctor at their six week checkup only to find they were pregnant again. The stories went on to caution new moms about our fertility after giving birth implying we could get pregnant from contact as simple as hand holding. I could not imagine going through another pregnancy that soon so the easiest thing for me was to put a closed sign on the diner.

The busy schedule of a working, single mother served as a wonderful chastity belt as I found myself extremely sleep deprived and over eighty pounds heavier. Sex was the furthest thing from my mind. After months of denying myself physical contact, it became the norm. I figured, it might be a great idea to attach a purpose to my freedom so I decided to label it as abstinence. Due to the fact I was not following any specific, prescribed religious doctrine guiding my decision, I could not call it celibacy. Whatever it was to be called, it meant I would be forced to control my body and risk losing many men because of my choice.

One thing is for certain, when you make a decision to discipline your body, you sign up for a neon green sign on your forehead with big, orange blinking letters saying, "I'm trying to live right. Please come and mess it up." Men began to come out of the woodworks when I decided to make my bold choice. Phone numbers I tried to delete always seemed to pop back up when my phone would undergo a reset. Nights seemed to get longer and longer while my bed seemed to get bigger and bigger begging for a male body to fill it. The first few months, it didn't seem to be so impossible to manage, but after six months, the cravings returned and with a vengeance.

Now, there were some immediate benefits to my decision. My menstrual cycle seemed to come more regularly and without any complications when I stopped engaging in sex. My yeast infections subsided and I no longer went looking for my period each month in the daytime with a flashlight. I was confident I was not exposing myself to disease or pregnancy and those two things brought instant clarity to the importance of keeping up my good work. Although my friends thought I was crazy and could not believe I had been able to survive so long given my past, I was proud of myself for choosing me in a real way.

Aside from the physical benefits, I enjoyed to mental break my sexual hiatus provided. I no longer had to wait for the call after the activity wondering if I had again reduced myself to someone's physical dumping ground. I no longer had to torture myself realizing I had done things with a man I should have been saving for my husband. I could look at myself in the mirror again and although at first I didn't recognize this new creature staring back at me, I wanted to get to know her. Perhaps I could grow to love her. I already knew I respected her.

I felt like an alien again because I went through the entire first year feeling I had to prove to people I was not lying about how long I had gone without penetration from a man. (Notice I specified the word penetration) I found myself fixated on the approval of others which took me all the way back to the origin of my sexual promiscuity. I finally recognized the flaw within myself which was my need to prove things to other people. I needed to prove to them I was changed. I noticed it was just like all the times I had performed my circus act of trying to prove to the many men I had entertained that I was worth their time. I had given them my body over and over, I didn't have anything to show for it except the honor and privilege of watching them choose the other girl right in my face. I had been a world class clown! I vowed to continue my discipline but to make sure I included my mind and thoughts in the equation because it needed some discipline as well.

It has been encouraging to share my journey with my friends and even my former students who jumped into a life of sexual expression only to find themselves faced with some of the same pitfalls I knew loomed just around each corner. Before I knew it, women were pulling me into quiet corners wanting to know more about the reasons for my decision. Even in my transparency, I could feel my freedom coming as I released myself into each of my conversations. I felt I was giving each one of my colleagues permission to be selfish with their gifts and my words gave them power.

To discipline yourself can be lonely as many of the phone calls will cease when a man finds out you don't intend to be loose with him. I have found it a good practice to let a man know my goals early as many feel as if you are not making a connection to them if you don't allow them to control your body. In this place, you are forced to have conversations and build real relationships. In cases where the man and I decided we did not want to pursue anything romantic, because we had not exchanged anything other than meaningful conversation, we could walk away wishing each other well. When it is all said and done, when you can control yourself, the world is truly at your fingertips for you are no longer bending to everyone's will yet establishing space for your own.

chapter 30

"Know Your Worth and LIVE accordingly"

"As I innocently and naively light up the world in my own little corner, I realize no one can see things quite the way I can. No one can inspire others to greatness through song, dance or words like me and for that, my stock rises with each opportunity to live a life based on the popular saying, "carpe diem."

−C. Frazier

Chapter Thirty
Know your worth and LIVE accordingly

We must live a life that is not geared towards living today but our existence after existing and exiting the earth. We must think of our footprints that will long exist after our existence come to its ebb. We must get reasons for existing. For what reasons are you existing?
— **Ernest Agyemang Yeboah**

Perhaps one of the most liberating catch phrases I learned prior to turning 35 was the fact that men "aren't worth the paper they are printed on." When I first heard it, from a quiet, little woman who sat near me in a conference for budding entrepreneurs, I chuckled as if I instinctively knew exactly what she meant by this revelation. Behind her words, I was confident she had done the appropriate leg work and that her conclusion could be taken to the bank, cashed and invested because it oozed with an assurance I hadn't seen in a while. I imagined, based on her flawless demeanor, she had dated men far superior to those I had chosen to spend hours of my life which I could, regrettably, never get back in pursuit of something more meaningful. I thought of her marvelous menu of men as carefully tasted fine wine swirled around at the bottom of her Olivia Pope-style goblets of crystal custom made to her liking and, in that moment, I was envious of her. My mind began to formulate its own moving picture which included her being summoned by a regal black car to a restaurant or jazz brunch. She would meet her Galahad for an intimate evening of stimulating conversation about stocks and rental properties. In contrast, it was like night and day when compared to my infrequent trips to TGI Fridays where I had enjoyed enlightening discussions of football and baby mamas. What a life she must have led prior to our untimely meeting!

While I noticed everything from her perfectly curled hair to her carefully designed ensemble which was clearly indicative of her attention to trend and fashion, one thing I noticed was the absence of the circular validation on her ring finger. Surely with all of her attention to perfecting herself as a woman she could not possibly have been outside the circle of painted ladies who lunch discussing things like china and exotic vacations. But, alas, she was a lot like me, still trying to figure out another avenue by which she could drive her way down the street of sanctification and arrive at the doorstep of delightful happiness known as marriage. I began to think about the process involved with the printing of our currency and wondered if there could be any parallels between its design and defining my own worth.

The process for making the simple currency we shove into our pockets, purses and billfolds is not one that happens as easily as we have been conditioned to believe. I often imagined money being manufactured much like the duplications from an office printer. One would simply send the file to the printer sitting in the adjoining office supply room and BOOM, bills would begin to duplicate themselves for our enjoyment. However, after more research, the procedure, by design is purposed to function so intricately it is almost impossible to reproduce outside of the process outlined by the treasury. In fact, from the onset, the process of producing currency begins as intentionally as the paper selected. No one has ever spent money printed on simple reams of paper found in the boxes cleverly lining the walls in the neighborhood Staples. As I am sure, if it were that easy, the value of money would be completely obsolete and an alternative entity would be necessary. In fact, the paper used for currency is defined as "a special blend of 75% cotton and 25% linen to give it the proper feel. It contains small segments of red and blue fibers scattered throughout for visual identification.

Starting in 1990, the paper for $10 bills and higher denominations was made of two plies with a polymer security thread laminated between them. The thread was added to $5 bills in 1993. This thread is visible only when the bill is held up to a light and cannot be duplicated by photocopiers or printers. The inks consist of dry color pigments blended with oils and extenders to produce especially thick printing inks. Black ink is used to print the front of the bills, and green ink is used on the backs (thus giving rise to the term greenbacks for paper money). The colored seals and serial numbers on the front of the bill are printed separately using regular printing inks. After learning of the foundation set for each individual bill, it became clear to me that each bill, while simplistic to the average cash-toting individual, would never be appreciated for the intricacies involved with its perfection. Man, what a revelation!

I bypassed the statement made by my female companion insinuating men stood alone in their devaluing assumptions. However, in my quest for self-discovery, I had to stop and evaluate myself from this perspective. The very fabric of my being had not been purchased with mere pennies, but a special blend of percentages which when added together still had not managed to equal 100%. I realized I had never considered the things which made me, innately, who I had become as a 30-something year old woman. How could I fault the men around me for not being worth the time and energy it would take to create something as simple as a dollar bill if I had never considered myself to be worth the same effort? How could I live a life of worth if I had never evaluated my own individual price?

I was not sure what I was worth because I never took the time to evaluate what it had taken to create me. Sure, I knew it had taken my mother and father and all of that biological stuff which defined the formation of each human form but, metaphorically, it had taken so much more. I wish I could say I was sure I had been conceived in love. I wish I could, with some heir of superiority, stand before a crowd of people and declare I had been born of a man and a woman who had made a conscious decision to join together in holy matrimony and all of that jazz, but my truth was a bit less like a picket fence and more like a steel trap. As I got older, the velvet shade had been drawn from my family's stage and what lurked beneath was a reality oh too familiar for most. I had been born to a man and a woman who I would love to believe loved at one time, but who had fallen into an agreement to do what was right and proper. You see, during their day, there was no such thing as "hit it and quit it," or "smash and pass." Thank God, during the time in which my parents conceived their children, it had been ingrained in their fabric to do what was culturally responsible which was to give children a name and a home. I can say with pride that my parents did the best they could do to provide us with something they valued; family. However, with that provision, I was not so sure they had taken into account the importance of creating a fabric for our family that would prove indestructible and irreplaceable. I had never learned my value and could not walk in the confidence of the woman I would become.

From what I can remember, I never knew anything was different about my family structure. One man, one woman, three girls and even for a time, a cute little dog named Chancey. If I had to define my blend at that time, I would say we were 60% church, 20% family and 10% education.

Things in my home were simple; Daddy and Mommy made the rules, we followed. Our lives were routine which included school and work from a certain time, dinner at a certain time and church at a certain time. I never thought anything of it because it was all I knew and all I was allowed to be around. However, when the threads began to unweave themselves, it didn't seem so normal anymore. My fabric no longer seemed unique, and after the divorce, it seemed just as cheap and shoddy as everyone else's. We were imperfect just like everyone else.

So now, at 35, what I think about the worth of the paper I am printed on, becomes more relevant. Much like the currency paper, I had to revere the unique fabric intertwined to make me the person I am as a unique blend. Much like the dollar bill, I am a blend of specialized components uniquely combined to form something never created before. Believing that I have been designed with a specific purpose in mind insinuates a belief that my life has been orchestrated from the onset and for some, this would be a good thing, but for me, it has caused frustrations knowing I never had a chance to live a life of complete and utter happiness. In fact, I was always destined to go through life the hard way. I would be that flower that would grow out of the concrete. Not an encouraging realization but man, what a truism it is. While it was easy to balance the percentages of the U.S. currency genetic makeup, for me, my fibers weigh differently from day to day, week to week and year to year. Most of the time, I am 70% fear and 25% faith leaving 5% to brokenness or happiness on any given day. On other days when the stars are aligned in my favor, my balances shift like the scales of justice and I feel as if the entire world is spinning on the tip of my index finger.

The comfort I have found has been in the red and blue fibers of my visual identification. The crimson fibers are my creativity and ability to express myself artistically. Those fibers, when held against any light, always seem to illuminate and everyone around me is able to see them, as well. As I innocently and naively light up the world in my own little corner, I realize no one can see things quite the way I can. No one can inspire others to greatness through song, dance or words like me and for that, my stock rises with each opportunity I was afforded to live a life based on the popular saying, "carpe diem."

Working perfectly with those crimson and fiery fibers are the cerulean specs cleverly sprinkled in the most inconspicuous places. Those delicate dots are the remnants of my fears replaced by my faith as fortified through trials and triumphs. In 35 years, I know the identifying names of each spec and each one tells a unique tale only I can narrate like an African griot. Each immortal epitaph is etched with an embossed memory of how I found myself facing impossible mountains for most of my life, how I plummeted into pits of promises only to find myself clawing my way up slippery walls of woes back into a light assuring me of an endless search for love. My fibers, when in their most secured form, make me pretty awesome to those who gaze from afar, but through my eyes blinded by my own ambitions, are mini comic strips of lifeless litanies looking for liberation.

So, the lesson at 35 is to know my worth. The lessons of life and how we survive them make each of us priceless and if I am going to live a life according to my worth, I have to be worth every penny of the process it has taken to make me who I am. Although far from perfect, my pursuits, at best, are noble as I have journeyed tirelessly for one reason and one reason only; to love and to be loved by those who have held my currency in their hands, folded it neatly and has invested it time and time again. Those continued investments continue to make me priceless and I have to live as if each bill I dispense into this world stimulates the economy and stabilizes the world.

chapter 31
"Pay it Forward"

"From the age of 33 to 35, I decided to deprive myself of sexual intercourse for reasons I will share in another chapter, but I was lucky to find myself surrounded by other women who had made the same choice to pull the cookies off the grocery store shelves. In effort not to go crazy and/or just start walking up and punching random people in the face, we elected to find other equivalents to our past sexual excursions. Keisha found the Vanilla Chai Tea at Dunkin Donuts and the sheer ecstasy the small paper cup could bring to her life prompted me to run to the nearest location to get my own hit of the new crack."

—C. Frazier

Chapter Thirty One
Pay it forward

Our job on earth isn't to criticize, reject, or judge. Our purpose is to offer a helping hand, compassion, and mercy. We are to do unto others as we hope they would do unto us.
-Dana Arcuri

I love Dunkin Donuts. Not the one back in the 90's but this new model is heaven on Earth as the owners and operators have obviously embraced the changing times. What solidified our love affair was the introduction of "sex in a cup" by my friend Keisha. From the age of 33 to 35, I decided to deprive myself of sexual intercourse for reasons I will share in another chapter, but I was lucky to find myself surrounded by other women who had made the same choice to pull the cookies off the grocery store shelves. In effort not to go crazy and/or just start walking up and punching random people in the face, we elected to find other equivalents to our past sexual excursions. Keisha found the Vanilla Chai Tea at Dunkin Donuts and the sheer ecstasy the small paper cup could bring to her life prompted me to run to the nearest location to get my own hit of the new crack.

The cost was cheap. For only $1.99 per tax, the lovely drive thru worker would bless me with a hot, steamy, wet cup of utterly delicious creaminess. As the warm liquid found its way across my lips, rolled over my tongue stimulating each taste bud, it then made its way down my throat until it reached its final destination in the bottom of my stomach. For what seemed like hours after, I would allow my body to replay the highlight reel of each moment of pleasure provided to me by my sexual cup of Chai. After that first encounter together, I needed it, every day. I thought of it while I was at work. Sometimes I would bring my finger to my lip and allow it to tickle my top lip, then my bottom and I would frantically watch the clock for when I could leave my building, fight traffic and meet my boo at our designated place.

One Wednesday morning, I had been fighting all night waiting to make it to the next day because I needed to feel the Chai inside me one more time. I hurried to dress, get my daughter off to school, grab my lunch and supplies and head out the door. Due to the location of the nearest store, I had to take an alternate route to work. Now, given the fact I was on a final warning for tardiness, I made the sacrifice to be with my boo for a few minutes. It seemed as if every elderly person in the world had decided to pour themselves onto the roads in an effort to prove they were still competent enough to operate a motor vehicle. They crept along with nowhere to be at any given time and they were determined to be stopped by every traffic light on the short stretch of highway. I believe on that day, I put together some of the most creative combinations of curse words known to man ignoring the etymology of each one and its part of speech. If I had a pellet gun that day, each one of those auditioning for the new and improved version of the Golden Girls would now have a permanent pinhole behind their ears.

The line inside the bustling Dunkin Donuts was absolutely disrespectful that morning. It had wrapped itself around the building and each car seemed to be cemented in its position. The cars moved at a snail's pace while the clock above my dashboard seemed to be moving at warp speed. Several times I considered backing out of the entire exchange but my greed and desire left no room for rational thought. I finally elected to park my car and hope the inside ordering process would be less taxing. When I entered the store, the intoxicating smells punched me in the nose and I knew I was in the right place at the right time doing the right thing. I was starting to formulate my lie for work so I could justify what was sure to be another infraction against my attendance record but I had come too far to turn back now.

The line moved swiftly. It was almost as if everyone was on the same mission and intended to get their fix and make it to work in time. The process resembled an assembly line with an orchestrated routine including ordering, paying and retrieving. It was perfect and I might make it to work on time after all! When it was time for me to place my order, the cashier was quick and efficient and turned to shout my order back to her waiting minions almost before I could get it out of my mouth. I reached down into my purse for payment and I knew I was only a few precious moments from my love. I had already began our foreplay as he was being mixed and scooped right before my very eyes. He was getting ready for me.

My fingers began to rummage through my purse. Corner to corner, front to back in search for my wallet. I had to be too excited so I steadied myself by propping my bag on the steel counter in front of me. I then took to using my fingers and my eyes to find the one thing standing between me and what I had come from. Alas, it was not there. My mind began to replay my last few interactions involving monetary exchanges and I realized exactly where my wallet was. I had spent the previous evening working out in the gym and wanted an after workout smoothie. In my desperation to elevate my blood sugar levels, I had chunked my wallet in my gym bag and it was waiting outside in the car. As I explained to the cashier I would have to go back out to the car to get my wallet, the disappointment was deafening. As I turned to make a mad dash to the trunk, a voice rang out in my chaos and said, "Ma'am, don't worry about it. Just put it on my tab."

All breath escaped my body as my eyes focused on my savior. My hero came the form of a pudgy, brunette with a beaming smile on her face. She said to me, "Girl, it's one of those mornings." As I nodded in agreement, thanked her over and over again with my boo thang in hand, she gave me one request, "Pay it forward."

I must admit I never watched the movie, "Pay It Forward," and to this day I haven't gotten a chance to add it to my DVD rotation. The one thing I have learned from the film shared by many of my friends is the power of influence. The overarching theme of investing in someone else in hopes they could continue to trend therefore creating a community of people living outside their personal bubbles seemed ingenious. Pretty simple concept but if done right, one that could change the entire culture of our world. It was a fact, I began to ponder the concept and I came to the conclusion it was one that should begin at home.

My mother often talked to me about the women in my family and the ways in which I exhibited some of their passions. I realized through her stories many of the women in my family had made some very interesting choices over the years. In fact, my great grandmother had cut her toe off because of a pesky hangnail. As the story goes, she tried everything to heal the wound but found herself toiling day and night with pain unbearable to her after months and months. She lost faith in doctors as each sab they prescribed provided temporary relief to her ailments. One day, she decided to take matters into her own hands, literally. According to my mother, she retrieved a razor and sawed her own toe off her foot. After she completed this task, she bandaged herself and went on about her business. Now, this story was one that always stuck with me as I imagined my great grandmother sitting on the floor in front of the television one night sawing through her own flesh and bone all to rid herself of a cut on her foot. What tremendous focus it must have taken. Now, my mind connects it to the movie, "Saw," when the main character found himself facing an impossible decision to free himself from his shackles by cutting of his own foot or sitting in his bondage while his family faced impending doom.

Now, my mother's point to the story was that the women who had come before me had demonstrated an ability to survive pain both voluntarily and involuntarily therefore setting a foundation of power and strength. The torch had been passed to me as their offspring and although life might not call for me to cut off my toe, it might call for me to severe other things in my life. My job was to do the cutting for myself and my kids and to then teach them how to cut for themselves. With each individual story of heroism regarding each woman in my bloodline I realized I would not be the woman I am if it had not been for each of their challenges, accomplishments and sacrifices. They had paid it forward.

So, my adult life began with meeting a sorority sister at a barbeque one Saturday. As a new ATL transplant, it was important for me to get my feet wet in a new city and she presented me with an unlikely opportunity to give back in a major way. She asked a group of us if we had ever been on the step team while in college. For me, my foundation with step began when I was 15 years old and participated in a step routine celebrating Kwanza. I had developed a love for the art form and continued to choreograph routines all through college. I eagerly shared my resume with her and found myself agreeing to provide a local team with a tryout routine for the upcoming school year. I traveled across town one Tuesday to a little middle school tucked down a long, winding road. After reporting to front office and being introduced to the team sponsors, I felt I was doing a great service as I realized those who would be in leadership over the team had a ton of passion for kids but lacked the skill and talent of the sport.

I remained through three days of instruction with a cafeteria filled with beautiful girls all hoping to be chosen for that season's team. The girls ranged in size, shape and color but all seemed dedicated to take on the task. When I arrived the second day, the crowd was thinner than the day before as girls began to give up on believing they were good enough to make the cut. I was discouraged to see so many children who had already bought into the belief that things worth having would come easy for them. I was even more motivated to stay and change the course of their lives.

After the audition process, we invited fifteen young ladies to be a part of the program. For weeks, we established routines with them they had never seen before. They were required to check in with the school sponsors each morning to make sure their hair and attire was neat and clean. If it was not, they would receive tips on how to look their best at all times. When I arrived in the afternoon from my 9-5 job in the Hospitality industry, I would take up their food journals and discuss healthy eating choices. In a short time, our program grew from clapping and stomping to a platform for life-changing decisions.

Year after year, I found myself charged with the support and guidance of hundreds of young ladies. I finally landed a job in the school so I could be closer to my purpose. The kids now had each of us at their fingertips. We began to take them across state lines showing them things they had never seen before and allowing them to display their talents on grand stages. They enjoyed college tours and their parents supported our focus on academics and etiquette. With each group, we added more and more benefits to our performers. Then, it happened. I got pregnant and I had a decision to make...would I be able to remain with the program now with a baby on the way?

On top of being pregnant, I was not married. Standing before young, impressionable young ladies with a protruding belly and an absent wedding band forced me into a corner. After speaking with my principal and the parents, I decided I would show them my struggle in hopes they would not follow in my path, but if they did, they would see a woman could still manage a career, motherhood, education and service to others.

Now, after investing over 15 years into the sport of stepping, I have found that I have paid it forward. My daughter reaps many seeds I sowed into other young ladies. She has been fortunate to have coaches in her various cheer, volleyball and church programs who have taught many of the lessons I taught years and years ago. She has never been injured and her world has been exposed to new experiences through her talent. I have learned a valuable lesson about paying it forward in your family and in your interactions by watching others pour into my child in such a mighty way. Never underestimate the importance of doing good things for others knowing it will return to you when it matters most.

chapter 32

"No Day Is Promised"

"When someone stands before the congregation to sing for me, to lament their love and affection on me, I want the song to be the sweetest cake ever tasted with a drizzle of snow on top. I want everyone to know that with each day, the only promise I had been given was that God would grant me a day I had never seen before and a day I would never see again."

–C. Frazier

Chapter Thirty Two
No day is promised

Live Today! Do not allow your spirit to be softened of your happiness to be limited by a day you cannot have back or a day that does not yet exist.
— Steve Maraboli

The 21st day of October in the year of 2014 was a day I never wish to live again. The morning had been pretty normal for a fall day; crisp air, light traffic and all my students seemed focused on the lesson. I had worn the wrong shoes, opting for a heel I had not familiarized my ankles with so I felt a slight burning half way through the day but it was nothing I couldn't handle. The commute home in Atlanta traffic was surprisingly light and I was proud only one 18 wheeler had almost side swiped me as opposed to the normal five who all enjoyed playing a human version of pinball. My daughter's homework was pretty normal and dinner was quick and easy. For the majority of the day, everything seemed to be pretty standard.

I had actually just gotten home from teaching an indoor cycling class and was asking my daughter to help me wash up the dishes from an earlier dinner when my cell phone began to ring. I remember being sprawled out on my couch still sizzling from a hard class and my fingers fumbled toward the end of the sofa to retrieve the vibrating box. As I haphazardly answered the call, I had no idea the news that was waiting on the other side. In retrospect, I think had I known what I would be told, I would have never answered it at all. For once I answered the call, my life was forever changed.

"Hey, Risse. Whatcha doing?" the voice asked. At first, I didn't think anything of the call and replied with my usual witty answer involving a brief description of how much time it would take for me to put my body back together with chewing gum and duct tape after punishing it so badly in the gym. I went on to explain how I had only taken a small step toward ridding myself of the fire my thighs continued to ignite each day during normal activity. In fact, I was probably putting on my most comedic routine ever when the voice cut through my cunning jargon like a knife.

"Tia's gone."

There was a deafening silence for what seemed like hours and the voice said, "Risse, Tia died today." I didn't move. I don't remember breathing. I don't think I blinked or even shuddered and the words continued to travel through my bloodstream. In typical fashion, my mind began to scramble for any phonetic equivalent phrase to replace what I had heard. Perhaps she had said, "Tia's fried," or "Tia's a guide," or even "Tia has pride." Anything else would have made more sense to me in the crevices of my brain which were now smoking out of my ears. The more I tried to rationalize, the more the heat began to rise from my toes. I wasn't sure what had happened, but I knew it was true and there was nothing I could do to fix it.

For the first few minutes, I remained calm urging my bearer of bad news to be very sure about the information she had been assigned to deliver across state lines. I urged her to consult her source before she contacted anyone else to authenticate the news for it was sure to devastate too many people for her to afford to be erroneous. She was sure...I knew she wouldn't have called me if she weren't sure...it was real; the realest words I would ever hear for the realest hurt I would ever feel.

As I listened to the fragmented details she had compiled, a million smiles ran through my head. I remembered jokes, relished in plans for fame and fortune, tortured my soul with hugs playing over and over again in my heart. She didn't know much nor could she elaborate, but the outcome would forever be the same. Tia and I had just corresponded the day before, all was well, all was normal. How could she be gone? She couldn't be.

I was instructed to begin the phone tree with my linesisters, many of whom I had not spoken to in years. I wouldn't be calling for updates on their children's developmental processes, or even the status of pending wedding plans. Instead, I would be calling them to punch them in the face with the news that another one of us was gone forever. Call after call, hang up after hang up, my heart was but mere shreds by the end of the night. I felt helpless not being able to see their faces, I had never felt so far away from their hearts in my life. I couldn't gage their responses but trusted their assurance that they were okay and we would get through it together. I never moved off of the couch yet my tears married sunrise with an imminent depression of the days that would lie ahead.

When I woke the next morning, I was confident it had been a horrible mistake. Maybe someone had mixed up the information and planned not to be upset with the person who had spread this vicious rumor; I just wanted it to be over and to get back to my life as it had been. When I logged on to Facebook, the snowball had begun to form into a colossal-sized weapon of emotional destruction as throwback pictures of her and the lives she had touched began to flood my timeline. It was like everyone had received the memo and we all were left to our own coping mechanisms. With each post, I could decipher the size of the hole created in everyone's hearts; the holes for some would be plugged with less effort but for some, their hole might never heal.

That day at work, my sunshades were my force field. I immediately reported to my supervisor what had taken place but I vowed to be strong enough to make it through the day. I would need days off to attend the services so I wanted to be productive until then. Being an educator means having hundreds of eyes on you at all times so I elected to share with my students the enormous tragedy happening in my life. Some of the kids shared their personal connections while others left their support on the pages of handcrafted cards saying, "Tea is forever a tiger." I remember having to leave the classroom over twenty times the first part of the day because I simply couldn't breathe. All I could hear over the explanations of compound sentence structure was her laugh. It was so clear and distinctly hers. It banged in my ears almost as loudly as my broken heart to the point I had to go home for the rest of the day.

For the next few nights, I planned to make the trip home. With the help of my little sis, Mick, who covered the cost of my ticket and my linesister, Courtney, who would get me back, I knew I was going to have to face it head on. Then the call to sing at her services came and it was more than I could take. How could I serenade my friend? I knew the notes would never come out right because my heart would bleed through each bar. When I was told Tia had already planned out her service outlining each job, true to her personality, I knew I would have to find the strength inside to finally say goodbye.

On the ride to the service, the girls who were now grown women exchanged humorous anecdotes of college times; times when life was truly good. We laughed. About thirty minutes from the town where the services were to be held, I was encouraged to run through my songs. My tears choked the notes and the words came in gasps. There was nothing anyone could do but encourage me to do my best and to make her proud. No matter what, I would make her proud.

We arrived at the church extremely early. I mean, NO ONE was there yet, not even Tia. I walked around the back of the church with my sisters making sure we had as much together as we could. Then, the hearse arrived. She was inside. I knew her spirit was gone, but that shell that remained had once been the home of one of the most ambitious, charismatic, hardworking people I had met in my entire life. Inside that shell had been a heart of purity which saw me during a time I had been hiding from myself. She had drank whiskey with me in the middle of the day after a hard test. She had planned university programs with me into the wee hours of the morning in an effort to make things better for the African American students on campus. She helped me glue flowers and pick up food and clean up the park and paint the schools and read to the kids and tear down the club. I didn't know of her, I knew her. And I loved her.

I tried to walk into the church where I knew she had been propped inside but I just couldn't go inside. I would get to the door and I just couldn't walk in. Instead, I found myself in the waiting room behind the choir stand. In that time, my sorority sisters and linesisters began to gather. My pain must have radiated because each of them prompted me to be strong. I had nothing. It wasn't until Tia's younger sister, Jessica, came to the door and told me to come in that I was able to move. I knew in that moment if no one else in the world understood how I was feeling, it was her. If she could be strong even with her unborn baby inside her, I had to find it somewhere on the inside.

When I walked up to the casket, my eyes were closed so tightly I could see purple fireworks behind my eyelids. When I opened my eyes and peered into the box, I finally let my chest relax and the breath that escaped my body was clean and open. I would never breathe the same again for I had finally found a way to let her go. I told her I was present and accounted for. I told her I had made it to be right by her side. I told her I would sing to her and I would make her happy. She looked too final. It was almost like the most perfect benediction to the most enlightening sermon ever delivered. She was there, but she was gone, too. She would never be again and as I had loved her in life, I would now have to learn to love her in death.

As I sat in the choir stand facing all the various faces, I suddenly didn't see them anymore. All I saw was me and Tia sitting in that Dallas restaurant we had visited only a few months before discussing everything from relationships to real estate. I sat with my friend and we had talked about what we wanted for each other and I could sing to her this one last time and then let her go. As the notes billowed into the atmosphere, I imagined her catching each note and adding it to the bag slung across her bosom. I watched her gather each note, each frame, each stanza and I smiled. I never wanted for forget that moment with her, and I knew she would take it with her into her forever.

I still miss her. Sometimes, I text message her just because my heart needs to feel connected again. I never thought anything could and would hurt me so badly but when you love someone and realize they have blessed your life, it's okay to miss them and wish for more time to have them play a role in the motion picture of your life. While no day is promised, for each day that is, we must take the time to gather each note, each ray, each blade, and each petal. With each passing day, life is a series of chapters separated by 24 hours of memories to create and traditions to build. When someone stands before the congregation to sing for me, to lament their love and affection on me, I want the song to be the sweetest cake ever tasted with a drizzle of snow on top. I want everyone to know that with each day, the only promise I had been given was that God would grant me a day I had never seen before and a day I would never see again. With that promise before me, for Tia, I will remember to sing.

chapter 33

"Sometimes you have to fact your mountain"

"My day on Stone Mountain showed me just how many people had and will experience a mountain in their lives. My mountain just happened to be the passing of my mom but all of our mountains will be different."

–C. Frazier

Chapter Thirty Three
Sometimes you have to face your mountain

Even hope may seem but futile,
When with troubles you're beset,
But remember you are facing
Just what other men have met.
You may fail, but fall still fighting;
Don't give up, whate'er you do;
Eyes front, head high to the finish.
See it through!

-Edgar Guest, 1881 - 1959

There were many things I hoped to experience as a resident of Atlanta. I visited the legendary Club 112, I made my way to the popular New Birth Baptist Church and I dined at Gladys Knight's Chicken and Waffles on several occasions confirming I had experienced some of the highlights of ATL living. I did not find it important to visit Stone Mountain until I had been a tax-paying citizen of Georgia for over 14 years. My invitation to face the beast came as an outing to celebrate Labor Day and I figured I had nothing to lose.

Only months prior, I endured the loss of my dear mother and the weeks in between seemed much like a blur of my feeble attempt to put the pieces of my life back together. I had lost my desire to do much and I realized my friends were doing all they could to connect me back to a world I had found spinning out of control. When I put on my shoes that morning, I was tempted to grab my headphones, but for some reason, I didn't want to drown out the sounds of the world. I wanted to allow the chirps and croaks to climb into my ear canals in hopes they could write my new song. I settled for a water and jumped in the car destined to conquer the mountain.

Everyone must have planned to tackle the mountain as opposed to firing up the barbecue pit because the park was dripping with fitness freaks adorned in various ensembles. For some, they pulled out their best Nike thread, while a few dressed in khakis and polos. I certainly was not fixated on everyone's attire, yet how eager they were to get going on their journey to the top.

The first few steps on the mountain were not what I expected. Almost immediately, the path stretched upward in a steep direction and my first few steps felt like looming death. My daughter and friend seemed to be unbothered by the steps and I began to feel like a loser for being unable to start out strong. I began to watch people twice my size breeze by me and kids over 20 years my junior moving even faster. Although my mind wanted to go faster and climb harder, my calf muscles told a different story. My friend offered me as much assistance as she could by showing me how to stretch the area and even stopped to massage the cramps beginning to take hold with each elevation. I think we all realized we would be in for a trip that would take much longer than we had anticipated but as I picked myself up off a rock I used as a resting seat, I made a declaration to all who would listen; "I will not quit. I will get up to the top. I have to."

Halfway up the mountain was a pavilion where each climber could stop and regroup their thoughts about life. During our brief stop, I could hear many people contemplating going back down the mountain while others discussed how they could shave some minutes off their time by going a bit faster. I didn't say much but in my mind, I was confident I was not the only one having a tough time but I was one of the ones who would finish the job. I got up off the bench and began to climb again.

The sun began to announce itself with much more passion as the second leg of the climb began. Its beams bounced off the smooth rocks with a blinding brilliance revealing beautiful specks of shiny minerals. At one point, I stopped and turned around only to see how high up we had gone in a short amount of time. The view revealed the beautiful Atlanta skyline dancing in the distance and the world seemed so far away from the vitality of the mountain. One thing was for sure, I was not closer to the end than I was to the beginning so I continued to put one tired foot in front of the other determined not to become a victim of the mountain.

The final quarter of the mile was the hardest. A climber who was on her way down the mountain for the second time provided me with some advice, "Don't look up. Just keep going." What I didn't realize is her advice came from a place of knowing the intimidation of the final steps ahead. At one point, the mountain appeared to disappear into the clouds revealing an unknown end to our journey. I decided to take her advice and looked down at my feet willing them to move although we remained at war with each step.

Toward the top, I could hear people cheering and congratulating others on reaching the apex. I wanted to hear the same cheers after working so hard to make it to the same finish line so I began to push even harder. Once at the top, there were no cheers from the others, yet I didn't care. I could hear my daughter say, "Good job, mommy," and her words were as sweet as candy. I had done what I felt was impossible and lived to tell the story.

However, as I sat at the top of the mountain and looked out into an endless sky, the message was clear. My journey wasn't about Stone Mountain, it was about my life. Grief, much like this large compilation of stone, had presented itself as a mountain in my life. When my mother first passed away, my legs immediately began to strain and cramp. I had no idea what I was expected to do or what my life would look like without my best friend. I began to stop early on and I felt I was not in a space or place to withstand the daily challenges left as precious gifts of despair.

Much like the pavilion, the loss of a parent becomes a secret rite of passage for those of us invited to a secret fraternity of fear where are all forced to pledge in pain and cross in chaos. During the grief process, it is common to rest with those who want to escape the process so they hide or run from it as long as they can. Others decide death is God's way of building their character and they look for ways to challenge themselves to be stronger than ever before. I, on the other hand, elected just to keep going for it was the only decision I could make and remain diligent.

The last leg of the mountain was symbolic of my daily push to make it from 12 to 12. Many gave me advice in hopes I would learn from the strategies they had developed on their own journey. Others struggled alone drowning out the panting of other beneath the beats of popular music streaming from cordless headphones. I had grabbed on to the handrails at the steepest point of the mountain much like I had grabbed onto my family and friends hoping they would give me the support I would need. In my final stretch, it was just me and my mountain of grief ascending straight up into this unknown place I would now call home for nothing would ever be the same again without my mom.

However, on the way down, I saw a different message. As we began to come off the top of the mountain, my legs no longer ached. For some reason, the change in direction relieved the pressure and I began to jump from rock to rock. The rail I had used on the way up for support was now a hindrance so I elected to depend on my own strength to get down. On the way, I passed others on their way up whose faces shown the same terror and strain I had known only a few moments before. I found myself cheering them on and wanting to put a smile on my face to show them once they made it to the top, the descent would be nothing.

As we passed the areas I had faced with pain, they now became stepping stones to the completion of my challenging task. I felt my strength coming back and began to move faster toward my starting point. When we reached the final stretch of the mountain, I heard another climber take a fall behind me. I looked back and almost kept going knowing there wasn't anything I could do from a medical perspective but before I knew it, I was headed in her direction to be there to support her. When she was strong enough to keep going, we all finished the climb...together.

My day on Stone Mountain showed me just how many people had and will experience a mountain in their lives. My mountain just happened to be the passing of my mom but all of our mountains will be different. I noticed people from every age group, every race and every ethnicity facing the mountain at the same time. For each of us, making it up the mountain meant something different but no matter the lesson, mountains are meant to be climbed and conquered. Although this mountain is not one I will beat in one day, I know it is not insurmountable. As long as I have family and friends to push me upward, there is no mountain I can't climb. Don't miss the lesson! The courage it takes to make your climb defines your life. My climb defines me as a conqueror.

Each day, I miss my mother more that words can express. The empty hole in my chest seems to drown me one day, and the very next day, it suffocates. It has been virtually impossible for me to grasp my emotions and arrest them. Instead, I wait patiently for the moment grief decides it wants to bring me to my knees. My faith has been shaken to the point of concern given the fact God has been my balance since I was 12. Somedays, I wonder how God could have ever loved me if he taught me how to love, gave me the perfect person to love, only to take her at a time when I needed her most. I still struggle with that. However, each day I climb hoping, crying, fighting, praying, wishing, bargaining, pleading, begging…all the while still depending. Although I can't see the top of this mountain, I know when I get to the top, she will be there to hug me again. She will be there to remind me of my power. She will be there to laugh with. She will there to cry with. She will be there to always believe in me. She will be there to comfort me. She will still be there praying for me. When my climb concludes, she and I will be home…together…FOREVER. I love you, mommy.

chapter 34

"Go Get It"

"There is an understanding that work must be done to reach the end goal, but the agreement in our spirits is to always reach the goal."

–C. Frazier

Chapter Thirty Four
Go get it!

If you don't go after what you want, you'll never have it. If you don't ask, the answer is always no. If you don't step forward, you're always in the same place.

— Nora Roberts

During annual student introductions at the opening of my 11th year as a professional educator, one of my 7th grade students said one of the most profound things I had heard in a long time. When asked to share one unique thing about herself in front of her classmates, the young scholar replied, "What makes me unique is I was born dying." This statement flew over the heads of every student in the class who I am sure were still mentally enjoying their summer vacation but for me, it almost took my breath away. The reality was, my scholar had just set the stage for a long personal session with my inner being. I made a decision to analyze her statement further and apply it to my own life.

Now, don't get me wrong, students in the modern-day classroom say all manner of things on any given day. It is not uncommon to hear them discussing the latest dances, popular fashion or the "artist of the week" penetrating their brains with pointless references to drugs and intercourse cleverly disguised by up-tempo beats. On any given day, their conversations would mimic that of their parents clearly demonstrating the inappropriate conversations taking place in their presence. One thing was for certain, inasmuch as they could speak and act like the adults in their lives, they needed permission to do everything. Whether it was the restroom or the need to get out of their seat, they were conditioned to elevate their hands and seek the approval of their instructor to do the things they freely did each day once beyond classroom walls.

During the school year, we often found it a challenge to get our students to think for themselves. On each assignment, they would need very specific explanation of each directive to the point they would simply have to fill in the blank to earn an A. There was little to no room for personal discovery and each child depended on the instructor to tell them what to say, how to punctuate and what resources to reference. It disturbed me that we were breeding a generation of young adults who would never be aggressive about life simply electing to have someone spoon feed them their future and they would then ask permission to ask for seconds. None of them would simply GO GET IT.

When my daughter was about two years old, I found it very easy to entertain her. She wasn't interested in many of the expensive educational toys most magazines had suggested I purchase to prove I cared about my child's academic development. Instead, she was the most in love with the tops of boxes. She fancied shoe box tops and would sneak into my closet, retrieve her friend and bring it to me. I would tell her to put it back after balancing it on my head or pushing it across the floor for her to chase, but she could play with her toy as if it was the greatest invention on Earth. Each day, she would make a beeline to check on her friend and nothing could stop her from her fun.

As I began to rearrange my closet with the changing of seasons, I unintentionally relocated all of my shoes to the top of my closet to make room for storage containers at the bottom. After working hard during one of my "duty free" mommy weekends, I was excited by my newfound organizational skills. When my daughter returned home, she entered with a baby doll in hand from her aunt. I was excited to see her taking a liking to another friend however, my happiness was short-lived as she sat her new baby on my bed and went straight for my closet. As my sister and I talked in my living room, I realized my baby girl had been in my room for quite a while. I decided to check on her and found her in a frightful position.

My daughter did not appreciate my decorating skills and had found her old friend now out of her reach above three leveled rows of hangers. In her desperation to be reunited with her security blanket, she had taken matters into her own hands, as opposed to asking me for her assistance, and climbed on top of the storage containers to bring herself closer to the top shelf of the closet. As she reached higher and higher, she would evaluate the distance between her climb and the carpet below. A few times, her facial expression read fear but the reward was far too tempting not to keep going. As the containers began to wobble beneath her, she continued to steady herself and reach higher and higher.

Although I finally had to pull her off the top container, I pulled down her trophy. She held it tighter and smiled brighter knowing it had not come easy to have it in her grasp. It was then and there my daughter taught me a valuable lesson about life. No matter how far out of reach your goal might be, the right person will see your willingness to work hard to have it in your grasp and give you the final push you need to reach your goal.

The concept of the "go get it" approach to life is best captured in rapper, T.I.'s chart topping song. The anthem was popular with the gym rats fighting for perfect bodies, however, the lesson easily transferred to all aspects of one's life. The message was simple, losing is not an option. In all areas of our lives, we must have an attitude that we are determined to pay the price to win in the end. There is an understanding that work must be done to reach the end goal, but the agreement in our spirits is to always reach the goal.

As a spin instructor, I have met many people who have changed my life whether they ever knew their impact or not. One, in particular, began to refer to himself as my manager blanketing me in support I needed to endure my own health journey. He began a series of video chronicles of his own personal fitness journey on Facebook giving a real look at the ups and downs of fitness. He would end each clip with, "Live, love, laugh, lose weight." What seemed like a simple affirmation was loaded with an underlying understanding of what it would take to truly accomplish the task at hand. Each of his subscribers, including myself, stalked his social media realizing if he could remain so focused despite his occasional pitfalls, we could certainly continue to push through our own. His "go get it" attitude screamed out in every post inspiring each of us to put on our Tupac music and get pissed off at the stumbling blocks we continued to allow in our lives.

My daughter, even in her own innocence, had done a great job of teaching me the lesson I would encounter years later in a different form. She had shown me the tenacity it was going to take to accomplish things like two advanced degrees as a young, single mother. She had shown me the sacrifice it was going to take to help establish a statewide organization with little to no background on how to run a non-profit. She provided a reference for me when I stepped out to start my own business just to make ends me during unemployment. There have been so many times I had to reflect on my own "go get it" approach to life. I had to ask myself, "Are you doing all you can do to get those things you KNOW you deserve in life?"

As I leap into real adulthood, I realize I have to tap into my "go get it" spirit more than ever now. After losing my mother only months before completing this work, I had to clock into that same spirit that always burned in her. She always went after the things she wanted and knew God had promised in His word to give her the desires of her heart. Even before she transitioned home to be with her father, she had a plethora of plans outlined in her daily planner and checkpoints to hold herself accountable for the dreams she had confirmed. Her deposits had been paid and her plans had been made showing me that same "go get it" drive I found deep inside had been planted there by the one who loved me best.

In life, there is no excuse not to GO GET IT. The only limits on your life are the ones you allow. God has placed unbelievable power in each of us as indicated in His word. He has made promises of prosperity and good health to each of us who keep to His plan. If you are to truly embrace the God in you, you must get up, get out and do something. Today is your day, yesterday is gone never to be seen again. Get moving and GO GET IT!

Chapter 35

"Love Your Body and Teach Others to Do the Same"

"Who are you? Without the gimmicks and the fake additions, do you recognize yourself? When you see that person, have you accepted them for what they are?"

–C. Frazier

Chapter Thirty Five
Respect your body and force others to do the same

When you are content to be simply yourself and don't compare or compete, everyone will respect you.
— **Lao Tzu**

No one ever wants to talk about the time they lost their virginity. I mean, who wants to admit to the foolish decision many of us made entirely too young to fully understand the meaning of such an act? The truth is, the way in which we lost or will lose our purity speaks volumes regarding our future actions and reactions as it comes to our interpretation of our body and its worth. When I was 15, I found myself in a situation where my boyfriend had taken my virginity from right under my nose. Literally. He was only 16, one year my senior and it was almost as if we had been arranged like an old African marriage. His brother had married my sister so technically, we weren't related, but trusted to be in each other's space. I'm not sure how things had even evolved over the years. I remember sharing letters in the mail from one city to the next. He would always write in a green pen and his mistakes would be minimal. As a lover of Literature, I found this a rarity compared to the degenerates I sat next to each day in class who always struggled with there, they're and their. To have a guy who understood the pairing of a singular subject and a plural verb made him more and more attractive by the minute.

For about two years, we had carried on a fictitious love affair; if you can call a long distance Pen Pal sort of arrangement between elementary and middle school kids an affair, and I could always make the girls at school jealous by talking about my boyfriend that lived in another city. My best friend, Angell, seemed to live vicariously through me and often inquired about my letters. She would beg me to bring them to school and share them. I would and she would even advise me on the proper way to send my love through the mail in response. As the years went on, the topics became more advanced, the terminology shifted from being about baseball and cheerleading to detailed outlines of a clearly more advanced young man. As I continued to nurse scraped knees from bicycles, he was entertaining a much more advanced agenda.

The summer before my sophomore year in high school, my mother agreed to allow me to stay with a family member for the summer. Seemed like a sweet deal; I could be near my family and they could trick me into being their personal, underpaid nursery service. Seemed like a win, win situation for everyone; I think. As a reward for my indentured servitude, I would be allowed to join them in the country where her husband found his roots. I would get an opportunity to ride horses, see them mate and even eat freshly slaughtered hogs. During that time, my Pen Pal and I were finally able to see one another. He was driving at this time and we would enjoy trips to Wal-Mart to retrieve items for his mother. We would walk up and down the street talking and laughing about nothing and everything at the same time. Life was good, I had a real boyfriend.

He, too, had become a slave to his family becoming the babysitter for each of the adults as they hung out in the local clubs on the weekend. We both were too young to identify the manipulation but we just enjoyed finally moving past words on a paper. He and I had been babysitting the children for our families one faithful night and somehow, he wound up in the bed with me and two small toddlers. It felt nice to be so close to him. During the day, it always seemed like we had eyes on our every move, largely because we always had someone's child with us, but for a time, we could have some alone time to pretend we were grown.

Being with him brought out a lot of desire to pretend to be more expressive than I had ever been in the past. He wanted me to talk to him more, kiss him more and share with him more. My first year of high school had taught me a lot about the things I "should" have been doing with boys my age. I, a proud tomboy, had just come into the more girlie side of myself, yet I was not yet totally convinced I was ready to sashay like the other girls who graced my school hallways turning the heads of the varsity football players. I secretly wanted them to look at me when I walked by but, when they did, the glance always had a "little sister" feel and was followed by a directive to pass a flirtatious message to one of my friends. This time, it was different. This time, the boy was looking back at me and the only person I had to do was pass a message to myself.

I had made the decision to allow him to kiss me like I had never been kissed before one night as we were watching over the children when the adults went out to celebrate the 4th of July weekend. He and I had bid one another goodnight and his mother gave him clear instructions to remain in the living room. He responded with a frustrated, "Yes, ma'am." He looked like someone had taken the wind out of his sails and I watched him settle the children in on separated sections of the couch. I took two of the kids with me and set off for the adjoining bedroom. I had drifted off to sleep when I was nudged out of my sleep by his cold hand.

I remember the soft touch of his lips, the wetness of his mouth and the passion that escaped from each thrust of his tongue. I felt I was too young to understand or even comprehend it at the time, but I knew what it felt like to be desired by someone else and the feeling seems familiar. As I continued to indulge in his kiss, I felt his fingers in the depths of my navel. He tickled it softly and drew small circles around it as if he were playing a child's game. I felt gorgeous and perfect in that moment. The sound of his breath was a soft pant as if he was tired from a light jog but he continued to define my womanhood with every touch.

I felt the ridge of my panties being pulled away from my hips and the youngest child moved abruptly in an effort to find a more comfortable position in the now crowded bed. I felt selfish for sharing such an innocent bed with such a guilty pleasure but this was the touch that had always peaked my curiosity. I only hoped the dreams invading the child's sleep would occupy enough of her psyche to keep her from stopping what was happening only inches away from her. As he continued to softly slip his warm, moist hands into a place no one had ever been, my breath was almost non-existent as my heartbeat quickened.

In my mind, the same touch he had given my lips would transfer to my most private place. I wanted him to look at me in a way no one had ever looked before. I don't know why I wanted it to be him, in that moment in time, I wanted him to see me; look at me and give me the approval I needed. His hands ran down my legs which were no longer tightly gripped. The quadrilateral muscles now felt like soft mounds of permission granted to his touch and as his hands delicately coaxed my thighs apart and I felt an excitement in the pit of my stomach that escaped my cognitive ability to connect. The soft tickle of his fingers against my inner thighs coupled with his soft kisses made me wonder if this, finally, was what love felt like. Never did I plan for it to be anything other than a simple exploration of my body, but I quickly learned the consequence for any female who allows her treasure to be discovered.

In one quick motion, I felt a stab in the depth of my secret place. I sat up in disbelief wondering what had shattered my window of wonder only to connect with a sinister smile on the face of my prince charming. "What did you do?" I asked in a whisper remembering the presence of the two children who remained deep in their sleep. I also kept in mind that his mother was only a few rooms away sleeping in her own bedroom with the infants. She had, undoubtedly, ignored the sound of him creeping into the spare bedroom of the trailer from the living room where the three 6-year-old boys laid, now alone, as their protector lay at my feet…smiling.

"It's okay," he reassured in a calm and proud tone. "You're not a virgin anymore. We can do it now." He brought his hands from under the covers which once shielded me from sight only to reveal blood dripping from those same, soft fingers that had prompted me to let down my protective shield. I looked at the blood knowing it wasn't a sign of my cycle, yet a grim realization my life would never be the same. I looked at him, this boy with a look of simplicity, and felt as if I was gazing at a stranger. I searched for the familiar look in his eyes to ease my confusion but there was nothing behind his eyes other than childish naivety and greed.

"What did you do?" I asked. His reply was one that echoed through my conscious for many years to follow. His response to my question insinuating my refusal to accept my own responsibility in my decision making process told me I would never again be able to blame another for my choices. His answer was simple; "I did what you wanted me to do."

As an adult, I have learned just how precious our body is and how comfortable we are with punishing it as often and as harshly as we can. I thought about how many people in the world spend thousands of dollars placing holes in various parts of their bodies. The growing number of individuals declaring their individuality through ink shoved under a layer of their skin proves we are in the business of damaging ourselves. When I consider the number of self-inflicted gunshot wound victims or even those who self-mutilate themselves, it makes me wonder if we have ever truly seen ourselves a "beautifully and wonderfully made?"

My daughter and I decided to escape our everyday routine one holiday and traveled to a spa located North of the city. The spa was a huge building loaded with pools, saunas, steam rooms and smaller areas dedicated to treating the entire body. When I did research on the origin of what seemed like a normal practice for other ethnicities, I learned that the process of relaxing, exfoliating and massaging the body at great length serves a vital role in how we view our bodies. In the spa rooms, the men and women are intentionally separated and women are free to enjoy steam rooms and whirlpools with the only requirement being a cleansing bath and complete nudity.

When we arrived, we had every type of cover up known to man stuffed in our rolling suitcases. As we checked in, we were told it was against the rules to wear clothing in the wet areas. I must admit, knowing my body is FAR from where I wanted it to be before agreeing to bear it all, I heard my daughter began to panic. She was dead set on leaving and if she had to stay, she had made up in her mind she was going to remain in the areas where she could remain comforted by her shorts and tanks. I realized, neither of us had developed a love for our bodies. We both yearned to hide behind lockers and duck into the water when all heads were turned. However, it was then I wanted to teach my daughter a valuable lesson to love her body and embrace the process of ridding her temple of impurities both inside and out.

Once inside, I tried not to look around at the other women but I could not help it. I did not look around at them to be sexual, yet, I admired their confidence. It was almost as if many of them did not realize anyone was nude. They were minding their own business and releasing their own freedom into the atmosphere free from care and judgment. What I noticed, however, was the fact that all of the Caucasian and Asian women walked around in pure bliss no matter their imperfections while most of the African-American women held on to the tiny towels still fighting to hide as much as they could from people who weren't even looking. I saw the same horror in their eyes as I had seen in my daughter. We all stood afraid of accepting our bodies and having those around us to be forced to respect it as well.

The movie, Coach Carter, asked a profound question over and over again; "What is your biggest fear?" For most, our fear is to be different in what we consider to be a negative way. For an African-American, we not only have to be comfortable with our shapes, but we also have to be comfortable and accepting of our own skin knowing it defines us. For many of us, we have allowed the definition others have placed on our skin color to cause us to feel inferior. For others, we have allowed that definition to propel us to greatness knowing we have to fight over additional hurdles to be not only equal, but extraordinary.

As a woman of any race, our breasts, hips, lips, hair and skin color define us each day. We braid down our locks and hide them beneath synthetic strings manufactured in a warehouse all for the purpose of redefining who we really are. Women inject foreign substances into their lips, cheeks and forehead trying to redefine themselves in the eyes of a society that was not created to love them. How can we tell our children they are beautiful when they see us alter every part of our appearance each day? After we are done painting, priming and pulling ourselves, do we even recognize our own image?

At 15 when my boyfriend told me he only did what I wanted him to do, was he right? Did I want him to violate me? Did I want him to travel into my body without fear of consequence? Did I set the stage for him to take certain liberties where I was concerned? If I am honest with myself, I can admit that from my conversation and my presentation of who I was, I did not force him to respect me because I didn't respect myself. As an adult, those same behaviors continued until I took the time to learn what it would take to truly respect me and now, I won't accept anything less.

Who are you? Without the gimmicks and the fake additions, do you recognize yourself? When you see that person, have you accepted them for what they are? Our bodies are precious. Not only are they susceptible to breaks and illnesses, the inner being, although sheltered by bones and flesh is our temple, is the most delicate part of us all. As an adult, protect you, define you, love you and respect you. If you do that, others will have to follow suit.

The Afterward to My Foreword:

These are the days that must happen to you.

-Walt Whitman

Stumbling into church that Sunday was the moment I now realize saved my life or what was left of it. I don't remember combing my hair although I am sure I brushed my teeth out of routine but I just can't seem to remember if I had even thought about combining my hair. I really didn't care how I looked and I couldn't see myself anymore, anyway so it didn't matter much to me how the world saw me through its jagged lenses. I mean, I had been a walking zombie for weeks and everyone around me continued to compliment me on my natural hairstyle, big and bright earrings and ethnic selections which must have fooled everyone into thinking I had finally tapped into my inner Black Panther and was abandoning my European influences. The fact of the matter was, when my hair was in an afro, I didn't have to match, coordinate or care much about my presentation. Everything was considered thoughtful and relevant as if I stepped into the world each day to make a political statement against the way my people had been marginalized. If that's what people wanted to believe, I didn't care anymore because I was counting the days I had left to live and when my feet crossed the threshold of the church that cold, Sunday morning, my feet felt as if they had large cinder blocks attached at both ankles. It was almost as if some invisible force was trying to keep me from going in but in that moment, I needed God to be what He was supposed to be in our lives. I needed God to be my savior and to save me from the worst enemy I could ever face; myself.

"I am so embarrassed about my life that I can barely look at myself in the mirror," I shared with my mother one day. I realized I no longer cared what people said about me because I had become my own, personal judge and jury. I had done so much I perceived as "wrong" in my life I was ashamed to even stare into my own eyes for they now held so much pain and inner turmoil that I couldn't bear to be reminded of it anymore. At only 34 years old, I had deemed myself one of the most horrible individuals to walk the Earth. I had given up. So, during that period of time, I avoided all mirrors; I often dressed in my bedroom away from any possibility of catching my own image in any reflective mirror or window.

I struggled with putting my testimony to paper for many years. My mom often encouraged me to face some of my demons and release them into the atmosphere. She thought it would be therapeutic for me but I was too busy trying to forget some of my past indiscretions so to put them to paper meant they would be forever recorded and therefore given life over and over again. I wasn't sure that I ever wanted to face that person ever again once I had rid myself of her. I was sure that I wanted to bury her in the deepest darkest hole and hope that she would disappear into an unknown abyss never to be seen or heard from again. For many years, I wasn't ready to be honest and accept that fact that I had to be that horrible person to move toward that woman God intends for me to become….until now.

I started writing a book in September of 2013 for reasons that might not make sense to most. I put my season of wilderness in the pages of this book not for money, fame, fortune or even attention. I put my testimony to paper for one reason and one reason only….because it was the only way I could save my own life. I came to a point and place that I realized that my story of trials and triumph were bursting out of each one of my pores and before I completely self-combusted, I would have to get it out. That morning when I stumbled into church, those words were tucked neatly on the front seat of my car in plain sight in case I…

If I had to provide a backdrop for what it means to live, imagine a young woman who found herself smack dab in the center of a deep, dark wood. The ground underneath was cold, hard and rocky and her feet were bare. She was surrounded by large, looming trees that seemed to reach toward her like the limbs you see on spooky Halloween cartoons around October. The sounds were a mixture of howling, barking and the sobbing of many tormented women and there was a distinct sound of clawing; almost like nails on a chalkboard. Above her, the sky peeked through vacant patches of the trees but a blanket of humidity slowly descended over the crown of her head. If you can imagine this scene, then you have experienced my vantage point as I faced two of the toughest years of my life which ultimately led to my decision to want to stop living.

I never thought I would ever consider suicide. Suicide was something for white girls who hadn't made the cheerleading team or whose parents had forbade them to be with the rebel who lived on the wrong side of town. It was almost like their ultimate temper tantrum for not getting their parents' attention when they had cut their hair or wrecked the car. I remember watching various Lifetime movies and the one I felt was the most shocking was entitled, "The Pact" which found two families coping with suicide of a loved one. I watched that movie over and over and began to assign each character to my own family members. I imagined what they would say, how they would blame themselves and, for that matter, the time it would take for each of them to recover from what would seem to be a selfish decision on my part. I imagined my sister, Renee, would take the news of my death the hardest feeling she had failed somehow. She would wonder what she could have done differently and would be upset with me for not feeling she was strong enough to carry my load as she had so many times before. My mother would rival her at the pity party questioning me about giving up and wondering where I had learned to give up the fight of life because she had given me the tools to withstand any storm because she had given me Christ. She would call on my grandmothers for guidance and beg God to show Himself mighty and bring me back from the dead in some reenactment of Lazarus's revival.

I had never heard of any black person who would be weak enough to take their own life. After all, we had been built on the ideology that each one of us was built on the bones of slaves who had endured unimaginable challenges in life but preserved through them all. If they could survive over 400 years of servitude, surely I could deal with the issues in my life. But, in my mind, the idea of living any longer seemed like its own death sentence. I seemed so far removed from such a life being I had never experienced anything other than Girl Scouts as a rite of passage so I didn't quite make the connection to a world that had brought me nothing but mind-numbing pain and a people who had never stopped to cultivate the little black girl whose nose remained in a book as a way to escape reality.

"To live" means to experience life, and to truly experience life, you have to open all your windows to your soul according to something I read once. The idea of opening up seemed like the most impossible move for someone like me to make after so many pitfalls in life, but if I was ever going to live and to live life with any sort of purpose, I would have to release my hurt, shame and condemnation. There is no way to live a life filled with anything worth having if one never opens their hand and heart to receive life. I learned the only time, prior to this realization, I had ever been truly open to receive life was when I took my first breath in the world. When I took in that breath, I drank in life and possibilities and happiness and uncertainties and fears and dreams and disappointments and hatred and insecurities and accomplishments and knowledge and children and songs and birds and talents and death at the same time. Now, I knew I had to open myself up again for a new drink, one that would be the cleansing refreshment to save my life.

One Friday night, I kissed my daughter, packed a bag filled with her favorite jeans with a matching hoodie with bright pink and orange plastered on the front. I made up some bogus lie and dropped her off to a friend for the night promising to come and pick her up the next morning. As she exited the car, I couldn't even tell her I loved her because I felt it would be a lie given the fact I had planned to never see her again. I wonder if what we all assumed would be possible, you know... where I could look down from the clouds and check on her from time to time. I sure hoped I would be able to peek in on her much as I had been doing the past few months as she struggled with allergies. She continued to walk toward the door excited to see her friend who was just beyond the doorframe and I hoped she wouldn't turn around but, just as she always had done, she turned and said, "I love you, mommy."

As my car bent the corner and I allowed my car to turn at its own will, I thought about the cars passing by. Surely some of them contained families coming home from dinner. I imagined they had enjoyed reminiscing about the holiday spent with family far away from any stresses of the world. I could see them scrolling through their cellphone picture galleries and even venturing to social media to relive each moment of the season all exchanging their own memories and smiles. I realized just as those cars whizzed past, my opportunity to have such conversations had flown by just as quickly as my mind had conceived its possibility. The temperature in the car began to drop and I felt as if I was suffocating so I decided to crack the window on the passenger side. The wind entering the car began to reverberate and it seemed as if I could not find the balance between what has happening on the inside and the elements attacking from the outside. It was almost poetic at that moment to have wars raging all around me and the fact I could not seem to bend them to my will only made me drive faster.

As my phone began to ring and my mother's picture illuminated the screen, my fingers skated across to drag the ignore button into its defining position. As a mother, I knew what was happening; my mother had tapped into my world with that mothering instinct and was reaching out to settle her own spirit. I didn't want to think about the horrible thoughts going through her head so I just continued to drive. The lights from ongoing traffic began to dance across the sky like a hypnotizing waltz as my car began to drift in and out of the traffic lanes. The sound of angry horns seemed to mock me as I jerked the wheel left and right, the right and left. I dared the cars around to hit me, after all, they had all just finished perfectly prepared meals with a photo-sharing session about the holidays. They didn't care about me so why should I care about them?

The phone continued to ring from the passenger seat. At this point, the calls were alternating between my mother's face and my sister's home number but the sound of wind, the dancing of the lights, the symphony of the horns, the weaving of the cars and the rings of the phone seemed to create a beautiful ballad, the sound of my last ride. I wasn't afraid anymore, there was nothing to be afraid of. This was my life. Its ending and it beginning.

So, the night I found myself driving to anywhere, wedged mentally in between everywhere and nowhere, I felt my life slipping through my fingers like grains of sand. As each particle fell from my fingers onto the naked Earth below, I saws my hands with little left to hold and it all seemed like it was the right thing to do. But...I slid my other hand beneath my hand with fleeting dreams, goals and ambitions escaping forever and I wanted to hold on just a bit longer. The hand below was catching every single drop with a power and persistence I thought was gone forever. Suddenly, I wanted my forever back and I wanted to fight for it like never before. I was exhausted, I was afraid, I was blind, I was deaf, I was unsure, I was doubtful but I was still alive and as long as I was still alive, I still wanted to live.

If life is to be drank, I want it to be the sweetest wine perfectly aged to marry all flavors together with great success. If life is an aroma, I want it to permeate my nostrils with traces of cotton candy and apple Jolly Ranchers. If life is a sound, I want to hear the soft chorus of a Catholic choir with a piercing chord of an operatic soprano. If life is to be a touch, I want to feel like a soft blanket swaddling a newborn baby and if it is a picture, I want it to be a vision of vibrant colors splashed against an organic canvas. I want to LIVE.

The lesson at 35 is to make a bold decision to LIVE in the moment, for every moment and about every moment. Life, by design, is going to challenge each person to their own level and in those moments, it's imperative to hold on to those things work living to witness. For me, I had seen the face of love in my daughter and it still was not enough to curve my thoughts of suicide. I heard the voice of God and it had been a still, small voice but with the clanging cymbals of calamity, I had trouble holding on to His voice. What saved my life was simply, wanting to LIVE; for me, not because I was sad about what it would mean to someone else if I made a different decision or because it wouldn't be fair to my family. The only reason I am still here is because it was right for me. I made a life decision to LIVE.

This book is dedicated to my mother, Ellen Marie Shields Frazier, who taught me to be the woman I am. She loved me past my faults and gifted me with Christ. I could not have finished this book without your strength and I know it is already blessed. I miss you every day but may you live on through my words. Together forever.

To my father, Clarence Frazier, Jr., you are my hero. I live to make you proud and I hope this piece does just that. Thank you for teaching me how to be strong in all things. Here is the return on your investment. Enjoy!

To my daughter, Casey Camille. You are the ham to my burger, the ice to my cream and the pop to my corn. There is no me without you and no "oui" without us. As long as you see me, I will always be beautiful, powerful and relevant. You have taught me what love really is for you love me effortlessly and inspire me to play with butterflies. Never change who you are. Your Maw Maw loves you...little sweetie.

To my sisters, Angela, Michelle and Sierra, may we forever find ourselves immortalized by these words. To my nieces, I have set the bar. Now, it's your turn to RUN!

Ms. Clarisse Frazier is currently a professional educator living in Atlanta, Georgia. Her next book, "Sleeping With My Father," is in its drafting stages and is set to be released in December 2017.

www.ingramcontent.com/pod-product-compliance
Lightning Source LLC
Chambersburg PA
CBHW070730160426
43192CB00009B/1377